Acclaim for Gregg Olsen's
The Deep Dark

"[Olsen] brings his considerable narrative skills to bear in this true-adventure tale. He tells the story in remarkably vivid detail, forcing the reader to experience the horror of the deep dark and to feel the exhilaration of the successful rescue."   *—Booklist*

"Powerful and haunting."   *—Seattle Post-Intelligencer*

"Excellent. A fascinating look inside the dangerous world of mining and mining culture."   *—Library Journal*

"Olsen has the narrative chops for this story.... In his gripping treatment, stocked with vividly drawn characters, one finds a metaphorical elegy for America's doomed industrial proletariat."   *—Publishers Weekly*

"Gripping."   *—The Oregonian*

"Spellbinding."   *—Daily Olympian*

"A spectacular piece of journalism. *The Deep Dark*...is written toughly and bravely...with the compassion of a writer who cares to know the truth."   *—Missoulian*

"An exciting, vital, memorable book."   *—Salem Statesman-Journal*

"A powerful narrative."   *—Vancouver Columbian*

"Riveting, page-turning, and gut wre

The Deep Dark

Disaster and Redemption
in America's Richest Silver Mine

GREGG OLSEN

THREE RIVERS PRESS
NEW YORK

Published in the United States by Three Rivers Press, an imprint of the
Crown Publishing Group, a division of Random House, Inc., New York.
www.crownpublishing.com

Three Rivers Press and the Tugboat design are registered trademarks
of Random House, Inc.

Originally published in hardcover in the United States by Crown
Publishers, an imprint of the Crown Publishing Group,
a division of Random House, Inc., New York.

Library of Congress Cataloging-in-Publication Data

Olsen, Gregg.
The deep dark : disaster and redemption in America's richest silver mine /
by Gregg Olsen.
p. cm.
1. Silver mines and mining—Accidents—United States.   I. Title.
TN311.O53 2005
363.11'96223423'0979691—dc22
2004.14165

ISBN-13: 978-0-307-23877-1

ISBN-10: 0-307-23877-6

Printed in the United States of America

Design by Leonard Henderson

First Paperback Edition

In Memoriam
Jack Olsen
1925–2002
Author, mentor, and friend

Author's Note

HEARSES WERE IN SHORT SUPPLY IN KELLOGG, IDAHO, IN May 1972. A pickup hauled a dead miner to a hillside cemetery slashed with freshly turned earth. Another arrived in a station wagon. Still others waited on an assembly line to meet their maker. Just after the tragic outcome of a fire that trapped almost one hundred hardrock miners in Sunshine Mine, my salesman dad passed through Kellogg on his way home to suburban Seattle. He saw the coffin in that pickup bounce up and down, threatening to pitch out onto the road. That bumpy ride was the culmination of a cruel eight-day wait—a vigil, both stoic and shattered, that was captured in the media. For outsiders, the serial funerals were the end of the story. For those living there, resolution has not been so easy. In the world of hardrock mining, a volatile place of explosions gone awry, cave-ins, and fortunes made and lost overnight, nothing has ever been easy.

Northern Idaho was the epicenter of America's hardrock mining industry. Within the region were the nation's largest, deepest, and most prosperous silver and lead mines. Bunker Hill had more than 180 miles of tunnels honeycombing the craggy mountains faced with yellow tamarack. The deepest was Star-Morning at 8,100 feet—

halfway to China, locals insisted. And the richest, Kellogg's Sunshine Mine, had given up more than 300 million ounces of silver—one-fifth of America's total output. When ore prices were good, Sunshine was a treasure trove of staggering wealth.

In good times, the most ambitious and, some would say, luckiest miners—those who had the very best contracts with the company—drilled and exploded their way to paydays of $1,000 or more a week. In less prosperous eras, during labor strikes or when operations were cut because high-quality ore was scarce, families only just squeaked by. And yet, no matter how long the downturn, men stayed because mining was about being a man as much as it was about bringing home a paycheck. Fathers like my own put in long hours and worked hard. Driving from Seattle to Montana several times a year and back again, my dad covered a substantial sales territory. But his job was air-conditioned. Highball-lunched. Miners didn't push paper. Their work was the type that we mimicked when we played at being men—firefighters, policemen, soldiers, and the rest. Though we were destined for desk jobs, we still pretended to catch the robber. We fantasized about blowing up a mountainside. Dirt clods were bombs. Nobody played at being a sewer-pipe salesman, my dad's occupation.

MORE THAN THREE DECADES AFTER THE FIRE, I WENT TO meet the people whose faces I had seen in the news when I was young and had first understood that for some, being a man meant your job put your life on the line. I checked into the Sands Motel in Smelterville, a fading town buried in the mire of a past from which it took its name. Today there is no smelter. Beyond the Wayside Grocery and the Happy Landing Bar, there isn't much of anything at all. The Sands' front-desk clerk, a young woman with a pleasantly askew smile, said I'd have to jiggle my key in the lock.

"Your room is twelve, but the key tag says nine. It'll work."

I went upstairs, twisted the key, and stashed my bag. A few minutes later I was in Kellogg, the heart of the Coeur d'Alene Mining District, driving past McDonald's and the Super 8 Motel. A multi-million-dollar gondola and ski slope, the crown jewels of an attempt to turn the town into a tourism center, beckon riders to the top of Silver Mountain. Those who live there feel it is too little, too late.

Kellogg has always worn its good times with brisk sales of new cars, its bad times with vacant storefronts. Soaped-out windows and ample parking on the main street reveal a town in the midst of another, deeper economic dip. At 10:00 a.m., the busiest place in town is a tavern called the Long Shot. A queue of graying men, beaten and battered by the elements underground, commands the barstools from one end to the other and cigarette smoke hangs like a canopy. While some involved in the Sunshine fire fled, many more, like the men at the bar, stayed—miners to the end. One woman runs a Kellogg pool hall while her ex-husband lives in a Smelterville neighborhood wrapped in Cyclone fence and lined with ancient RVs, their bumper stickers recalling a past when all were younger and their billfolds heavier. The woman can't shake the days of uncertainty and tragedy from more than thirty years ago, and still wells up with tears at the mention of the fire. But her miner ex-husband gets right to the point.

"I wanted to get out of there alive," said the man, now in his late fifties. "I'm sure all of the guys felt the same way."

Another miner shares the bond of survival with the Smelterville man, but seldom sees his old pal. Their lives, however, remain parallel. When they walk through Kellogg, people still regard them with mixed emotions. *Why them? Why did they survive?*

Back in my room at the Sands, I wondered about their lives, how different the place might be if so many hadn't perished at the same time. A Top 40 band played downstairs and the music thumped like a bruising fist against the wall of my room. I followed the music downstairs. The patrons were mostly in their twenties, about the same age as the youngest who died in the fire. Fewer of them work in mining today, though some who do call it *mineral extraction*. They are not as tough as their fathers were. Sons seldom follow their dads deep into the darkness for a seesawing paycheck and a chance at a hard-fought dream. Some lie and say they are smarter and mining is too dangerous; there are other ways to make a so-so living, better ways to get an adrenaline rush. Those are excuses born of a catastrophe that vanquished the soul of a town and hastened the end of a distinctly American way of life. Every day, people remember the date, May 2, 1972. It is their local "when Kennedy got shot" touchstone. It rewrote the lives of everyone, and even now its extraordinary legacy of unity and divisiveness is palpable. It is as if the smoke never really cleared.

Gregg Olsen
Olalla, Washington

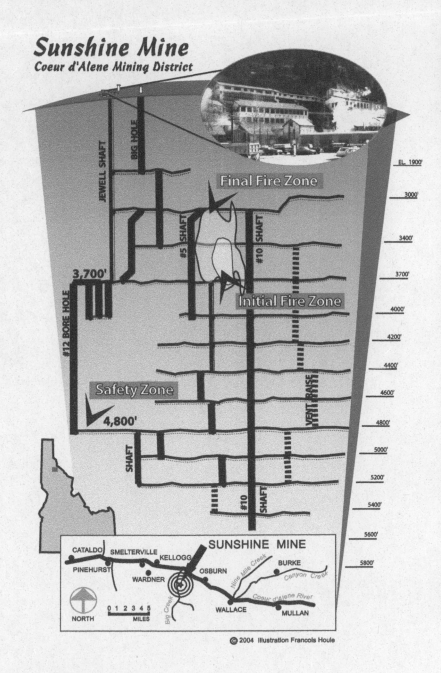

Sunshine Mine
Coeur d'Alene Mining District

Final Fire Zone

Initial Fire Zone

Safety Zone

JEWELL SHAFT

BIG HOLE

#12 BORE HOLE

#5 SHAFT

#10 SHAFT

VENT RAISE

SHAFT

#10 SHAFT

3,700'

4,800'

EL. 1900'
3000'
3400'
3700'
4000'
4200'
4400'
4600'
4800'
5000'
5200'
5400'
5600'
5800'

SUNSHINE MINE

CATALDO   SMELTERVILLE   KELLOGG   OSBURN   BURKE

PINEHURST   WARDNER   WALLACE   MULLAN

Big Creek   Nine Mile Creek   Canyon Creek   Coeur d'Alene River

NORTH   0 1 2 3 4 5 MILES

© 2004 Illustration Francois Houle

Prologue

NOT FAR FROM WHERE A MINER GUTTED THE EARTH, A thin haze curled through the hot, moist air and fluttered teasingly. At first the wispy cloud hesitated and hugged the edges of the stope, the blasted-out chamber where men extracted muck, rock, dust, and silver-laden ore. Then it swirled onward, deeper into the void. In the beginning, the miner who first smelled it might not have paid much attention. At depths of more than a mile, smoke was a constant element of the subterranean environment. Engines that crushed and carried muck, and blasts from ammonium nitrate and nitroglycerin, released thin smoke throughout the mine every day. The scent of burning tobacco also permeated the air. Deep underground, on the hunt for silver in the famed Sunshine Mine near Kellogg, Idaho, close to two hundred men were in grave trouble.

The fingernails of the miner who first noticed the smoke were cracked. His busted-up hands were calloused from rotating rock into position through a heavy steel grate over a chute that sent everything crashing down into hungry cars on the track level below. The man's eyebrows were coated in dust, and the grime of his sweat ringed his neck. He worked on the 5,000-foot level—the figure designating its depth below the surface. He wore coveralls so stiff from ore dust and drill oil that his pant legs remained tubular when he took them off at the end of his shift. On his head was a miner's hardhat; its lamp shot a beam through the dark emptiness that awaited him at every turn. He looked up from what he was doing and realized he was in danger. His gaze still fixed on the oncoming smoke, he reached for the valve of the oxygen cylinder on a portable cutting and welding cart. He felt for the hose.

Initially, most men working underground passed off the smoke as a motor fire somewhere down the drift where others were mining silver ore. That happened all the time. By the time smoke made its way through the mine's vast ventilation system, its source had usually been extinguished. No one worried about a fire getting out of hand because of the mine's notoriously wet floor and sodden rock walls. In some places the mine floor was a gritty layer of mud; in others, coffee-colored water stood ten inches deep. The very geology that brought the men so deep into the earth also lessened the worry of fire. Hardrock mines were blasted through mountain walls of solid metamorphic rock to reach slightly shimmering veins of gold, silver, or copper. Unlike coal mines, hardrock mines had no naturally occurring fuel to stoke a fire.

Men working up on the 3,700-foot level observed a slim channel of blackened air start to seep through vents used to feed fresh air into the mine. They attempted to seal it off. Working quickly, the miners piled up what they could find—wood, a steel drum, and scraps of the bric-a-brac that collected in the mine. Not all of them would get out on the hoist to the surface. Only a handful could make each trip, a thousand feet up, then a long walk to a second hoist, then up again to a tunnel toward daylight.

As the veil became a dark and lethal shroud, the miner who had been working near the welding kit bought himself some time. The others began to slump to their knees as if pins that held joints together had been yanked out. But he opened the valve and put a rubber tube into his mouth and sucked like a baby, consuming the contents of a tank of clean, smokeless oxygen. Even with limited knowledge about combustion, the man correctly deduced that there was something poisonous in the air. It couldn't be the smoke alone—there was so little of that. He drew in more oxygen as the canister hissed.

Like the petrified figures of Pompeii, a bunch of men were frozen in their places. A coffee cup rested on one man's knee, his body limp on a crate that he had used as a chair. Others were stiffened in their attempts to save their own lives. One fell running, his arms and legs stuck in full stride.

As darkness slowly devoured the shrinking space of the underground, the last man standing in that part of the mine threw his hardhat to the ground, its light still casting a thin line through thickened air. He watched his fallen friends as they began to die, their skin taking on a reddish hue as carbon monoxide replaced oxygen in their bodies. His blood pressure skyrocketed. Panic seized him. The others were dying or dead, en masse, from something no one could see. A group of motionless men lay by a telephone with a direct line to the surface. Even in death, one clamped the receiver in his hand. Down in the mine, where cap lamps were eclipsed by ever-thickening smoke, the miner took in measured gasps, certain he was about to die.

EIGHT MONTHS AFTER THE FIRE, IN DECEMBER 1972, THE U.S. Department of the Interior declared Sunshine Mine safe to reopen. The closure had cost the Idaho panhandle communities of Kellogg and Wallace more than $3.2 million in wages, and the country's mineral supply about $11 million in silver, copper, and lead. That was nothing, of course, compared with the human loss.

There were clues everywhere that something catastrophic had taken place. Most of the reminders came in the form of who was no longer there. Unclaimed street clothes still hung on hooks near the showers in the men's dry house. No one was sentimental about a greasy pair of Levi's and a frayed chambray shirt with mother-of-pearl snaps. But there were other signs, too. Deep underground in the mine, some of the rock was now coated in thick, black, velvety soot. In other places, rock with its foot-thick vein of high-grade silver and lead had turned molten and oozed like a lava flow, until it cooled into a thick, bubbly mass that resembled the shiny bark on a fallen cherry tree.

On one of the deepest working levels, there was another memento of the fire.

Near a battery barn, not far from the station where the men gathered to yak and wait for the ride up after shift, a miner noticed that when his cap lamp was turned off, the silhouettes of three bodies would reveal themselves in a ghostly glow. Johnny Lang, a stope miner and one of the men who'd worked on the rescue and body-recovery crew, heard about the eerie phenomenon and went to take a look. He switched off his light and stared down at the damp, smelly ground. And he saw them. Three men had been splayed out there, arms and legs akimbo like fallen soldiers caught unawares and shot in the back. The only part of the human forms that didn't reveal itself through the darkness was their feet.

Must be the rubber from their boots, Lang thought. *It kept whatever leached out of them from pooling there.*

The scene at once disturbed and fascinated. How could this happen? What was it in a man's body that would glow like that? Lang wasn't a biologist, but a miner with a high school education. He wondered if a man's body contained phosphorus. Or had foul secretions fed some kind of subterranean mold as the dead silently waited to be sacked up and taken from the mine?

This is the damnedest thing I've ever seen, Lang thought. *It just isn't right.*

He turned on his headlamp and left for a niche blasted out of rock that had been outfitted with a bucket for men to use as a toilet. Adjacent to the shit bucket was a drum of miracle lime used to cover excrement until the bucket was full and was sent out of the mine by the nipper. Lang scooped up a shovelful of lime and returned to the place where the three men had fallen on the day the mine coughed smoke through its miles of drifts and raises. He scattered the chalky powder. It fell like sugar off a spoon and melted on contact. He wasn't trying to erase their memory—which he knew could never be done. It was just creepy and wrong to leave the eerie traces of those three men in the sodden muck. He leaned his shovel against the drift wall and went back to his stope to blast out some more rock, going after more silver.

BOOK ONE

When Darkness Fell

If It Can't Be Grown,

It's Gotta Be Mined.

—BUMPER STICKER
SEEN AROUND THE MINING DISTRICT

One

MORNING RUSH HOUR IN THE IDAHO PANHANDLE WAS A stream of primer-splattered bombers and gleaming pickups on big tires that pushed the cab halfway to the sky. All were driven by miners hurrying to get underground. Many rode together so their wives and girlfriends could use their cars to run errands during the day. Some smoked and nursed hangovers with coffee as they planned their day underground: how much they'd have to blast, and how much muck they'd haul out. Some of the best of them took the Big Creek exit between Kellogg and Wallace. Around a sharp curve on the edge of the Bitterroot Mountains, buildings congregated among the steep folds of stony terrain bisected by the rushing waters of Big Creek. A giant green structure clad in sheet metal was planted as though a twister had dropped it in on the edge of the parking lot. A few other buildings flanked the green monster, though none was nearly as commanding. On the other side of the creek was a backbonelike array of metal and wood-frame buildings that included a mill, dry house, machine shop, warehouse, hoist house, assay office, electric shop, drill shop, and compressor shop. The most visually pleasing edifice was the personnel office, a two-story, variegated redbrick structure with a peaked roof and a walk-up pay window. A sign proclaimed that the property belonged to the Sunshine Mining Company, but the biggest billboard faced the mine yard. In demibold letters it read, TODAY IS THE FIRST DAY OF THE REST OF YOUR LIFE—LIVE IT SAFELY.

Sunshine has long been legendary, even sacred, among miners. Maine brothers Dennis and True Blake discovered what would become Sunshine in 1884 when a soft glint beckoned from an outcropping on the eastern ridge of Big Creek Canyon. Assaying indicated tetrahedrite, a superior silver ore, and not galena or lead, which was scavenged by other area mines. For a couple of decades the former farm boys worked underground by candlelight while mules hauled out ore and dragged it down Big Creek Canyon on skids. They quietly made a small fortune, calling their discovery the Yankee Lode. Later, in 1921, when they sold their stake to Yakima, Washington, interests, it was renamed Sunshine Mining Company.

IT WAS ANOTHER DECADE BEFORE SUNSHINE CAME INTO ITS own, when, at a depth of 1,700 feet, an ore vein of astounding breadth—23 feet—was discovered. In time, the mine would give up more silver than any other mine in the world, a distinction it would hold for decades. In addition to lead and copper, it was also a leading producer of antimony, a metallic by-product primarily used to harden lead. Sunshine's triumph was the result of the development effort led by the go-for-broke, risk-taking owners from Washington State. Most silver mines followed veins from outcroppings that eventually became stringers and petered out. Outside of the Coeur d'Alene Mining District, it was a rare operation that extracted ore at depths greater than 1,000 feet. Not only did Sunshine have viable ore below 1,200 feet, but in the decades that followed, crosscuts chased high-grade ore bodies all the way to the 5600 level. Sunshine by itself was far richer and produced more silver than all the mines on the fabled Comstock Lode *combined*.

Idaho mines shared more than just their luminous underground Dagwood sandwich of lead, silver, and zinc. Labor strikes, chronic absenteeism, and pumped-up wanderlust made the workforces somewhat fluid. Tough and experienced miners moved freely among Galena, Lucky Friday, Star, Silver Summit, Bunker Hill, and Sunshine. But even as itchy-footed as miners could be, every man had his home mine. It was the mine to which he knew he could always return.

AROUND THE TIME BOB LAUNHARDT, FORTY-ONE, BACKED his '68 maroon Chrysler Newport out of his Pinehurst driveway, the sun had risen, leaving the sky awash in luminous Maxfield Parrish hues. The men of Sunshine's graveyard shift were leaving the mine. As safety engineer, Launhardt made it a practice to get underground as early as possible—before the day shift rode down to their working levels. He liked to get a head start on the day. Tall and lanky, Launhardt had dark, wavy hair that he combed back with a slight swoop. Black-framed glasses made him look like a schoolteacher, or maybe a middle-aged Buddy Holly. After a five-year absence, Launhardt returned to the district in February 1972, bailing out of another job going nowhere, wanting to reconnect with a part of his life where he felt worthwhile. He was quiet and thoughtful, the kind of man who got lost in a crowd, yet Launhardt believed he stood out because of his fierce dedication to the safety of the men of Sunshine. No one questioned his passion for his work. It was apparent in every move he made. Many, however, found it difficult to connect with him on a personal level. Guys he'd known for years never even got his name right. They called him Bob *Longhart*. Part of the distance was the result of his personality, but it was also his status as a salaried man. Miners saw Launhardt, other managers, and office workers as outsiders. The fact that Sunshine's owners were now New Yorkers who hadn't blasted a round in their lives didn't help. Yet managers and bean counters were necessary. Silver mining was, after all, a business—and a dangerous one, at that. As safety engineer, Launhardt was there to make certain that each day every man who went into the mine came out alive. That involved working with national and state labor agencies and the U.S. Bureau of Mines (USBM) to ensure that safety regulations were in place. It meant seeing that equipment was up to date and miners were properly trained in evacuation and rescue techniques. Guarding miners' lives was a crucial job because so much could go wrong. Government statisticians and mining district undertakers frequently acknowledged mining as the most perilous job *on or under* the earth. Some assumed the safety engineer's position existed solely to meet government regulations, mitigate the risk of union complaints, and dodge civil lawsuits. Some mine managers considered it little more than a necessary nuisance. The workers themselves understood that there were ways to avoid injury, but they dismissed many of those measures. Many considered risk and danger essential to the job's mystique. Launhardt, a bespectacled Goody-Two-shoes among his peers, believed that if he could get men to think before they blast, to wear safety glasses, to cool it on the horseplay, just maybe he could save a life. His biggest challenge in 1972 was the same as always: *How do you convince men that accidents are unacceptable and unnecessary?* For Launhardt, who had once studied to be a Lutheran minister, promoting safety became as important as preaching the word of God.

There were many reasons for his vigilance, and all were damned good ones. Sometimes men fell down shafts so deep that nothing remained but bloody clothes and serrated splinters of bone. Rockbursts or airblasts, however, were the most feared of district hazards. Those occurred when the stone ceiling exploded under pressure and sent slabs of rock the size of camping trailers down to pulverize men into biological splat. Other times, it was the floor that gave way. The lucky ones were buried alive until someone could move two tons of rock to free them. Although Sunshine had its share, the district's Galena Mine was considered one of the worst, if not *the* worst, for rockbursts. Anyone who'd worked there longer than a month experienced the sudden and frightening reaction of rock giving way to pressure. Old hands knew that as long as the rock was talking—making characteristic popping and grinding noises—they'd be all right. When it got quiet, that was the time to think about moving to a different location or taking lunch early. Whenever it was quiet underground, look out.

In the battle being waged by men with jackleg drills against the fractured and folded metamorphic world of the underground, men frequently lost. Every man knew there was no guarantee he'd ever see daylight again.

Launhardt knew some accidents had more to do with human error—little mistakes that miners made doing things they did right every other day. Veteran miner Stanley Crawford's accident was a case in point. Crawford had been setting charges on some blocking in a shaft, as he'd done countless times. He set four fuses, but only three blasts rumbled through the mine. Crawford was confident that two had ignited simultaneously, thus obscuring the distinct sound of a fourth explosion.

"I'm gonna go look," he said.

His partner didn't like the idea. "Stay here and have a cigarette. We can check it after dinner."

But Crawford was impatient and insistent. As he bent closer to take a look in the smoky air, the charge ignited. It was the last thing he ever saw. His eyes were blasted from their sockets like a pair of soft-boiled eggs.

Sunshine's safety engineer knew the inherent reasons for Crawford's mistake. The greater the danger, the more reckless men became. It was a mix of laziness, tempting fate for the buzz of adrenaline, and just plain ignoring the obvious. More men were hurt and even more died because someone decided to push something to a new limit. Miners sometimes took the extra step toward trouble. *Trouble could be a rush.*

Some health hazards were slower in catching up with the miners. Airborne silica turned lungs into wheezing dust bags. Corneas were trashed by gritty dust belching through the working areas, forced along by the man-made cyclone of ventilation fans. The omnipresent dust that bloomed inside the working areas after blasting consisted of near-microscopic particles of lead, tetrahedrite, and razorlike pieces of silica from the quartz that frequently hosted the veins being mined. After each round was blasted, the air thickened with gray dust. Miners breathed it all in. Some tried to deplete the cloud through the judicious use of water over a muck pile as they were slushing out their stope, the working area whose name was a bastardization of the word "step" from the days when mining was done in a stairstep fashion. But water only goes so deep—no more than six inches—and men and machines stop for nothing. They didn't wear any kind of respirator or paper filter, though common sense would indicate that such precautions might help. Some of that was the result of tradition and ignorance, but it was also that Sunshine's underground was so hot that it was difficult enough to breathe even without a barrier across your mouth. Breathing a little easier underground at age twenty was paid for at age sixty, when scar tissue from abrasive dust caught up with a man's lungs. More than one old miner ended his days with an oxygen canister, a metal mongrel trailing on a leash with every step.

The steam-table heat of the mine and the repetitious work of mining machinery also created inescapable peril. Hands, wrists, and legs cramped up to such a degree that men looked like aberrant sand crabs, with arms all bunched up and hands locked in claws. One miner cramped up while waiting at the station for the cage, the underground elevator system. When the cage arrived, he couldn't stand up. His legs had turned into rusted C-clamps tightening around the bench. To beat cramping, some ate potassium-rich bananas. They thought a banana, not an apple, kept the doctor away. One miner opened a pickle jar, drained all the juice into a glass— and chugged the briny solution in two gulps. The light-green-tinged liquid tasted like shit, but the salt did the trick. In the mid-1960s, Sunshine installed enormous ventilation fans that improved conditions, but for those guys working underground, it still felt like being in Panama in the middle of August.

Most miners became astute at reading their bodies. Before the onset of a headache—when a dull throbbing alerted a man before the pain jumped into a sledgehammer on the cranium—was the only time to stem the inevitable cramping. Salt tablets stored throughout the working levels were the preventive, of course, and miners ate handfuls all day long. Wait too long, and fingers, toes, and other body parts started to curl, and nothing short of a bath in a vat of Morton's would cure a case of heat cramps. A man in his teens and twenties could handle it better than an older miner, but even youth didn't guarantee immunity. In the underground, nothing did.

Chronic heat-related indigestion was also an underground scourge. Men had to drag themselves to the station to get out of that hot, stinking hole, sometimes feeling sicker than they ever had in their lives. One Sunshine miner got so ill from the heat that he vomited all the way from 4600 to the 3700 station. As strong as they were, men had been shaken like paint mixers all day long underground, and they arm-wrestled with 115-pound jackleg rock drills in their stopes and rained sweat from every gland. One miner chomped Rolaids like Beer Nuts; another carried a bottle of sickly pink goo that he swigged with the same gusto as a whiskey shot.

Two variables ensured that underground accidents could and would come to pass—the earth was unstable and men took chances. Launhardt knew how men thought underground because he'd worked there. *I've done this before. I can do it again.* Injuries were an accepted cost of the business. Broken ribs and cracked skulls were the hidden costs of grandma's silver tea set, the film in a young family's camera, or the precious metals used in electronic components. Timber framing and five- or six-foot-long rock bolts were rarely enough to permanently shore up the guts of the earth. That realization was a thorn in his side. Launhardt knew that there were very few things that he could personally do to eliminate injuries from a fall of ground or rockburst—the greatest source of serious injury or fatality. Changing behavior when tradition, history, and male bravado had entrenched it was beyond his influence. Instead, Launhardt would preach safety to those who took an interest, and he'd see that lifesaving equipment was in working order. And when inevitable calamity occurred, he would suit up with the rescue team to extricate a miner from a two-ton tomb. If the accident involved a fatality, federal USBM and Idaho State Mine inspectors would arrive to conduct what was seen by many as nothing more than a cursory examination. Safety violations were cataloged and a narrative of the accident was captured on inspectors' clipboards and they'd move on. Up through the 1960s, there were few teeth to whatever laws were on the books, anyway. If an operator could make an easy change to improve underground safety without too much expense, it usually got done. If it could be put off, it was.

Mine-shift bosses and foremen saw safety as the safety engineer's responsibility with their own focus solely on production. Launhardt wanted the foremen to lead by example and—though some were exceptions—the foremen just didn't buy it.

"Now wait a minute here," one shift boss told him, "I'm not going to go around with all this babble you're giving these men. It's not my job. It won't do any good. The men are going to get hurt regardless of whatever you tell them."

Launhardt was profoundly disappointed by the dismissal. He'd preached safety with so much true belief that he expected that the concept had made at least some gains the years he was away from the district. He hoped there was the same prevailing momentum in mine safety as there had been in other dangerous industries. *Just maybe,* he thought, *these Sunshine miners have let the importance of job safety sink in. Maybe there's been a change in attitude.* It took him less than a week back at Sunshine to see the futility of such hopes. Nothing had changed.

A FAMILIAR MAXIM AROUND THE DISTRICT THAT HAD THE distinct ring of truth was that miners work hard, play hard, and fuck hard. Everything miners did was hard. Physically demanding jobs, dangerous jobs, brought a greater need for blowing off steam. Nothing was kept inside, and no rules needed to be maintained, period. Like soldiers, miners were a lifelong fraternity. Most had grown up together and had dads or uncles who worked underground. Sure, they fought, as brothers do, and certainly there were the kinds of rivalries that pitted one man against another. But in reality, when push came to literal shove, miners were Johnny-on-the-spot. Pity the newcomer, the logger with a tough-guy attitude, the out-of-towner who came to cause trouble. Miners who were at odds with each other a minute before would chuck all their disagreements and draw battle lines around the outsider.

Launhardt was just a man who wanted to do his job and do it well.

But as far as the men busting rock were concerned, Launhardt was not one of them. He was a guy who kept track of what they did *wrong*, wrote it down, and passed it along to the boss. The boss would come and make sure some irritating violation was corrected. All it did was slow down the process.

Every time the garage doors opened across the yard from Launhardt's window, it was a reminder that his cautionary words, his best intentions, were frequently ignored. Launhardt could feel his adrenaline percolate as one of a pair of ambulances came into view. Shoved right in his face would be the sight of a "basket case," a miner strapped into a Stokes stretcher, being put into the back of an ambulance for the ride down the mountainside.

As the calendar peeled toward May 2, the scene was played out with alarming regularity.

Two

MEN WENT MINING FOR MOSTLY THE SAME REASONS. They needed a job, had no other options, or fell into it because their dads and granddads had been miners. And while the supply was usually there, district mines as big as Sunshine had to duke it out for the manpower needed to keep things running. Bill Steele, Sunshine's hiring agent, knew every man, every reason, every goddamn story ever used to get work—and get out of it. On the morning of May 2, Steele, a square-shouldered military type, looked at his bedside clock and knew he wasn't going to lift his head from the pillow. A cold had knocked him down like a gust of wind. As men across the district prepared to head to Sunshine for another workday, Steele was probably the only one in the company who could name each one of them. Steele had taken the recruiting job in the early 1960s when Sunshine management dumped his predecessor because

19

that man was more interested in the bottle than in working. More than two hundred men had applied for the position and, tellingly, all but three were disqualified for poor attendance. Steele never missed a shift, shaved every day, and talked more than a magpie. Keeping men coming into the mine sometimes required persuasion, even wiles. At the time, the hiring office was in a little building that had been the barbershop in the days when rootless tramp miners roomed in the boardinghouse, drank at the Big Creek Store, and left the mountainside only when they fell off it. It was nothing for Sunshine to hire ten or twenty men a day, because that many would quit at any one time. Steele started each morning in the shifter's shack where bosses—shifters—rattled off manpower requirements.

"Bill, I need four miners."

"Bill, I need two."

"Bill, get me a couple laborers."

Almost every day, Steele would return to his office, slide open the hiring window, and view the motley lineup. Many faces belonged to seasoned miners and were quickly hired, though Steele knew they'd be leaving soon. That's just the way it was. Men rolled into town without a penny in their pockets. If they were any good at all, they'd have a job, a hot meal, and a room—all inside of a couple of hours. Some faces belonged to working miners' sons. By the early 1970s, many in the district had seen a lot of good times, times where dumping a shift was seen as no biggie. After all, miners working on a contract were making as much out of their stope as they wanted. Steele learned that the best prospects to fill the employee labor pool frequently came from outside of the district, especially the Midwestern states. There he found young men who'd been stuck on a farm in Bumfuck, Nebraska, earning $200 a month, plus room and board. When Sunshine's hiring man explained the pay scale of a laborer, it left young men slack-jawed.

"You can make about $250," he said.

"Sounds good. For the month?"

"No. That's for a *week.*" ·

The farm boys were astounded by their good fortune. That the work would be harder than anything they had ever done, and would likely rewrite the trajectory of their lives, didn't matter. *It was more money than their fathers ever made.*

New hires were sent to Sunshine's warehouse for boots, a hardhat, a belt, and a pipe wrench—the essentials for the underground. After that, they were directed to Wallace or Kellogg for a physical examination. Doctors documented blood pressure, height, weight, and the disclosure of any possible past injuries, but they also paid close attention to the condition of a man's lungs, back, and hearing. If a man's eyesight warranted glasses, it was so noted and stipulated that he should wear them underground. Exams were quick. A man could get in and out in twenty minutes. Hired in the morning, medical once-over by lunchtime, the new hire was at the mine for the afternoon shift. Some, however, never made it that far. Every now and then, Steele saw new Sunshine-issued boots and belts in district hock shops.

No matter how much they made—$700 clear for gyppo or contract miners and even bigger weekly paychecks for men sinking shaft— plenty couldn't make the money last until the next payday. There was a stinging irony to that, of course. On Fridays, Steele handed out paychecks that were more than what he made in an *entire* month. Yet by the following Wednesday the same guys would be leaning on the paywindow shelf, begging for a draw to get them through the week. Steele heard it all. Sometimes they'd say a kid was sick and had to see the doctor; other times they'd just put it on the line that they were flat busted. "I just gotta have it. My old lady's really on my back. You gotta help me out here." When he was feeling tenderhearted, Steele would fork over the dough a day early, keenly aware of the danger in doing so. Next time, the hard-pressed miner might beg for his check on Tuesday.

Every week contract miners gathered to pick up their gyp sheets—forms kept by the Sunshine office that showed just how much rock they moved by the cubic foot or by the ton, depending on the contract. Even more important, the sheets put a dollar figure to their efforts. This wasn't done in secret. The sheets were fanned out and handed over in a free-for-all that let everyone know how much money a man made. Status came with the money. And top miners were never shy about saying how big their checks were or how they were going to blow their cash.

Gyppo miners hated it when Sunshine adopted its "bank system," which held gyppo money until a job was done. Anything beyond a double day's pay was put in an account managed by the company. Sunshine held on to the dough until the entire stope—two hundred feet, level to level—was mined, thus completing the contract. Mine managers positioned the program as something good for miners, who frequently and frivolously wasted paychecks on toys and booze. But in actuality it was simply a way for the company to improve its cash flow and keep the best gyppos from tramping out to work at another mine. Walking away from the job could mean walking away from a small fortune. Gyppos working especially tricky stopes were the most irate about the system. It could take a year or more to get the money they earned. The system, they insisted, was about controlling the men who put their lives on the line and made a bunch of money for guys who never sunk a jackleg's steel into a wall of rock in their lives. With the bank system, the most a guy could bring home was $48 a day— no matter how much he slushed out. And to make matters worse, if a miner got mad and quit, he forfeited whatever remained in his account. The union fought against the provision but failed.

Some guys got around the bank system by "high grading" or

stashing some particularly rich chunks of ore into their buckets and selling them to a processor, thus cutting out Sunshine. Irate contract miners hid good veins and came back later. They'd timber over it, wash it down, and cover it with mesh or mats—anything to make it look as though a stope was either depleted of decent ore or downright worthless. Sometimes they'd rework the area after hours or on weekends, taking whatever they could haul directly to processors. Some of the most respected Sunshine miners did that a time or two. A very few made it a general practice and earned more money that way than they did mining for the company. A man could make some cash and say *fuck you* to the company at the same time.

WITH A YOUNG WIFE, THREE KIDS TO FEED, AND BARELY enough cash to get him from here to there, Wilbur "Buz" Bruhn needed a job. In mid-1962, the curly-haired man with a Vise-Grip handshake stood in a Seattle unemployment office and studied job listings on a board. A placard indicating Idaho mining operations were short on muscle caught his eye. Bruhn had recently mined for quicksilver in Guerneville, California, and dug for iron ore in Minnesota as a teen. The next day he zipped across the state and got in the queue with another two or three dozen other scruffy job seekers at Sunshine's Wallace hiring office. Despite the optimistic job flyer in Seattle, it didn't look good. The line was at a standstill.

I'll never get a job here, Bruhn thought. *Now what am I gonna do?* But just before packing it up for more uncertainty in Seattle, Bruhn noticed something. Every now and then a man would slip into the office and leave looking satisfied, even cocky. He followed their lead.

"You have something for me?" he asked.

The hiring man looked up and regarded Bruhn with unmistakable wariness.

"You ever work in a mine?"

Bruhn said that he had, and the man seemed faintly impressed.

"Come back Wednesday. I'll have something for you then."

Bruhn wasn't about to be put on ice. "If you ain't got a job for me today," he said, his voice booming as he made his play, "you ain't going to have one for me come Wednesday."

The man smiled a little and proceeded to fill out a card.

"Put this in your pocket and don't say nothing to nobody," he said. "Just walk out."

Damn, I got a job. With a few bucks and that little card in his pocket, Bruhn went looking for a place to crash. A Wallace madam had a good chuckle when he asked for a weekly rate at what he thought was a hotel but was actually a whorehouse. He footed it over to a hotel that boarded miners in a ramshackle warren of spartan rooms. He had cash for the night, but no money for food. An easygoing woman running a café in the basement agreed to feed him that night and even make him a sack lunch for work if he'd pay her back on payday—something she did for a handful of miners every shift of the week.

A few days later Bruhn's wife, Ginny, and their children joined the newest Sunshine miner and moved into a two-bedroom apartment with a kitchenette on the east side of the district. They'd never had it so good. When Ginny paid the bills, there was still money in their bank account.

AFTER SERVING AS AN ARMY MEDIC, PINEHURST NATIVE Kenny Wilbur trailed his dad to the cell room of Bunker Hill's zinc plant, where he stripped plates of bluish-white cadmium. It was a repetitive and low-paying job, so when summer warmed the valley, Wilbur headed for the Idaho woods to hook logs on the jammer. Working as a gyppo in a lumber camp could earn a man half again a day's pay or more. When fall weather arrived, Wilbur went underground at Sunshine Mine. At first the young man reveled in that kind of back-and-forth rhythm which so many district men embraced as a good way of living. After a couple of years, however, Wilbur, who had a young wife and an infant son, saw it was not the way to sustain a life with responsibilities. In 1969 he became a permanent Sunshine employee, though he knew his connection to mining was tenuous. The bug hadn't bitten him. His carpool buddy couldn't stop yammering about mining, and Wilbur wanted to talk about hunting or fishing. *About anything else.* After spending all day underground, he wanted to get his head out of the dark hole and into the light.

Wilbur noticed right away that longtime miners paid a huge price for that fat weekly paycheck. He even played a little game, asking veteran miners their ages. When they said they were thirty-five or forty, Wilbur stifled his shock. He watched as the older guys worked harder and harder, faster and faster, until heatstroke knocked them down in a clenched, fetal position. A veteran miner might think he was running a mile in a darkened sauna, but he was only walking. Men who had once been gyppo miners with big incomes and balls the size of grapefruits no longer had much stature. Miners knew the fragility of their place in the mine. All they had to do was look around at the men older than forty-five to see what most of them were doing underground or on the surface. If they hadn't shown some kind of indomitable presence, some leadership, most who could no longer mine plummeted in the hierarchy of Sunshine— even though they knew a hell of a lot more than the young guys with quicker reflexes and greater muscle mass. It was like the pro-football player who was stuck selling insurance or new cars; their glory days were known but irretrievably lost.

"Holy smokes," Wilbur told his wife, Judy, one day after work, "these guys look like they are twenty years older than they are. This ain't good. I don't want to do this forever."

Kenny Wilbur wanted the kind of job that made him *more* valuable over time, not *less*. He put his name on the list to be an electrical apprentice at Sunshine. Get a trade and get out of the mine was his plan. On May 2 he was still in the mine, waiting on the list, looking for a way out.

EVERY NOW AND THEN IT WAS NEITHER TRADITION NOR necessity that took men into the earth's crust for money. For Californian Bill Mitchell, a marine serving in Vietnam, the road to Sunshine came in the form of love letters from a Smelterville girl. Bill Mitchell wed Vicki Johnson in 1969, and the Bay Area transplant rustled a job at Sunshine and bought a house on Riverside Avenue, a street of modest homes on the eastern side of Kellogg. Right away, Mitchell felt the pull of the underground. Certainly the subterranean was different from what he'd imagined—unlike, say, *Journey to the Center of the Earth*, with James Mason and Pat Boone wandering around twinkling masses of glittery crystals. A hardrock mine was a man's world, created by men. It was gray, dark, damp, and grimy. Yet everywhere Mitchell looked, men earned an income as big as their ambitions. He embraced that kind of accountability and freedom. He alone controlled how much money he brought home to his wife and, later, his two daughters.

Across the district, Buz Bruhn, Kenny Wilbur, and Bill Mitchell downed some coffee and dressed for work. Bruhn carpooled from his little red house in Mullan with three other miners he'd known for years. Wilbur rode in with a buddy from Pinehurst. Mitchell, the closest to the mine, drove east from Kellogg. In less than five hours, everything each knew about hardrock mining would change forever.

Three

BOB LAUNHARDT WAS WELL SUITED FOR THE SERIOUS demands of his job. Meticulous by nature, he was the kind of buttoned-up guy who alphabetized and organized most aspects of his life—from his garage tools to his sock drawer. Organizational acumen aside, Launhardt had a miner's soul and was no stranger to the underground, having worked at Sunshine from the mid-fifties to the midsixties. That's what brought him back. Launhardt didn't leave in 1967 because he was dissatisfied with his work or wanted more money. He left because the New York owners didn't see the relevance of a proactive safety program. They didn't want anything to get in the way of production. Giving safety-minded employees an electric can opener as a reward for days without any dangerous incidents without really addressing the larger issues of mine safety wasn't enough. Rather than feel underutilized at Sunshine, Launhardt quit the company to sell insurance for the Lutheran Brotherhood in Spokane, and then went off to Seattle to work as an executive headhunter. Four years after he left mining, Sunshine contacted him with an offer to resume his old duties. It took a little convincing. Eventually, Launhardt saw it as his chance to return to something he loved, but, even more, as an opportunity to start over. He understood the connection the men had to the earth and its hidden wealth. He knew the thrill of hitting a vein that would pay out for weeks and how it felt to work so hard that your muscles passed the point of soreness and ceased aching. Launhardt wasn't an underground lifer, but he understood those who were. Moreover, Launhardt recognized he was no longer one of the army of men who blasted away the innards of a mountain. As safety engineer, the six-footer was now *office* rather than *underground*. A little awkward and deeply religious, Bob Launhardt stood out underground and in the mine yard. Perfect grammar and a clean-shaven face always did.

It wasn't that he was smarter or even more educated than those underground. There were plenty of men with college degrees busting rock, who wore belt buckles the size of dinner plates and drove midnight-blue pickups to hunting grounds on the weekends. But those men had adapted to the culture of the job and the district. The physical side of the work felt good. The strain of the mines felt better than the stress of the office—for which there were seldom tangible results. Desk jobs would never feel right to most miners.

Underground was, quite literally, a world unto itself. It was a realm that fed on competition and practical jokes, the likes of which were seldom seen in any other industry. It was a place of nicknames that were frequently so entrenched that when Blackie, Skinhead, or Doc died and his given name was announced, few fellows knew it was the pal they'd talked to every day. A hoistman earned the name Greasy for playing dirty tricks with the thick black smear used to keep his hoist cable shipshape. His bit was to rub cable dope on the phone receiver and laugh like hell when a fellow picked up the line and blackened his ear. He'd conceal a greasy gob inside the yarn of a mop head and tell a new hire to start swabbing the floor. When he really wanted to get to someone, Greasy would slide a little cable dope on the blades of a man's windshield wiper and wait for the next rainfall. Another hoistman's favorite ploy was to pretend to relay an urgent message to an unsuspecting miner. *Have to return the call immediately. Right now.* The miner would dial the number and get the madam of a Wallace whorehouse. Magic Markers were also put to creative use. Men caught napping woke up to find handlebar mustaches or chin whiskers on their faces. Cager Stan "Talky" Taylor got up after one lunchtime nap to thunderous laughter. Etched on his balding head was a four-speed gearshift.

While dressing at the end of a shift, guys sometimes got a jet of Right Guard sprayed onto open sores, to unbearable and stinging effect. A hoistman who used a Norelco razor was notorious for dumping his whiskers in drying socks, making a miner's feet itch the next day like he had the world's worst case of athlete's foot. Some tricks were classic and played over and over—dinner buckets nailed to the station floor, the cat-food sandwich trap set for a miner who routinely helped himself to the wrong man's bucket. But, boys being boys in the fraternity of mining, nothing got a bigger rise than the mix of humiliation and sex. Easter-egg-dye tablets were tucked into hip pockets or the fly of a man's underwear to turn his butt or genitals green or red. One wife refused to have sex with her husband until he "got the purple off his pecker" after a dye job. One hapless fellow was held down while a band of miners ran duct tape from his chin to his scrotum—and then peeled it off, leaving a hairless racing stripe from "chin to hose." Getting greased was undoubtedly the most humiliating of the common pranks. One new miner dodged the practice for quite a while, but made the mistake of telling a buddy,

"No one can grease me." Soon after, four burly fellows pinned him down, pulled down his diggers, and rubbed cable dope over his genitals. The thick, waxy grease had phenomenal staying power. Most learned the hard way: *The stuff has to wear off.*

Miners referred to their horseplay as grab-assing, and occasionally things went too far. In addition to stunned pride, miners turned up with broken bones and gaping wounds. Bob Launhardt was put in the position of having to write up some of those antics as safety violations. That pushed him further away from the brotherhood of miners. In truth, Launhardt's reserved personality made it difficult enough for a close relationship with others anyway. He hunted elk and deer with a couple of pals, but those relationships didn't last. One of his buddies left for another mine, and another died when the battery hood of his motor caught a muck chute and swung back, slicing his head from his neck.

ON THE MORNING OF MAY 2, AS HE HAD FOR THREE MONTHS since his return to Idaho, Launhardt drove from Pinehurst through Smelterville and five more miles southeast of Kellogg, to the spur at Big Creek. Filtered sunlight reflected off his windshield as he went up the mountain and past the row of miners' houses that marched up toward the company gate. He was troubled that morning by something he'd read in the *Kellogg Evening News* the night before. It was a scathing letter from the local of the miners' union, the United Steelworkers of America:

> I do not know whether you are aware, that now we have more favorable laws for the protection of underground workers in this state and a more active department for the enforcement of these laws, that several mining companies in this state absolutely refuse to abide by the law and the abatement of orders of the Idaho Inspector of Mines office.

Launhardt took the comments personally because he took his responsibility to heart. He parked behind the mine offices. It was forty-five minutes before the day shift would start filing underground. After changing into coveralls, heavy woolen socks, yellow hard-toed rubber boots, and a hardhat, lamp, and battery, he met up with Jim Salyer. A no-nonsense fellow with angular features and a head of sandy hair, Salyer, fifty-one, was the foreman in charge of development efforts on the 5400 and 5600 levels, where Sunshine was searching for new ore bodies. By the early 1970s there were additional pressures on mining companies throughout northern Idaho to ramp up production. Mineral extraction was no longer merely the interest of the small towns where shafts were sunk. Mining was going corporate, and pressure to perform was increasing with every quarterly report. Sunshine's owners wanted the silver mine to pay out, and a stiff-armed push was on.

Four

EVEN IN EARLY MAY, FRAGMENTS OF THE SNOW PACK WERE scattered like broken dishes over the mountainsides adjacent to the mine. Icy water drained from the dirty white deposits into Big Creek and gushed under the mine bridge before joining Elk Creek and the south fork of the Coeur d'Alene River. The weather was a yo-yo in May. Days sometimes hit the mid-seventies, with nights plummeting to freezing as the elements battled over whether it was winter or summer—the seasons that rule the district most of the year. On the eastern edge of the thirty-five-mile-long valley, water dammed up by beavers was smoothed flat, and stalks of cattails with the last tufted remnants of coppery fur stood battered but upright.

But more than any place on earth, mining districts were about what lay beneath the surface, what couldn't be seen by the day-tripper passing through.

Mine engineers recorded the world below, but such schematics were a blend of reality and wishful thinking. They depicted an orderly place. In a mine map, drifts often run in straight lines, and raises poke from one level to the next in a perfect, logical trajectory. But no mine is so tidy. Men develop mines with muscle, jackleg diamond drills, and explosives. And as much as they would like things to go exactly as planned, the subterranean has a will of its own. Rocks break, fractures form, and routes are adjusted. To the layperson, the concept of a tunnel speaks of a streamlined and uniform tube. In a hardrock mine, the height and width of a tunnel or drift vary considerably. A drift might start out spacious enough for a Peterbilt, but a hundred yards later it may be just big enough to accommodate an MG. It only has to accommodate a muck car and a man train. Bulkheads along drifts are patched with wood and plastic or polyurethane foam to control airflow and to keep the face from splintering off any dangerous rock. Steel mats are bolted to places that appear especially perilous. Massive timbers shore up intersections or cross-drifts.

The Jewell, a timbered, four-compartment shaft, was not only the gateway for men and machines, but it was also the mine's single most important source of fresh air, the life-giver of any mining operation. Jewell was the surname of the supervisor who sank the shaft back in 1934, though most assumed—obvious misspelling aside—it commemorated the wealth deep in the mine's gullet. The Jewell dropped from the surface to the 3700 level. Sunshine was a web of passageways that, if accurately depicted, would look more like a near-blind grandmother's worst crocheted potholder than a grid made with a ruler. Drifts or tunnels followed ore bodies set off by bands of snowy white quartz that, in the bright light of a motor, appeared as swirls of silver tetrahedrite folded into a metamorphic meringue. Spaced every two hundred feet, horizontal drifts were intersected by vertical cuts called "raises" that led miners from one working level to the next. Around every turn of the underground maze were old stopes that had been emptied of ore and gobbed—packed with waste rock and trash—to protect against collapse. By the early sixties, most Idaho mines had switched to backfilling mined-out voids with sandfill, a slurry of water and tailings, the by-product of the milling process that chemically and mechanically separated precious metal from waste rock.

Safety engineer Bob Launhardt considered Sunshine no more convoluted than any other district mine, although it did operate with multiple shafts. The Jewell Shaft was the main way into the depths of the mine, and it carried miners and other underground workers in a single-drum chippy hoist; muck and equipment traveled the Jewell in the larger double-drum. The Jewell bottomed out just below the 4000 level, but its role was to get men and machines to the most important levels, 3100 and 3700. If the Jewell was the way into the mine, 10-Shaft was the route down to the current production levels. The deepest level being developed was 6000. The 200-foot-spaced drifts that followed the veins were fed by 10-Shaft. They no longer were identified by descriptive names like Yankee Girl or Chester Vein but with numbers and letters to mark their location. Men took 10-Shaft from 3100 to the deepest working level of the mine, 5600. By 1972, the route to 10-Shaft from 3100 was seldom used. The 3700 level was preferred. In fact, most Sunshine miners had no familiarity with 3100 whatsoever.

A mile's train ride east of the Jewell, 10-Shaft was powered by a 900-horsepower double-drum hoist that carried ore and waste muck from lower levels to cars that ran on a track to the Jewell. The double-drum configuration also allowed for two single-deck cages. Each deck held nine men—one deck coming and one going on a counterbalance system. On the 3700 level, a single-drum chippy hoist had a four-deck configuration that transported forty-eight men at full capacity. Cages had next to no clearance from the jagged shaft, maybe four inches at best. Both the shaft and the cage were gated, a necessity given that one slip was a rocket ride downward. The conveyance's trajectory was steadied by four-by-six-inch mahogany guides bolted to timbers that defied gravity with rock bolts and timber spikes. To ride the cage was to experience a seemingly endless free fall, a long, dark descent through a great empty space. Men traveled at about 900 feet a minute; muck and supplies hurtled at about 1,800 feet a minute. Speed depended on three things: the state of the equipment, the government's regulations, and what kind of night the operator had the night before. Sunshine cages had an excellent safety record; not all mines in the district did. In October 1936 at the Morning Mine in Mullan, a hoist cable snapped, the backup safety dog catches failed, and a cage with ten men plummeted downward. The cage was forty-three feet tall before the accident. When the crew recovered it, it was a six-foot steel sandwich spread with a paste of dead miners.

Clustered around the station at 10-Shaft on 3700 was a cavernous space that served as a warehouse, a shaft repair shop called "the chippy doctor's room," and, a little farther down the drift, a pipe shop known as the "08" because of its proximity to the defunct 8-Shaft. All were lit by dangling banks of fluorescent tubes.

6:15 A.M., MAY 2
Fourth of July Pass, West of Kellogg

THE KITCHEN MEN—DELMAR, THIRTY, HIS EIGHTEEN-months-older brother, Dewellyn, and their fifty-four-year-old father, Elmer—drove in from the western town of Coeur d'Alene and the surrounding area where most of the Kitchen clan lived. Delmar, who lived the farthest out, near Hayden Lake, was always the last and first link in the family carpool. As the only nonsmoker of the three, Delmar kept the window cracked no matter the weather or the season. The men in the '65 Ford on the morning of May 2 were mining elite. For some in the mine, the name Kitchen was revered for the fear it evoked among lesser miners. Challenging a Kitchen was a fool's death wish. Led by Dewellyn, the pecking order of any mine started with a Kitchen and went down from there. Men underground would pass their lunch hour by betting on who could bend a timber spike, a long, pencil-thick nail. The best at the challenge was nearly always Dewellyn. He'd take out his handkerchief, wrap it around the spike, and turn it into a horseshoe. Others practiced with spikes for hours, trying to make them give. Few could.

Guys in the Shoshone County Mountaineer Motorcycle Club admired thirty-one-year-old Dewellyn, although not so much for his riding ability, because he was only so-so at that. Fellow riders were spellbound by Kitchen's casual display of his Samson-like physical strength. One time Kitchen and a buddy were out riding a steep hill, their motorcycles sputtering up the incline. Kitchen had enough, got off, and put his motorcycle up on his shoulders and *carried* it to the crest. He was going to win that race, and if it meant packing his motorcycle up the hardest part of the course, so what? That's what muscles and stamina were all about. The Kitchens were solid blocks of grit and don't-fuck-with-me attitude. If there was a tougher man, a harder sonofabitch than the Animal, as Dewellyn was respectfully known, he'd yet to make his presence felt anywhere in the district. Kitchen was Mullan miner Buz Bruhn's partner. Bruhn had seen with his own eyes what the Animal could do. One time they were working on a raise prep that involved putting in upright fourteen-by-fourteen timbers. The timbers were so massive that a motor was used to lift them into place. Kitchen sized them up one morning and told his partner that he thought he'd be able to lift one and put it into place. *By himself.*

Sure, pard, thought Bruhn, a man who'd paid a printer twenty dollars for a fake birth certificate when he was sixteen so he could join the Marines. Bruhn, thirty-nine, was no slouch himself when it came to physical strength. He'd known Kitchen for years, but wasn't sure *any* man could move those massive timbers. Bruhn offered a hand to get one lifted, but without so much as a grunt, the Animal dismissed the help and took it the rest of the way. His forearms were a pair of fire hydrants, stout and bulging under the taut sheath of a grungy T-shirt. He picked up that timber as if it was a campfire log.

This guy's a walking winch, Bruhn thought.

The morning of May 2, in a routine followed by all the men of the mine, the Kitchens checked in with the bosses at the shifter's shack, a corrugated sheet-metal building with a peaked roof facing the portal. Overhead, the cables of the hoist ran from the hoist room to the Jewell's headframe, where huge steel wheels and massive pulleys with cables supported the cage—the vertical transportation system that miners always told outsiders was like a high-rise building elevator.

The Kitchen boys made another play for working on 5400 on Tuesday. They had been bugging their foreman for the past week or so about the heat on 5000 and how they'd prefer to go work on the cooler 5400. Their father, Elmer, was down there, and the three Kitchen men thought it might be good to work on the same level.

"I'm not going to argue with you guys no more," the foreman said. "Just go down to the 5000 and finish what you're doing. All you have to do is slush it out and you're done with it."

The Kitchens knew how to pick their battles, at least when the boss was calling the shots. They backed off.

From the Jewell station they took the cage down to 3700 and scrunched up to fit into the tight and low confines of the flame-orange, battery-powered train for the mile-long ride to 10-Shaft. Guys sat on benches two abreast facing each other. So tight was the fit, men interlaced their legs for the duration of the ride. Some smoked, some talked, a few even slept as the train lurched through the drift, its wheels scraping against the rails and screeching as it ran along a drift, parallel with the ore body. At the station, another cage was waiting to ferry the miners to their working levels. Delmar and Dewellyn got off on 5000 and passed through two air doors on the east side of the shaft, where they were working a raise prep with their respective partners. Elmer continued on down to 5400.

Five

BENNIE SHEPPARD AND GLEN SHOOP HAD BEEN REPAIR-ing shaft guides on the 3400 level off 10-Shaft. They were coming off an uneventful graveyard shift, typical of their routine of track and shaft repair. A little after 6:00 a.m., the pair made their way to 3700 station for the man train out of the mine. Foreman Ray Rudd ran the motor, and Sheppard and Shoop joined the others and got on. As the train passed an electrical substation, Shoop, twenty-one, turned to his partner and sniffed.

"Do you smell smoke?" he asked.

Sheppard indicated he did, but he pointed out Rudd had just lit a cigarette with a wooden match.

"That must be it," Shoop said.

But the scent niggled at Sheppard. He knew that a match's odor could be distinguished from most any other burning smell. Miners

39

had particularly acute olfactory senses. A man underground could tell the scent of a burning mahogany guide over one made of fir.

He shrugged. "I didn't smell any sulfur," he finally said.

The man train continued to the Jewell, and the graveyard guys aboard walked out toward the light of a brand-new day. Topside, near the portal, they came across foreman Gene Johnson and told him about the smoke. Johnson was a breath under six feet tall, but he had the kind of personality that made him seem even bigger, the way a blowfish can puff up. Those who worked under him sometimes considered it hot air. He had the ramrod gait and air of authority that broadcast immediately that he was a military man, a man deserving of respect. His dark, curly hair crowned a ruggedly handsome face, punctuated by dark eyes that could flash fire or charm whenever he needed to summon either.

Johnson promised to check it out. No one could say for sure if he ever did, or even had the chance.

SAFETY ENGINEER LAUNHARDT WAS HEADED FOR UNDER-ground Tuesday morning to inspect safety equipment, including any fire extinguishers and BM-1447 self-rescuers. Filter breathers of charcoal and hopcalite, BM-1447s were small lifesavers about the size of a tuna can, though twice as thick, with a rubber mouthpiece and nose clip. Used all but exclusively in coal mines, where fires were frequent and often deadly, the device chemically converted deadly carbon monoxide in smoke to harmless, breathable carbon dioxide. Launhardt had been the first to order Bureau of Mines–approved self-rescuers in the district about halfway through his first tenure as safety engineer in the mid-sixties. By the time Launhardt left for Spokane to sell life insurance, Sunshine was one of only two district mines to procure BM-1447 self-rescuers, the other being the Page Mine. Lucky Friday, Bunker Hill, and Galena—all big, busy operations—didn't have a single one.

When he'd returned to the district in February of '72, Launhardt had found many of the mine's self-rescuers in poor condition, if not completely worthless. In ideal conditions—when the vacuum-sealed lid was not popped, accidentally or intentionally, by a curious fellow testing the plunger on the opposite side—the units were supposed to last a decade or even longer. But not so, it seemed, at Sunshine. In a mine environment akin to a gigantic steam bath, moisture seeped readily into the self-rescuers' hopcalite chambers, turning the chemical to sludge and destroying its effectiveness. Storage was part of the problem. Leaky wooden doors had replaced the glass fronts on the storage cabinets he'd installed in the early sixties. Locking solid-paneled doors stenciled with SELF-RESCUER replaced shattered panels. Launhardt learned that during his absence, self-rescuers had rarely been replaced after being corroded or pinched by a few miners who'd take just about anything from the mine that wasn't nailed down, whether it was useful topside or not. New locks and solid wood panels weren't meant to keep men out during a fire, but only to deter the weekend auto-body painter who found the units good protection against the CO by-product of spray-painting. Besides, most miners regarded self-rescuers with little if any interest. The devices were viewed as unnecessary because metal mines had had little or no fuel to sustain a fire.

Many of Launhardt's trips underground lately had brought the same disappointing discovery. Ignored for years, some self-rescuers had been damaged in the hot and humid underground. Following an inspection on February 24, he wrote: "It is obvious that a serious problem exists in mine fire protection . . . according to the record card, the unit at #4 was last inspected on 2/5/68."

As he worked his way through the various levels in the last weeks of February 1972, the lanky safety engineer recorded which locations were in need of a new supply. He replaced what he could from the safety office's rather limited supply and discussed ordering more with his predecessor, Jim Atha. Atha ordered three dozen of the Mine Safety Appliance Company's W-65s—an improved one-hour unit that was in the works. But there had been a delay. The government had recently mandated that all coal mines use the newer, longer-lasting self-rescuers. To meet the requirement, the Pittsburgh-based manufacturer had diverted its production to coal mining companies. Sunshine's purchase order was on hold. Launhardt was as troubled by the quantity ordered as by the delay. He wanted every Sunshine man to have access to a self-rescuer. An additional three dozen would hardly do it.

On the morning of May 2, Launhardt was a man with little time to spare. He had a lot of ground to cover in the mine, and adding to his workload was a big project waiting on his desk. Launhardt was in the process of redrafting Sunshine's decade-old safety rule book, and its deadline loomed. The draft was due before the joint safety committee on Friday, and the following week it would be shared with representatives of the union for their comments. Launhardt and development foreman Salyer rode down the Jewell in a cage to the station at the 3700 level. The trip took less than five minutes, the cage traveling through the shaft at almost 1,000 feet per minute. From there, they took the man train for the mile-long ride to 10-Shaft. At 10-Shaft, they climbed on the cage powered by the chippy hoist. "Chippy" was the term used in the Coeur d'Alene Mining District to denote an auxiliary hoist, one that carried men and materials, not ore or muck. Sunshine's chippy could haul as many as forty-eight men at a time. The other hoist, the double-drum on the 3100 level, was used to haul muck, ore, and rock. The double-drum hoist was also outfitted with a twelve-man cage.

The chippy moved miners at a decent clip, between 500 and 750 feet per minute, depending on the hoist operator and the need to get the men down or out. Ten miners was considered a full load on a single deck of the chippy, but at that time of the morning Launhardt and

Salyer were the only two passengers for the ride down to the level Launhardt had targeted for inspection—5600. Launhardt's cap lamp illuminated the blur of the shaft's timbered walls as the hoist dropped into the darkness. Every 200 feet a strobe would flash as the cage passed through a lighted shaft station on its way down, about a mile underground in the deep dark of the mine.

A man's senses were bombarded underground. Sunshine, like all deep mines, was damp and musty, accented with the stink of powder smoke from explosives. Some thought parts of the underground where timbers rotted and sent off methane gas reeked like sneakers stored in a plastic bag, or like the foulest, wettest farm dog. Others—owners and top gyppos—smelled money. Beyond the intake air shafts, humidity at Sunshine was at 100 percent, and whatever odors percolated through the underground hung heavy in the moist air. Bob Launhardt, for one, could even detect the tang of specific chemicals found in the sandfill. All tailings, and therefore all mines, were unique in their odor because all companies used different chemical combinations to process ore.

Outside might be cold, but the underground was always hot. Outside dry, inside the mine, dripping wet. Fresh air versus the heavy smell of blasted ammonium nitrate powder. A thousand miner's lamps could never capture the light of the sun. It was easy for some to forget worries and phobias because their work world was always on sensory overload. All around were enormous pieces of heavy equipment that seemed incongruous, given the space around them. It was a ship in a bottle. Outsiders expect working in a mine to be claustrophobic, but that phobia was rarely the reason men quit. Certainly the back end of a stope could get tight, shrinking down to maybe six feet in height, but it wasn't nearly as tight a squeeze as coal miners faced. They were often forced to crawl to chase a coal vein. In hardrock mines, vast sections of the underground were blasted into cavernous spaces that miners referred to as "rooms." There were hoist rooms, machine shops, and storage places scattered throughout hundreds of miles of working levels. Underground, coffeepots with stains so deep and dark no bleach could clean them perked all day long, and newspapers and magazines were stacked with the precision corners of a neat freak. Launhardt knew of one hoistman who actually waxed the floor every week. Pity the miner dumb enough to enter without making sure his boots were clean. Another man whose job was to service a hoist carried a grease rag in one hand and a polishing cloth in the other.

Some guys figured they could almost live down in the mine, and it was true. In the days before muck cars and rails, mules actually *did* live underground. Stone corrals beneath the surface contained the animals used to pull carts of muck to the hoist. Once pressed into such service, most mules never saw daylight again.

THE DEEPER LAUNHARDT DESCENDED TUESDAY MORNING, the hotter the rock became. Each hundred-foot drop brought an increase of one degree. At the surface, just past the opening of the Jewell Shaft, the temperature held steady at about 55 degrees, whether it was a hot summer day or a frigid Idaho winter. At the deepest part of the mine, the 5600 level, it was a sweltering 127 degrees. Mammoth booster ventilation fans and refrigeration units pushed more than 130,000 cubic feet of air through the mine to keep the conditions bearable at the lower depths. Cold water from Big Creek pulsed through the mine and emerged as hot as coffee when discharged into a tailings or waste pond on the surface. Even with all that had been learned in a century of mining at that location, the cooling system was far from perfect. Miners knew where the hotspots were at Sunshine—or at any other hardrock mine, because all mines had them. Only unlucky or inexperienced miners got stuck working in the devil's breath. Whenever the ventilation system failed, temperatures rose quickly and the air grew uncomfortably thin. *Rapidly.* Miners working farthest from a ventilation or intake airshaft to the surface, especially those in Sunshine's deepest reaches, would be in unbearably sweltering conditions in less than half an hour. The air temperature would surge to rock surface levels. Enduring temperatures close to 130 degrees for any amount of time was very risky.

Miners heard bosses talking about the importance of ventilation. But for those guys underground busting rock, the very idea that there was some great ventilation system bringing air throughout the working areas was nearly a joke. Large fans—the kind that made hurricanes howl on movie sets—huffed and puffed air through the mine the best that they could. But the air in the stopes and raises sometimes forced the thermometer to 115 degrees. A 50-ton chiller was installed on 4600 to cool ventilating air, but it didn't do all that was hoped— or promised. Men working in the lower levels used whiz-bangs— blowpipes with broad nozzles punched with holes—to spray cool compressed air into stifling work areas. Many actually preferred stope fans shut off because all they accomplished was to blow hot air at them, dry them out, and sap them of their strength. Fans also kicked around dust, which was bad enough without the high velocity of a blower. Many times, a foreman would return to a stope to find fans off and the men using compressed air. He'd raise a big stink about it, ordering the fans turned back on. *The goddamn compressed air is to run the machines. The fans are to cool off the men!* The minute he'd disappear down the raise, the fans would be shut off again.

Besides a money-producing ore body, nothing was more important to the workings of a hardrock mine than fresh air. Before compressed air, men collapsed from what was assumed to be heat and exertion, but was actually oxygen deprivation. Even with compressed air, the air in deep mines was thin and replete with residual gases from blasting.

6:30 A.M., MAY 2
Smelterville

CONTRACT MINER RON FLORY STOPPED IN AT HAPPY
Landing in Smelterville, a town surrounded by a dead ring of skele-
tal vegetation from Bunker Hill's towering and noxious lead smelter.
Flory, a big man with a gate-jaw and a goatee, filled his water jug with
ice from the bar's icemaker before catching a ride with his partner
Tom Wilkinson. Over in Woodland Park, outside of Wallace, mine
sanitation nipper Don Beehner picked up three Sunshine miners in
his red-and-white Volkswagen bus. Buz Bruhn's Mullan carpool
pulled over to give a lift to a Sunshine miner hitching to work on the
highway to Big Creek. Though it was only Tuesday morning, day-
shift silver miners had already discussed what they would be doing
on the weekend—or even *that* day, instead of working.

Wilkinson, Flory, and the others changed from their street clothes
to their diggers in Sunshine's dry house, usually called just "the dry,"
an enormous building of lockers, urinals, toilets, and communal
showers. Wet boots, diggers, and towels were suspended on hooks
and raised up to the ceiling by chains and pulleys, making for a kind
of hanging garden of miner's gear, drying in the breeze of a forced-
air furnace. Each shift was bookended in the dry. It was the place
where the men lightened the prospects of the day ahead, or blew off
steam from a disappointing dig that had yielded fewer muck-car
loads than expected. An average blast typically dumped thirty to
forty tons of ore and rock to be hauled out; anything less was a frus-
trating money loser. More so than any other place outside of the
bars, the men's dry was the place where miners could get to know
each other. Snippets of life echoed through the mammoth room.
Sometimes there were fistfights and angry altercations. A few times,
things were revealed that no one expected. A man who had custody
of two preschoolers worked a shift opposite his father, the kids'

grandfather. Every day the dad brought the kids into the dry. They'd sit and wait under the hangers while the shift diggered up. Then their grandfather would come out of the mine, shower, change, and take them home. This routine went on for quite some time. One searing summer day, a cager asked the kids if they wanted to cool off in the shower.

One immediately peeled off his clothes and started running around, laughing and having the time of his life. The younger kid thought that it looked like fun, too. In a split second there were two kids laughing in the shower, which was fine, except for one thing.

The smaller of the two was a girl.

Men around the shower towers grabbed washcloths and frantically tried to cover up. All those months of men wearing nothing but shower shoes playing grab-ass flashed through the mind of the man who'd made the offer. *Who knew that tot was a girl? And she's been running around here?*

Wilkinson's best buddy, Johnny Davis, was among the men in the dry getting ready to go underground on May 2, his twenty-eighth birthday. Davis was local through and through. He'd graduated from Mullan High School, enlisted in the Army, and, like so many of his classmates, returned to the district and the mines. He'd started as a weekend smelter helper at Bunker Hill and had done a small stint for Hecla mines before coming to Sunshine in November 1967.

Wilkinson tried to cajole his pal into skipping work. If Davis said yes, Wilkinson was sure Flory would probably give in, too.

"You ought to dump shift. Let's go get drunk," Wilkinson persisted. "It's your birthday, man."

Davis was tempted, and it seemed that he was going to say yes from under his thick mustache, but ultimately family obligations won out. He was married and had a kid of his own and two stepchildren.

"Nah," he said, "can't do it."

Wilkinson was only mildly disappointed. He'd figured they'd catch up for a few beers after shift.

WHATEVER MEN OF THE DISTRICT TOLD OUTSIDERS WAS their reason for going mining, Ron Flory's reasons were twofold. Yeah, the money was good, but he loved it even more because between the cage rides up and down, every day underground was different. Every day he felt privileged to work in a world that few ever see. The underground was a mystery to topsiders. They saw it as a dark, dank, unpleasant world of rock faces and brutal sameness. Those who didn't know metal mining, or who didn't respect where the silver came from for their camera film or for the conductive strands of metal that fired the circuitry on their cars or TVs, talked trash about the underground. *Cold as stone. Rocks in your head. Dumb as a rock. Where the sun don't shine.* The miners, many believed, were a born-to-lose, scruffy rabble who toiled with a pick and a shovel because they weren't smart enough to do anything better where the sun *did* shine. Good gyppo miners knew better. And those who couldn't gyppo and plugged away as pipe men or water guys looked at gyppos with deserved respect and even awe. Men like Flory saw great challenges in working a stope, shooting a face down just so. Meeting the unknown head-on was one of the rewards of mining. Understanding what the rock was saying when it talked was more relevant than speaking three languages and knowing what wine went with steak. Flory knew which formations meant good money and, conversely, what clues signaled a difficult and ultimately less profitable stope. Besides mere muscle, it took skill and fearlessness to get a round drilled and blasted, muck pulled, and the stope bolted, and then to do it all again.

No one knew it, of course, but on May 2 a man needed more than strength and daring. Ron Flory, his partner Tom Wilkinson, and 171 others were on their way to discovering just what it took to be a Sunshine miner, the Marines of the underground.

SINCE KELLOGG AND WALLACE WERE SO INSULAR—CULTUR-ally, geographically, and economically—most boys simply grew up knowing that mines waited on the other side of adolescence. Mines weren't traps, but they were whirlpools of sorts. Close to the edge, with a father or an uncle going mining, a young man found himself leaning over, curious. Before long, he was inside. It was like that for Ron Flory. His family had shuttled between Montana, Washington, New Mexico, and Idaho as his dad, Richard, worked the tramp miner's circuit. Home, however, was always Pine Creek in the Coeur D'Alenes. A Nazarene churchgoing woman of tested resilience, Belle Flory had raised five children on her husband's wildly fluctuating paychecks. The Florys never had a TV, though they always had electricity—when many neighbors and friends didn't. Whenever the mines went on strike, Richard Flory waited it out while his wife stretched macaroni until it snapped. It was a hard way to live, so when she finally booted him out, few were surprised. Belle Flory didn't leave the district. She couldn't. None of her family could leave. Ron Flory's brother, Bob, had long wanted to move away, but he also found himself working at Sunshine. The district, he began to believe, was like one of those open crab barrels he'd seen one time on Seattle's waterfront. The containers didn't have lids because they didn't need any. If a crab tried to escape, the others would grab it and pull it back.

Ron Flory had his dumb-kid brushes with the law and two years of Army service behind him when he came home to a miner's life. His father broke him in at Nancy Lee, a Kellogg-owned lead and silver producer near Superior, Montana. The idea that he could do something else for a living never really entered Flory's mind. Mining was a dirty, thankless job that someone had to do, and he didn't mind.

The only thing that got to him was the never-ending nighttime. It was dark in the morning before shift, the work was in the dark, and after shift it was dark outside. He was a mole. Sometimes the only way around it was to dump shift during the week.

Partner Tom Wilkinson went mining later. He'd tried working at Bunker Hill, where his dad had spent most of his career, but poor eyesight kept him topside. Surface jobs were all right, but they didn't reap the kind of paycheck he wanted—not when he saw the other kids he'd grown up with trading in cars whenever the mood suited them. Wilkinson had seen his father try other jobs, but the old man had always kept coming back to the mines. With each injury, with each downturn or strike, there was always the possibility that the subterranean pull would weaken. The worst of it came when a timber fell on his dad and broke or seriously ruptured several discs. The old man went back, but it was a struggle. He ended his career topside at Bunker Hill. At five feet six and 135 pounds, Wilkinson wasn't a big man, nor was he a particularly smooth talker. He was a tad rough around the edges and probably knew how to party better than anyone else in Smelterville. He'd dropped out of school, had been raised in part by his grandmother, and had even done some time in a boys' reform school in St. Anthony, Idaho. Frances Christmann, the daughter of a veteran miner, didn't care about any of that. If Wilkinson was a bad boy with eight tattoos and a cuss-filled mouth, there was something gentle about him, too. She was woman enough to see it. They dated for a couple of years and married on May 20, 1956. In time they had a daughter, Eileen, and a son, Tommy.

Wilkinson worked five tedious years smoothing the running grain of centuries-old Douglas fir on a planing machine at a Smelterville mill. Making housing-grade lumber was repetitive, and the income from the job predictably flat. Wilkinson rustled a job at Sunshine in 1970, joining two of his brothers already there. Six months later, he and his old school buddy Flory were partners.

Six

Visitors tended to fuse together Kellogg and Wallace as rough-and-tumble, hardscrabble, and indistinguishable. But in reality, while the neighboring towns shared origins and economics, they were more rivals than twins. Kellogg was a company town that sprang from the silvery profits and spillover goodwill of the Bunker Hill Mining Company. The lead, zinc, and silver producer was best known for its lead smelter, with its towering stacks spewing smoke, and its strings of lights that made the place look almost Christmas-like at night. Locals referred to the company as "Uncle Bunk." With a long tradition of local ownership and philanthropy—founding the YMCA, building swimming pools, and funding youth groups—Bunker Hill was the community's largest employer and most generous benefactor. Uncle Bunk almost always did right by his men. Even after the Gulf Resources and Chemical Corporation acquired it, residents still clung to the belief that Uncle Bunk would always look out for them. If a miner—or an office worker, for that matter—worked hard, there'd always be a job and food on the table. But with the shift from local ownership to outsiders, the 3,500 citizens of Kellogg began to understand that unbending loyalty was foolhardy.

The stand-ins for Bunker Hill's absentee management were often too fancy for local tastes. They weren't interested in being a part of the Coeur d'Alene Mining District's insular world. Most executives' wives shopped in Spokane. Kellogg, most certainly, didn't have what the well-heeled desired. Even worse was the unspoken understanding that time in Kellogg was merely a stop on a career path. Outsider managers from Los Angeles or San Francisco or New York City were always temporary, with roots planted back home.

A masonry and terra-cotta village that had barely changed architecturally from its 1880s origins, Wallace was fortunate to be the hometown of several mining corporations—Hecla and Day Mines being the preeminent ones. As such, Wallace, with its population of 2,200, wasn't as dependent on the corporate types who came to scavenge at Kellogg. Wallace's companies actually *lived* in, and mixed with, the community. In a Wallace bar like the 1313 Club, it wouldn't be unusual to have two men in a heated argument over mining or even politics—the only thing remarkable would be that one man was a miner and the other a CEO.

Those who live in them know that rivalries drive small towns. When boys morph into men, home territory becomes sacred. In the mining district, the battle over which sports teams were better—*which town was better*—sometimes turned intense. Parking-lot posturing frequently led to black eyes and petty vandalism, sometimes worse. One time a pack of boys wearing Kellogg Wildcats letter jackets took a baseball bat to the windows of a Wallace High School bus, leaving a row of jagged holes and a parking lot that glittered like a

Vegas showgirl. The rivals were pretty evenly split in athletic prowess, allowing both towns to claim bragging rights. Most of the time, the Wallace Miners were the football team to beat, while the Wildcats had the upper hand in basketball.

In the 1940s and 1950s, Wallace billed itself as "the richest little city in the world." Kellogg would never dare such a Chamber of Commerce slogan. In fact, strangers knew Kellogg as the dirtiest town in America.

CAREER SUNSHINE MINER CHARLIE CLAPP KNEW THAT HIS rowdy son, Dennis, was a schoolyard fight away from a trip to St. Anthony's, and he wasn't about to let that happen. He moved his family from Wallace to Moon Gulch, seven miles from Kellogg. Dennis couldn't have been more pissed off, or more dejected. Though only in sixth grade, he was a Wallace kid to his bones. Kellogg reeked. Heavy, leaden smoke ensnared the town. Not only did Uncle Bunk's lead smelter put a gray lid over everything, but it encroached on every aspect of life—even those most sacred sports fields. The grounds staff made a valiant effort to keep the high school football field Foster Grant green, but to no avail. The smelter claimed the turf. The Kellogg track team had to huff and puff through smoke at home, and frequently did better on road trips outside the kill zone. Rivals hated playing on the Kellogg field of cocoa-powder dirt. Yet, for longtime residents, there was beauty in the discharge from the enormous smokestacks. It was a symbol of prosperity. Coming from poorer towns made it easier for most to shrug off the stink, or blink away the stinging air.

Football saved Dennis Clapp's childhood. At the time in a boy's life when nothing matters more, the Wildcats were the better district football team. Miners' sons battled on the barren Kellogg gridiron, dusting off and putting an end to disagreements their fathers had a mile underground. When Clapp graduated in 1967, he was a member of one of the biggest classes in Kellogg High history, with 299 classmates. And like many of his pals, Clapp took a temporary job at Sunshine while he contemplated what he'd do with his life. When summer ended, he just stayed put. *And why not?* He had cash in his pocket, and a cherry '57 Chevy that he buffed to a mirror shine. By working underground, guys like Dennis Clapp had the opportunity to make serious cash.

MINERS CHAFED A HEAVY BACK-AND-FORTH LINE BETWEEN the mines in Butte, Montana, and those strung through the Coeur d'Alene Mining District. In hard times, when certain metal prices dipped low, companies cut back on crews and sent men packing for other, more viable operations. Labor disputes also sent miners from one place to another. Even so, men on both sides of the state line were fiercely loyal to their roots and to the guys who came from home. Coeur d'Alene men always thought they were better miners than those fellows from Butte. In Kellogg and Wallace, working three days in a row was known as a "Butte ringer," as in "I got my Butte ringer in." District men figured Montana miners took off Fridays to get an early start on the weekend and missed Mondays because they were too hungover to make it to work. Montana miners made similar jibes at Idaho miners.

In the late 1950s some Butte mines faltered, while most of Idaho's held steady. Kenny "Ace" Riley, eighteen at the time, couldn't rustle a job where his father mined. When a referral came from his brother-in-law, already at Sunshine, Riley, a reed of a young man at only 135 pounds, fibbed about his weight on his job application and was hired as a miner's helper.

Before he left town, his dad offered a warning.

"Once you've mined," he said, "you'll never get out of it. It'll grab ahold of you."

The senior Riley's words were prophetic. Every day was an adrenaline fix, like a motorcycle on Lookout Pass at speeds above ninety miles an hour. *Take the turn a little tighter, go a little faster. Feel the air and watch the world blur right by.* Working underground provided a rush, with blasts shaking the mine, rock tumbling down, and the certainty that anything could happen. After a shift, in the back of a miner's mind there'd always be the thought: *Cheated death again today, and got paid pretty good for it.* Riley loved it, and life was good.

Competition was another draw of working underground. Men pushed it even harder, maybe even took a few chances that they shouldn't, because they had something to prove. And being the biggest, strongest, and toughest was the brass ring. A miner's identity, his reputation, was based not only on how much muck he pulled and therefore how much money he made, but also on the size of his balls.

When he was thirty, married and the father of five sons, Riley learned that the price of the rush could exceed its value. Sometimes devastatingly so. In March 1970 he was partnered with Bernelle Brown, a forty-two-year-old dreamer with a college education and a love for the big fat stack of cash that came with the mining life. It was a hellish 100-plus degrees in their stope on 4600, a wet atmosphere that sapped energy like a virus. At around 9:30 they opened a water line and let it run over their heads, shaking off the excess like dogs out of the river. They made small talk, smoked, and returned to drop more ore, but found that the chute was clogged. Lagging, or boards, had been carelessly placed across the chute by the night crew, but neither man knew it. Brownie started poking at the rock with a steel, and in a second, a thunderclap of rock and muck sounded as the world gave way to gravity and pressure. Riley lunged for Brownie, but no man could have been fast enough. Brownie, the muck, and the lagging under his feet swirled down the chute like a backed-up sink drain that had finally found relief, instantly killing the father of five. Neither man had worn a safety harness because both had believed the area was stable, and belts were too much of a bother anyway.

No one who lost a partner was ever the same afterward. The event kidnapped the survivor's psyche for the rest of his life. It was a footnote that never vanished. Whenever Riley heard the song "Swing Low, Sweet Chariot," he'd think of his fallen partner. For some reason, Brownie had been singing that song that day.

IF DANGER WAS A MINER'S HEROIN, MANY WHO WORKED underground were junkies. For Howard Markve, a week shy of turning twenty-nine, the suggestion that his life was on the line every minute underground became a compulsion. Standing on the raise climber's steel deck, two hundred feet above the track, a light from a cap lamp casts a beam into a darkness of rock, talking and popping. The raise climber's deck is the size of a dining table, and the miner standing on it doesn't really know, with complete certainty, which way that quarter-ton rock will fall, or if the rock that rains down will be small and just a nuisance, or like a load of bricks being hurled from above. Miscalculate a pivot, and a wife is a widow. It was that live-or-die thrill that held Markve, husband and father of two, spellbound. He understood how sky divers felt when parachute cords felt a little sticky.

At fifty-three, Bob Follette was considerably older than Markve. Most men his age had been exiled to the surface, but Follette wasn't ready to concede to the inevitable. He'd been a Sunshine miner since 1967, having first proved himself as a contract miner at the famed Homestake gold mine in Lead, South Dakota. Homestake miners like Follette, Markve, and Markve's father-in-law, Louis Goos, were among the best in the district. Homestake's rock was harder than Sunshine's, and pulling an eight-foot round there gave a man serious bragging rights. Part of what brought Follette and others to Sunshine was its reputation for putting contract miners above all others. Homestake bosses hovered like flies on roadkill, telling a man what to do and how he ought to do it. At Sunshine, not only was a man compensated with a decent paycheck, but he was left to do things his way.

On the morning of May 2, Ace Riley grabbed his dinner bucket and left Wallace for Sunshine, where he'd connect with his partner, a tough sonofabitch named Joe Armijo. Howard Markve and Louis Goos drove in from Wallace and Osburn. Bob Follette picked up his son, Bill, at the Rose Lake exit off the interstate. The younger Follette was partnered with Goos. They all met up at the portal to ride the cage to working levels.

7:45 A.M., MAY 2
Smelterville

HER HUSBAND HAVING GONE TO WORK, MYRNA FLORY finished her smoke and looked in on her toddler, Paul, nicknamed Tiger. She glanced at the laundry and planned her day. Though only eighteen, Myrna Keene Flory had the kind of weary eyes that told others she'd seen it all. She had been used and abused. She'd had a baby as a teenager. Though some would say she'd been scrunched up and dragged through a knothole, Myrna was still a fighter, the kind of survivor who had the ability to tap into hidden mental and physical reserves when circumstances required it. Myrna was born in Butte, one of ten kids of a West Virginia coal miner who'd made his way out west to try his hand at hardrock mining. In 1968, when underground jobs in Butte gave way to surface jobs associated with pit-mining operations, Myrna's parents had loaded up their belongings and moved to a little house on Riverside Avenue in Kellogg. Kellogg and the rest of the district was a job hunter's paradise. Every place with a halfway decent ore body was hiring. A job at the zinc plant or mining at Bunker Hill or Star or

Sunshine could be had by anyone with a little experience and the ambition for a regular paycheck.

During Myrna's teenage years, Kellogg was also a place where turbo-jetted hot tubs froze over in winter because miners couldn't scrape up the cash to pay both the utility bill *and* the snowmobile dealer. Months making ends meet were followed by spending sprees that promised never to end, though they always did. And while see-sawing bank accounts were a part of living in Kellogg, a few things remained constant, too. Each night when the sun dipped low, miners crammed into local taverns to drink away the day's profits and to talk about mining. From stools in front of beer-sloshed bars, men relived every moment of their hours in the dark.

There wasn't much for teens to do, except drink and party up in the hills or on a sandbar along the Coeur d'Alene River. Every day in the summer, carloads of kids went down the river from one keg to the next. It was a mining town with mining kids, and drinking was more than a right of passage. Parents played rough; so did the kids. A pretty girl with precision-parted long hair, Myrna had grown up with the belief that most miners' kids could drink an adult under the table. Certainly any adult from outside the district.

Throughout the district, it only took three things to be considered cool. A guy had to have a pickup, a gun, and a dog. A girl just had to have the guy.

Myrna Keene was sixteen and pregnant when she met Ron Flory, a twenty-six-year-old miner with the kind of booming voice that effortlessly cut through the raucous clamor of the underground. Myrna always knew she'd end up being a miner's wife; she just assumed that the man who had made her pregnant would do the right thing. He didn't. Ron Flory came along at the right time to pick up the pieces. In Myrna Keene, the shy miner saw a young woman, though in some ways she was still very much a girl. She needed a decent man to look after her. So did the baby. They married on

Christmas Eve 1970 in Coeur d'Alene. Flory made a good living, and whatever his very young wife wanted, she got. When he arrived home from the mine, he worked on their modest trailer or tinkered with his car. On the weekends they followed the music to the Happy Landing or to the Sunshine Inn's Jackass Room—named for the small burro that 1880s prospector Noah Kellogg said led him to a galena outcropping that founded the great Bunker Hill. The legend gave rise to a common refrain among out-of-district mudslingers: "What do you expect from a town discovered by a jackass?"

Though most men would be loath to admit it, Ron Flory loved to dance. Myrna never had to beg him to come out on the dance floor. As a big guy, a barrel-chested fellow with Popeye forearms that went white at his biceps, Flory could handle his booze. In turn, Myrna could handle *him*. The match was good. Mining was a dangerous wild card, and all young wives like Myrna knew it. And so when the mine siren called from the mountain, or when word got out that an ambulance had blazed up to the mine, Myrna joined other wives as miners' wives had done for almost a century. They waited. Some worried. Some agonized. And over and over inside their heads, as they fed their children and did their laundry, they'd think of their men: *Call me. Come home.*

Myrna and her older sister Garnita were close in the way that only sisters who'd survived rough times can be. They had other siblings, but the two had remained especially devoted from the days in Butte when Garnita Keene would help her sister get dressed, or brush out her pretty brunette hair. When she got older, and was no longer the kid sister with the hair in need of brushing, Myrna still sought out her sister as a sounding board. When both were living in Kellogg—Myrna, seventeen, and a just-separated Garnita, twenty—the two took up where they'd left off. They partied together and obsessed about their love lives. And whenever Garnita got into a cleaning binge, Myrna put dibs on anything her sister was going to throw out.

A tiny blond with cobalt eyes, Garnita Keene was the single mother of two little girls, living in an uptown Kellogg apartment and waiting tables at the Sunshine Inn to get by. She'd dated a few locals and did her share of partying. But when she met Sunshine miner Billy Allen, she knew she had met someone who stood out from the others. Allen was a good-looking guy of twenty-four, with a couple of small scars on the bridge of his nose and a head of thick, dark hair. More than anything, it was Allen's grin that hooked her heart. It was the kind of smile that was both sweet and sexy. Garnita and Allen made a pretty picture—trim, young, and alive. There was one complication, however. Allen was separated from his wife, who had taken their toddler daughter and preschool son back to Arkansas to live with her parents. Divorce papers had been filed in Shoshone County in late 1970, but neither side had taken the final steps.

On Sunday, Allen picked up Garnita for a drive along the north fork of the Coeur d'Alene past Kingston to a riverside roadhouse called the Snake Pit. His '67 Chevy Impala in a Cataldo transmission shop, he drove a borrowed pickup truck that in reality wasn't a much more reliable ride. They parked across from what was known by everyone in the district as "the black bridge," even though it was painted a dark shade of red, and went inside the Snake Pit for a couple of beers for the road. Allen was in a good mood. Fired up, having fun. Garnita half-hoped, maybe even deluded herself a little, that the young miner would eventually fall in love with her and forget about his wife. Actually make her the ex-wife. That Sunday evening, however, it was still as clear as it had been on other occasions: Allen was a long way from that. He was planning a trip to see his on-again, off-again wife and their children. He was back living at home in Pinehurst and sharing a bedroom with his younger brother, but his mind and heart were set on the future. Garnita just didn't know where, and if, she fit in.

Up the river, the pickup overheated and sent a bloom of steam into the chilly air, and Allen climbed down the muddy riverbank to fill a small container of water. Garnita offered to help, but Allen shook his head, waved her back into the cab, and flashed his smile.

"I can handle it," he said.

Two hours later, Allen parked in front of Garnita's parents' place on Riverside Avenue, where her children were sleeping in an upstairs bedroom. He leaned over and kissed her good night.

"Call you later," he said, driving away in a cloud of exhaust. And again, the smile.

Seven

ITS FAÇADE WASN'T IMPRESSIVE, BUT IT DIDN'T NEED TO BE. The Big Creek Store was a plain wood-frame building, low-slung, with windows trimmed out by a thick and crackled coat of forest green paint. A pair of gas pumps jutted from the weedy lot out front. The tavern and store was only one of many miners' hangouts in the district and was only really distinguished by its location. At just a few hundred yards down from Sunshine, it was the easiest place for the miner in a hurry to get a beer. It was also the social center of the Big Creek community. To the right of the front door was a twelve-foot bar with a candy counter and a cash register. Opposite the bar were a pool table and a handful of tables where miners would drink, play liar's poker, or just talk until they were sure their pissed-off wives had gone to sleep. At the back of the store were the living quarters of perpetually irritated owner George Dietz. Dietz served more draft than root beer, along with pretty tasty chili and cabbage rolls. After shift change, the place burst at the seams.

Yes, tough muthas though they were, arms wallpapered with blurry-edged tattoos and scars that wrapped around like wet jute, the men who lined up at Dietz's bar were surprisingly tenderhearted—especially when it came to their families. Whether they lived in town with a brood of five or had been on the tramp-mining circuit so long they hadn't seen them in months or longer—their kids came first. *My kid's doing this. My kid's going to college.* And so on, like grandmas with their photo album brag books, men climbed onto the Big Creek's barstools and yakked about their kids. They also talked about their cheating wives with tears rolling into a half-empty schooner one minute and the angry promise to even up the score with a Wallace prostitute the next. Mostly, however, they talked of mining. There was always someone to listen. From time to time the tavern became a good place for a fight. Dietz strived to stop things before they started, but many of his patrons thought it wasn't a good night if there weren't a couple of fat lips and some bruised egos. The source of most rows was the reason men went there every night. It certainly wasn't the women. It was mining. Who could pull a better round? Who knew better than anyone how to make the rock do exactly what was needed? Squabbles that started inside the Big Creek Store sometimes ended in the parking lot. The best skirmishes concluded with a trip to the ER or the Shoshone County Jail.

Among the very few who never set foot in that bar was Bob Launhardt. He wasn't a complete teetotaler, but close. Even when he was a pipe fitter, and among the lower echelon of the mining hierarchy, he stayed away from Sunshine's favorite watering hole. Had he spent some time there, he might have learned that the Big Creek Store was a training ground for future miners. Boys would sit with colas, listening to miners bitch about their women, brag about their mining prowess, and generally strengthen the bonds that made them more a fraternity than outsiders could ever imagine. By the time a Big Creek kid was ready to go to work, he already had the soul of a Sunshine miner.

IN THE SPRING OF 1972, BIG CREEK NATIVE RANDY PETERSON, twenty-three, had been among a group of laid-off Sunshine workers, part of the company's cycle of managing the ups and downs of the metals market. But by May 2, he'd been called back and was caging with a coppery-headed nineteen-year-old named Roger Findley. Peterson was one of the few who didn't want to mine. The son of a hoistman, Peterson had returned to Big Creek after a brutal tour of duty in Vietnam. And while there were other things the capable young man could do, Sunshine paid $1.25 an hour more than a previous job with the highway department. Even better, working underground meant actually working *less* than six hours a day because travel time from portal to portal was paid, as negotiated by the union. It was just too sweet a deal to pass up.

Even though Peterson and Findley weren't miners, they understood the pride of being one. It went beyond mind-boggling physical strength and relentless stamina. Certainly the hot temperatures of mines like Sunshine and Star were given their due by tramp miners from California and Nevada mines. A lot of those men just couldn't make the grade in northern Idaho mines. To be considered a miner in the Coeur d'Alenes, a man had to know how to drive a drift, run a raise, and work a stope. To be a *real* miner, a man had to drill, blast, muck, timber, bolt, and do it all in a day's work. Sunshine miners scoffed at their supposed counterparts down in Nevada. A man down there did only one thing. He might drill all day. He might load explosives all day. He was a cog in a process that kept him from really getting in there and mining. Being a Sunshine miner was being an all-around miner, and that meant working in most jobs before going mining. Running the cage was another step on the way.

Cagers and hoistmen usually came on shift a half hour before other crews showed up. First, in accordance with state and federal law, they'd test the cage by running the conveyance up and down the shaft. The first men down ahead of the working men—foremen, supervisors, and shifters—made up what was known in the district as the "meat run." Running the cage, or "caging," was nothing more than an elevator operator's job. Even so, it commanded a certain amount of respect. The relationship between cage tender and hoistman—one the eyes and ears of the operation, the other the machine-powered muscle—was crucial to any mining operation. Not only did they have to work completely in tandem, separated by thousands of feet of darkly lit shaft with men tethered in cages that hurled from level to level, but the best of them did so with a kind of finesse that recalled the great pitcher-and-catcher pairs of the major leagues. A good hoistman could read his cage tender's bell signals and know what kind of mood the fellow was in that day, or if in fact it was him ringing or another guy. Same with the cage tender. He knew by the way the hoist stopped at a level if his buddy was running it way up in the hoist room, or if some other guy had taken over while he went to the shitter. The squawker, a buzzer system, let the hoistman know what level they were at when a ride up or down was needed. The bells chimed when the cage tender wanted the hoistman to know just where they were going. It was all done in a rudimentary code. Sunshine's station signal for traveling to 3700 10-Shaft was three rings of the bell, then a short pause, then four bells, and another pause before adding one more ring for *up* and two more for *down*. The electric stroke bells on the main station of the Jewell were enormous and cast from brass. One hit 87 decibels and the other 93. No one doubted the hoistman who said he could hear the bells ringing in his sleep.

With lunch ten minutes away, Randy Peterson and Roger Findley listened politely as shaft foreman Fred "Gene" Johnson showed them how to do things *his* way with some timbers and fan lines before announcing that he had to head out to the Jewell. Working with Johnson always meant jumping to it. The sooner a guy came to terms with that, the better everyone got along. Peterson didn't mind Sunshine's most demanding boss. Despite Johnson's hard-ass persona, Peterson respected the shaft foreman because he knew his business.

10:45 A.M., MAY 2

Underground

SAFETY ENGINEER BOB LAUNHARDT FINISHED HIS MORNING rounds at about the same time brusque Gene Johnson left his two cage tenders. Launhardt felt good. He liked going underground, the daily reminder that there was directness and simplicity to metal mining. If his old man, a farmer, could see the tangible world of mining, Launhardt believed he'd completely understand the appeal and the simplicity. If crops failed, there was no money.

Growing up on a farm during the Dust Bowl years in Collinsville, Illinois, Bob Launhardt was one of five born to a taskmaster father and a sickly and sometimes emotionally chilly mother. Both parents were strict, remote, and deeply religious. Launhardt would later reason that they were only products of their own German Lutheran upbringing, one that drummed into their psyches a work ethic that made no allowance for the extras, like nurturing children. It was just as well. The Depression years were not for merrymaking, anyway. But in all fairness, his mother and father occasionally exhibited a kinder side. Bob's dad taught him to drive a tractor at six, and a car at nine. His mother was a terrific cook; her angel food cakes nudged the clouds.

For more than three years a field-cracking drought and coughing wind mowed over struggling crops, and the family's cash reserves dwindled to next to nothing. Praying for rain was an exercise in futility, but it was practiced daily. Chickens died and window ledges were covered with a traceable film of dust and poultry feathers. Launhardt's mother's asthma worsened during those years, but there was no real treatment besides confinement to an oxygen tent. The pressure exacerbated his father's remote nature, until it turned his anger outward. He repeatedly told Bob and his older brother that they were "not worth their salt," words that would echo in Bob Launhardt's mind for the rest of his life. Nothing he could do would make his father happy. Launhardt left home at seventeen and enrolled in a Lutheran prep school and seminary college in Missouri, with plans to be a minister. His future was his own plan, a personal road map that called for discipline with caring. His plan was on course until his uncle Bill, a gold prospector who had seen the country from Alaska to California, made an offer of a summer job in Idaho. That changed everything.

THE TALACHE MINING COMPANY IN ATLANTA, IDAHO, WAS in its declining years when Bob Launhardt, then nineteen, arrived to shatter rock in the summer of 1951. In its heyday, decades before, the Talache was the largest gold producer in the state—and one of the best gold mines in the country. It was located in a remote spot in the mountains along the middle fork of the Boise River. The little camp swelled and shrank over the years, following the availability of ore, the advances of metal recovery techniques, and the switch from donkeys to machines. Launhardt's first three days on the job were spent shoveling fallen rock from an exploration drift into a muck car and depositing the worthless load in the waste dump. Not exciting, but decent work. After each night's rest, Launhardt returned to find as much muck in his working area as had been there before his shift the previous day. It was mystifying. Finally, someone copped to the reason. They'd been working in a place of "rotten ground" where the rock above the timbers was so fractured that it rained pebble- and marble-sized pieces all night long. Sometimes bigger pieces, two hundred pounds or more, dropped, too. It certainly wasn't the safest job, but Launhardt was young and not one to complain, anyway. His next assignment there was no better. The Talache foreman had the lanky young man drilling and loading old—and volatile—gelatin dynamite into a new raise. He didn't offer any training, just a quick send-off.

"Here's your buzzy," he said, indicating a 104 Gardner-Denver drill with a telescoping leg that gave it its other nickname, jackleg. "Here's your drill steel. We'll bring you some powder this afternoon."

The foreman, with big, leathery catcher's-glove hands, pointed to the back of a darkened stope and told Launhardt to get busy.

"Just start drilling, son."

No mention of the importance of safety was offered. Just the command to get going.

The Illinois teen worked alone, drilling, blasting, and running the raise like some goddamn movie miner. When timbering, he'd lower a rope to track level and an unseen helper would tie on a five-foot timber and Launhardt would haul it up. He'd set it above two posts and wedge it into place. The pressure of the rock—quite literally the weight of the world—held it in place. No spikes were used at the Talache. Wedges of wood were shimmed into cracks and along pressure points to ensure a snug fit. It was only the grace of God and the work of men that kept mines like the Talache from collapsing.

Back then, Launhardt earned a passable $10.25 a day and rented a house for $10 a month. Electricity set him back $20—the cost of mining in a remote place and being at the mercy of those who made a living off miners. With his mother in a hospital oxygen tent with asthma, Launhardt sent most of his paychecks back home. He didn't need money, anyway. For a mining town, the place was surprisingly straitlaced and quiet. He made a few good friends, including a father-and-son team, Delbert and Duwain Crow. That fall he returned to Illinois for his second year in seminary and was assigned to his home parish. He soon realized the politics of running a church was not to his liking. He was a solitary figure, a man who didn't want to be enmeshed in consensus-building. He figured he'd serve in the Army and figure out his life. Launhardt notified the draft board only to find the Army wouldn't take him—he was legally blind in one eye. His uncle's words, which couldn't have made sense without the experience at the Talache, took hold. *Mining gets into your blood. No one knows why, but it does.* Tall, skinny, and excited by the adventure, Launhardt drove his '48 Chevy west, and when he hit Kellogg, he knew he'd made it home. He moved into the Crows' little house, two blocks from the post office. His first day at Sunshine was March 13, 1954. He started at the bottom, earning $13.70 a day.

Around that time, Sunshine was in the throes of a fight with the miner's union. The tradition of union and management unrest and distrust, in fact, was deep and bloody in the Coeur D'Alenes. North Idaho had been the site of some of the most brutal and divisive labor uprisings in American history. For a decade prior to the turn of the last century, the Coeur d'Alene Mining Wars had drenched the district in miners' blood. Miners wanted a bigger piece of the stake that was making mine owners rich. They traded their picks for rifles, hijacked trains, and bombed Bunker Hill's mill. But of all district mines during recent history, Sunshine probably saw the most discord between labor and management.

Since the 1950s the feds were convinced that communists ran the unions, and that Sunshine, in particular, was a hotbed of commies. Sunshine job applications required new hires to disclose whether they were affiliated with the Communist Party. When Launhardt was a new hire, there was talk among some of the men that he was an FBI plant who'd come to get the goods on the miners and their potentially subversive activities.

Once he was better known and trusted, a fellow pulled him aside. "You just don't fit in here," he said. "In a way, you're lucky to be alive. You're lucky someone didn't throw you down the shaft."

Launhardt shrugged it off. He felt luckier for another reason. He'd found the woman he'd marry.

WHEN JANET NOYEN WAS SEVEN, HER PARENTS, BILL AND Hazel Noyen, purchased the Wayside Grocery on Smelterville's main drag. It was 1946, and the town was in its heyday, with a movie theater, another market, a drugstore and soda fountain, car dealerships, and a nice little public park where kids could swing. Smelterville was packed with the kids of miners and loggers. It was a place where splashing in the milky water of Lead Creek—the runoff from tailings left by Bunker Hill and other district operators—came with a warning. Kids were admonished to rinse off after a swim and never to drink the water. But no one was afraid to play in it. In the beginning, Launhardt fretted over the green metallic finish of his car, a Chrysler convertible. Every now and then, acid rain would pelt Smelterville and Kellogg, mottling the paint on cars. Launhardt saw how others just accepted the air quality and the problems born of living in an industrial area trapped in a valley. Smelter smoke was an irritant to the upper respiratory system and bronchial tubes, but as far as anyone knew, it wouldn't kill people. Livestock, maybe.

Tall, blond, and very pretty, Janet Noyen certainly wasn't the first high school girl to have a crush on an older man. Launhardt was seven years her senior, a man with a steady job at Sunshine *and* a convertible with Scotch plaid upholstery. They met at the American Lutheran Church in Kellogg, where he was Luther League adviser. Handsome and brainy, Launhardt was the kind of man who listened and processed his words before offering an opinion. They married on September 2, 1956, and moved into one of the rental houses that barnacled the route to the mine. Not long afterwards, the Launhardts bought a house at the apex of an invisible triangle that ran between the two most important buildings in the community— the Sunshine Mine manager's house and the Big Creek Store. The community also included Sunshine housing, a neighborhood of forty-two company-owned residences, most of which were three bedrooms ("built for families") with appliances that included an electric range, a hot water heater, and a floor furnace. Sunshine leased the houses by the year, with rents averaging around $45 a month. By far the most extravagant of Big Creek's residences was the mine manager's mansion, a big white colonial built by the company in 1935. It had a maid's quarters, a kitchen with a paneled dining room, and a drawing room that always smelled of cigars and whiskey. Miners dubbed it "the guest house" because no one stayed there long.

The Launhardts settled into a nice, comfortable life. Janet ran the household while her husband worked underground as a pipe fitter up the road at Sunshine. She learned to deal with the dull ache of worry when she felt the rumble of a rockburst. Sometimes it felt as if a mini-earthquake shook the house, tinkling the dishes in the sink drainer and jostling the floorboards. Living in Big Creek gave Launhardt an even stronger dose of the daily rhythm of the mining life. Riding the bright orange Sunshine Mining Company buses with men from Wallace, Osburn, and Kellogg also provided the young pipe fitter with a better look into the lives of others caught up in the rhythm. Younger miners tended to drive to work, so the miners on the bus were often older down-and-outers, or those who just plain didn't own a car because they spent their money elsewhere. A few got in at one of the whorehouses in Wallace and Kellogg, indicating how they'd spent their nights. Boozy breath and talk of screwing some barmaid or waitress filled the stagnant air and shocked the former theology student. It didn't fit with his memories of Talache gold miners. The Sunshine crowd was nothing like those homebody miners. The men on the bus were seasoned tramp miners, and their lives were like their military or jail tattoos, ragged and colorful as hell. After shift, the men would leave Sunshine's parking lot, trails of cigarette smoke and cranked-up country music trumpeting the end of the day. And one after another they would slow down and rejoin the horde in front of the Big Creek Store. Launhardt pumped his brakes to squeeze past traffic, but he never stopped inside.

Bob Launhardt was a family man. In December 1957, his son, Rob, was born. Almost a year and a half later his daughter Julie followed. In 1962, baby Jeannie arrived. By then Launhardt had moved up the union ranks to chief grievance committeeman and finally president of the local. He was a good organizer and leader, and he did the paperwork that others couldn't be bothered with. When offered the safety job at the mine, he said yes.

On the morning of May 2, 1972, his inspection complete, Launhardt caught the cage to the surface and made his way to the showers in the shifters' dry. The cleanup was needed. Grime rolled around his collar, and his black hair clung to the nape of his sweaty neck. The trip underground had been extraordinarily swift. It was the only time he'd made it back topside before lunch.

Eight

THE LATE-MORNING ROUTINE ON 5000 WAS INTERRUPTED with an altercation between Butte transplant Ace Riley; his partner, Joe Armijo; and their shift boss, Bob Anderson. Riley and Armijo were angry that the stope they had been working was a loser, and they wanted another—one that would give up sufficient muck to pay out decent gyppo money. Riley, thirty-two, wasn't shy about making his point known, and his boss didn't care much for his attitude. Anderson refused to commit to getting them out of that stope without having to lose any pay. Riley and Armijo wanted action right then and there, but Anderson was more concerned about the day's production. He wanted them to get back to work and shoot their round. They'd talk about another stope later.

But Riley, a man with a deep bullfrog voice and an admitted hot temper, wouldn't let up. "There's no sense in taking that round today, or in doing *anything* more here."

Anderson turned away. Riley, his dark, wavy hair and long side-burns dripping with sweat, got angry and switched on his drill and turned his back. It was a kind of "fuck you, boss" stance that miners frequently employed. No man can argue when he can't hear a word. Anderson paid it no attention and left just before 11:00 a.m.

11:00 A.M., MAY 2
4600 Level

THE DAY'S TEMPO TOPSIDE WAS A LOT SLOWER ON THE morning of May 2 because it was the day of the company's annual shareholders' meeting. Most of the big bosses were gone. The men at the geology and engineering department took a little longer with their coffee and newspapers in the break room of the dull-yellow and blue building across from the administrative offices. They lingered, waiting for the paperwork to arrive from the shifter's shack with instructions about which stopes needed sampling.

Larry Hawkins, twenty-eight, was one of several Sunshine rock technicians, or "rock rabbits." A big man at six feet and 220 pounds, he considered his job every bit as vital to the fortunes of the company as mining ore. The company, which frequently scrimped on development work, needed to know where the highest-grade ore was coming from and how much it could expect. Hawkins's job was to map the specific location of ore bodies and to retrieve samples from corresponding headings. That required charting the length and depth of the stope and the width of the vein on graph paper. The angle of the ore body was also recorded. A little hammer chipped off samples that he put in a little white canvas bag and ticketed for the assay office.

Rock rabbits weren't always welcome. Some miners figured they'd become experienced enough that they could see or even *taste* the quality of ore in their stopes. They didn't need a damned scientist to tell them they were working a second-rate stope—or one that was going to make them a buttload of money. Most gyppo miners were annoyed that they had to stop to let the technician do his work. Stopping cost them money. A few were always ready to catch a smoke break. *Just one cigarette, though.* Any longer and they'd get aggravated, too.

When the paperwork came, Hawkins, dressed in diggers, went down to 4600 to climb down the raise to 11 stope on 4800. The morning was a little quiet, oddly so. It seemed that the miners on the station at 4600 had kicked back a little early. A couple of the guys had removed work belts laden with tools and cap-lamp battery packs. Another was sleeping. There wasn't much bullshitting going on. Hawkins tied up the cords of a sample bag and looked around. *Seems like some of those guys must have had a rough night,* he thought. It was a little early for napping, as some men did every day during lunchtime, from eleven to eleven-thirty.

Hawkins finished and rode the cage up to the so-called blue room on 3700. Nobody who worked at Sunshine was really sure about how the foremen's hangout came to be painted a hue somewhere between baby blue and the bottom of a swimming pool. Some thought the color scheme went back to the 1950s, maybe earlier. Whenever it was, it was clear that someone had had some extra paint and decided that nearly every surface of the blasted-out room should be coated in pale blue. A substation, cordoned off with chain link, took up one end of the fifty-foot space. At the opposite end was a fourteen-foot-long desk with several benches—painted blue, of course. Shifters met there, ate, and did paperwork. Fluorescent and incandescent lighting kept the whole thing illuminated with a cool glow in one of the hottest sections of the mine. Gene Johnson, Harvey Dionne, and the Bush brothers, Bob and Jim, were among the men talking and drinking coffee when Hawkins arrived. It was a ten-minute ride on a Mancha Midget, a small, passenger-only, battery-powered train used to travel through much of the mine. Running a motor brought a little rush. It wasn't the life-and-death excitement of mining a stope or running a shaft, but it wasn't completely devoid of danger. Reeling down a track at fifteen miles an hour was fun—like a Disneyland ride on eighteen-inch gauge rails. At the Jewell, Hawkins took the cage to the surface, the brilliant light of day pouring in from the portal.

11:30 A.M., MAY 2
3700 Level

SHAFT REPAIRMAN AND MECHANIC JACK HARRIS AND HIS partner, Keith Breazeal, finished tightening bolts on the head frame of a new borehole on the 3700 level and returned the length of the drift to the station at 10-Shaft. Some of the passageway was barely six feet in height, suitable for a mine car but not for walking without affecting a Quasimodo stoop. It was lunchtime at the mechanics shop, where a bunch of miners, motormen, and other laborers assembled to eat and talk about their mornings. At almost fifty, Harris was one of the older men underground. Harris had been a mucker, a motorman, a cager, and finally a shaft repairman on graveyard, then day shift. It was a good life, and for the most part, time flew underground. Time to start, time to eat, and time to go home. He and his wife and their houseful of eight kids lived just down the road from the mine. Big Creek and Sunshine—everything a man needed—was right there. A sentimental fellow, Harris never removed a ring that his mother had made out of a steel nut when she worked at a Seattle shipyard during World War II.

After eating, Harris and Breazeal waited for the chippy to load up with timbers before the ride to 4400 for offloading. Cagers Randy Peterson and Roger Findley finished their work, and Harris, Breazeal, and Delbert "Dusty" Rhoads, a mechanic, stepped on. Breazeal pulled a cart with an acetylene torch and an oxygen canister. When they reached 4400, Harris noticed a light wisp of smoke coming down the shaft.

"What the——?"

Peterson and Rhoads got off to source the smoke, and Findley, Harris, and Breazeal continued down to 4500 to see if it was coming from there. It wasn't a working level, but it was used by shaft repair crews as a staging area for timbers and supplies needed on lower levels of the mine. The smoke didn't appear to be coming from there, and Harris didn't think it was all that bad. He'd been in smokier places. It never dawned on him that the influx of smoke in the shaft could be coming from *above* them. They decided to go up to 3700 to continue their shift. A mine car there needed welding.

But when Harris pulled the bell cord for the chippy hoistman to raise them to 3700, nothing happened. It didn't move. The smoke started to thicken so much that the men began to choke. Findley sought relief with a deep drag off the oxygen line from Breazeal's little cart before ringing the bell for the double-drum hoistman. The chippy signal, he thought, was out of order. He belled a second time, but no answer. Not even the response—two long buzzes—the "take five" signal that indicated the hoistman couldn't move the conveyance just yet. Two buzzes always meant "Sit tight and I'll be right at you." Just dead silence. The men waited a few minutes before going over to the other side of the shaft, where the double-drum ran up and down in its separate compartment bringing in supplies from above, taking out muck from below. They planned to take the double-drum to 3700 to see what the hoistman was doing. They were willing to cut him a little slack. It was possible that the bell was out.

Harris squawked for the cage. A second later the cable began to move in that fast, reeling pace of a machine that at times seemed alive with its strength and force.

Cager Peterson appeared in the haze and pushed open the heavy steel-plate gate.

"What's going on?" he asked.

"We've got a fire somewhere," Harris said. He and his partner got on, shoving the cart with their welding gear into the rear of the cage. "Ain't down here."

ABOUT THE TIME ROCK RABBIT LARRY HAWKINS HEADED topside, foremen Gene Johnson, Bob Bush, and Harvey Dionne were guzzling the last of their coffee in the blue room when electricians Arnold Anderson and Norman Ulrich called out "Smoke!" from down the drift. The three foremen grabbed their lights and left to investigate. Smoke was coming from the 910 raise, a three-hundred-foot cut through old workings, long since mined out. Jim Bush and Harvey Dionne hurried to locate its source. Gene Johnson and Bob Bush went the opposite way, to 10-Shaft, to alert the crew.

Dionne climbed up a lumber pile to peer over the heading of the raise, a clearance of no more than eighteen inches. He twisted his head and fixed his cap light onto the dark gap. Nothing but black. He strained to see behind the wall. It was like staring into the empty blackness of a schoolkid's slate. He finally saw smoke—an enormous, undulating cloud—boiling behind the timbers. The source of the smoke was coming from the 910 raise. It had to be. Dionne climbed down, and he and Bush jumped on a couple of motors and went west down the drift, away from the smoke toward the Jewell. They met a muck train coming, and sent its driver back to close air doors while they continued on. Things were under control. Everything would be just fine.

11:30 A.M., MAY 2
Sunshine Offices

PERSONNEL OFFICE ASSISTANT BETTY LARSEN, THIRTY-NINE, was a short, round woman with auburn hair and nerves of Jell-O. At lunchtime, Larsen and other office women left the administration building for the employee break room in the immense green sheet-metal-clad building in the middle of the mine yard. It was a quiet morning, with all the bigwigs at the annual shareholders' meeting. Not that anyone took advantage, but they savored the freedom nevertheless. The women noticed smoke coming out of Sunshine Tunnel, on the mountainside north of the mill complex. Smoke also came from the big blue steel stack over a seven-foot-wide borehole called Big Hole. It exhausted air from the 1900 level to the surface.

"I've never really paid much attention," one of the women said. "Maybe there's always that much smoke?"

Larsen didn't think so, but she wasn't quite sure. She looked up at the smoke, puzzled but unworried.

Larsen, whose sole office skill was typing a brisk 105 words per minute, was another of the South Dakota newcomers of the 1950s. Like so many, Betty and Duane Larsen went on hope and faith from the surging sea of prairie grasses to the dingy towns of the Coeur d'Alenes. Betty thought Kellogg was a dump, a smelly place with no lawns, unpainted houses, and dirt that wasn't even pretty like the black soil of the Dakotas. Even the Miner's Hat drive-in, a replica of a hardhat with a working lamp as its omnipresent beacon, sat in a cloud of dust along the highway. Larsen also noticed that the scruffy men were pale-skinned. Farmers back home were clean-shaven and tanned from outdoor work.

"These men look like convicts," she told her husband when they first arrived.

"That they do," her husband said.

To a teetotaling Seventh-Day Adventist, Kellogg was one bar after another, with no shortage of customers. Back home, there were one or two drunks. Kellogg, she thought, was a town of drunks. Gambling, cards, and slot machines also reigned. And, fittingly, silver dollars were the favored currency. Some men lugged so many coins in their pockets that they nearly lost their pants. Before Kellogg, Larsen had never even *seen* a silver dollar.

By the time the office women finished their lunch on May 2, they assumed the fire was under control. Betty Larsen was sure that since there was nothing to burn down there, an underground blaze couldn't be a major calamity. When she noticed a company ambulance ready to go, someone told her that a victim of smoke inhalation was going to the hospital for treatment.

That's too bad, she thought. She hoped the fellow wouldn't miss much work.

Nine

A T TWENTY-SIX, JEWELL CHIPPY CAGE TENDER KENNY
Wilbur was still waiting for a chance to apprentice as an electrician and get out of the mine before he was an old man at forty.
After lunch Tuesday morning, Wilbur hung around 3700 kibitzing
with sanitation nipper Don Beehner, as the pair did at that time
nearly every day. Beehner was an easygoing guy who could talk
about anything, a trait Wilbur knew he put to good use when bar-
tending nights at the Wallace Corner. Beehner, who was responsible
for emptying the crude toilets and disposing of garbage underground, had things to do topside the last part of his shift. He usually
waited on the station while Wilbur unloaded the cage, then they rode
to the surface together.

A ringing phone interrupted their conversation. From 10-Shaft,
electrical foreman Floyd Strand told Wilbur there was a fire, and that

they'd been looking for its point of origin. It was getting so smoky, however, that a hoistman with a bum lung had been sent out on a muck car. Bob Scanlan was now operating the double-drum. Strand said they were going to evacuate the mine.

"Get the cages on the double-drum," Strand said. He seemed remarkably cool, without the slightest trace of alarm. "I want a cage there all the time."

During day shift, the double-drum was configured for muck, not men. Wilbur belled himself topside. He joined the double-drum hoistman, and the two of them went up to the collar, or top, of the shaft to pull out the pins and switch out to man decks. The exchange took a few minutes. When he returned to the station, Wilbur told a trainee to watch the men exiting the mine.

"Keep a count as best you can," he said.

No one had any particular anxiety about smoke. It just wasn't uncommon underground. At that time of day, clouds of smoke emanated from the cumulative blasts that miners reserved for shift's end. Such timing allowed the dust particles to settle before men returned to survey the success of a particular round the next day. There could be other causes for a little smoke, too—machines, cigarette smoking. Wilbur remembered how the power went out occasionally and the drifts clogged up with smoky air. That had happened four or five times since he'd been at Sunshine. Sure, guys coughed, but after a few minutes it usually cleared up and everyone was fine.

Miners can take a little smoke, he thought. *It isn't like it's going to kill anybody.*

11:45 A.M., MAY 2
4600 and 4800 Levels

BESIDES THE BELL SIGNAL SYSTEM AND THE SQUAWKER, Sunshine had an underground telephone system miners knew as the "red phones." With the exception of the telephone by the double-drum hoist on the surface, which was black and was merely *labeled* RED PHONE, all phones underground were indeed a dull crimson. The phones were a pager system and a party line, which allowed any man to pick up and hear what was being said. They were the old-fashioned hand-crank models, powered by two dry cells and mounted just outside the cage. They crackled from level to level and took some experience to operate.

Shift bosses Virgil Bebb and Charlie Casteel were talking on the station when the phone, the squawker, and the bell system went haywire. Casteel was in charge of the 4800 level, which connected with 4600. Some of the men working for Casteel would get off the cage at 4800 and head up to their stopes, depending on where they were in their work. Bebb, fifty-two, ambled across the station to answer the phone. It was a call from an upper level that there was a fire, but by then the call was moot. Smoke had begun to skulk into the drift. Bebb told a pair of miners to get the word out to the seventeen men working on that level that the mine was going to be evacuated.

At almost six feet tall and barely 130 pounds out of the shower, Dennis Clapp was a stick-figured young man with wire-hanger shoulders. He defiantly wore his sandy blond hair shoulder length, and braced himself to defend it when guys like Dewellyn Kitchen reached to tug it during the man-train ride to 10-Shaft. Sometimes he wasn't able to. Kitchen was quick. Clapp and his partner had been mining on 4800 for nearly four years, and were nearly finished with their stope. They'd worked their way up to 4600, just below track level. Clapp was drilling a round, his eyes fixed on the rock. Compressed air spun the steel drill bit and a spray of water washed down the cloud of dust. A cap lamp flashed and Clapp looked away from the drill. A worker down on track level called up that there was a fire in the mine.

"Someone needs to get back down to 4800 to tell Flory and Wilkinson and the Syndicate crew to get out," the man said.

Clapp hadn't noticed a thing. With the friction of the drill, there was always a tempest of smoke, burning oil, and dust. He volunteered to go down to Flory and Wilkinson's stope. Climbing down was easy, of course. But the thought of going all the way back was too much after a long morning of drilling.

It's closer going by the track than climbing back out of this, he thought.

DOWN IN A STOPE BETWEEN THE 4600 AND 4800 LEVEL, miner Ron Flory slid a cigarette from the protective case strapped to his hat with a slice of an inner tube. Both of the six-footer's well-muscled arms bore permanent reminders of his youth. One tattoo, a tarantula, had been started when he was sixteen and in jail for stealing gas and tires off a '56 Crown Victoria. A cellmate had drawn the spider and started outlining. After Flory was released, his sister pulled his skin tight and poked a sewing needle through a puddle of India ink to finish the tattoo. The other tattoo, a cartoonish image of a dagger, had seemed like a good idea when he was an eighteen-year-old Army private.

Flory and Wilkinson had started the shift barring down, scaling off loose rock from the opposite shift's blasts, before settling into mucking out the stope with a slusher, a compressed-air-powered scraper. Wilkinson put his entire wiry body into the task, feverishly pulling a pair of levers that pulled the muck into the chute and down to the muck cars lined up on the sodden tracks below. His arms were bare; a tattoo of a curvy come-hither woman moved with the muscles of his right forearm. He wore thick lenses that saved his eyes more than once in the days when safety glasses were seen more as a hassle than a safety requirement. Without them, Wilkinson couldn't aim a drill. Flory, a toothpick dangling from his mouth as always, called over to Wilkinson that he thought he smelled a little smoke.

"Slusher motor might be burned up," Wilkinson said, his voice carrying over the din of the machine.

Flory filled his lungs. "Smells like it," he said.

After giving their equipment a cursory review, the pair concluded that their slusher was all right. The problem must have been someone else's down the drift. Wilkinson went back to the machine to drag more muck to the chute opening while Flory took another drag on his cigarette. He wondered about the source of the smoky odor.

Maybe it was a generator on the battery barn. Or the battery on the motor.

FROM TOP TO BOTTOM, THE MANWAYS BETWEEN LEVELS were two hundred feet of ladders, offset so that a fall wouldn't carry a man all the way down to certain death. When Dennis Clapp finished the long climb down, he found Flory and Wilkinson back slushing.

"Hey! There's a damn fire," he yelled, flashing his cap lamp. "You guys are supposed to get on a motor and get the Syndicate crew out. Tell them to get the hell out."

If there was any real urgency in his voice, it was only because added volume was needed to ride over the normal racket of the mine, a never-ending grinding of metal machines, the sound of the slusher scraping loads of muck from the back of a stope, and the thunder of rock smacking rock. Clapp watched a thin haze curl through the hot, moist air. At first the wispy cloud hesitated and hugged the edges of the raise. Then it swirled upward. The young miner didn't like the looks of it. It wasn't because he thought it was dangerous. It was more like a nuisance he didn't want to face. The air had been clear on 4600, so he decided to go back up that goddamn two hundred feet of ladders. He'd be out early with a beer in an hour. That sounded damn good.

11:50 A.M., MAY 2

4600 Level

A MONTH FROM HIS TWENTY-FOURTH BIRTHDAY ON MAY 2, Terry Jerome was another man who had once figured there'd be something more than mining. A graduate of Kellogg High, he'd started as a summer helper with the intention of saving up enough cash to take classes at a junior college in Coeur d'Alene. By May 2, 1972, he'd been a Sunshine miner for two years and knew he'd be underground for the rest of his life. Jerome and his partner, Roger Koisti, were off of 10-Shaft on 4600 repairing timber on a service raise coming from 4400. Service raises were the lifeblood of the mine, carrying water pipe, compressed-air lines, and electricity from level to level. Without all that flowed through a service raise, no man could survive the conditions of a deep metal mine like Sunshine. The two men were at track level, replacing timbers that had taken too much weight and busted at the entrance to the raise, when they heard smoke was causing problems up above. They were told to alert other crewmen and get to the station. To save time and facilitate communication in places remote, dark, and noisy, miners used "air tuggers" to send notes from track level to the working areas above. Tuggers pulled cables connected to buckets that brought material in and out of stopes and raises where men worked two hundred feet above the track line. It was too noisy and too far away to yell for a man to come down.

Hearing was a casualty of the underground, anyway. The constant eardrum-splitting din turned many miners deaf enough that their wives had to scream to get their attention, and the sound on their TV sets was cranked up to window-rattling volume. Earplugs were required at Sunshine, but it was a rule that most ignored. A man couldn't be bothered with something as silly as earplugs. A few checked them out from the safety office, and others brought in cotton balls or wadded-up paper towels. Terry Jerome had discovered that filter tips from smoked cigarettes made serviceable earplugs.

He sent a tugger up with a note indicating there was a fire.

IT WAS QUIET AND SMOKY ON THE STATION AT 3700, 10-Shaft. Jack Harris couldn't even make out the faces of the guys sitting around waiting, but he knew there were a bunch of them. Pinpoints of light from their cap lamps pricked the blackened air. Some were in clusters; a few stood isolated. Yet, through the smoke, Harris could see the irrepressible Gene Johnson, a BM-1447 self-rescuer in his hand, directing traffic and giving orders. Johnson's brow narrowed to a tight V, and his mouth was a straight line. He ordered cager Randy Peterson to release the cage and send it back to 3700.

"Get every man into the cage that you can, and get up to 3100," Johnson said. "Give it a two-one-two and let it come back down."

The directive also meant that they'd be running only a single side of the double-drum. Running both was the rule on the system, which was counterbalanced—one cage or skip always going up, the other always on the way down. Johnson apparently didn't see that there was time for clutching in and out as in normal operations.

Jack Harris found a small reserve of self-rescuers on the station, but didn't bother to get one. In fact, most of the men sitting around waiting were without them. Chippy hoistman Don Wood sat on a bench with other hacking miners, trying to catch his breath. Wood said the smoke was overpowering in the hoist room, and he'd had to get out of there. Wood's departure was the likely reason Harris hadn't received a response when he belled for a cage from 4500.

ON 4400 THE LEAD MAN FOR THE SHAFT CREW WAS ROBERT Barker, a compact man at five-foot-six and 150 pounds. Barker's nose was a bit of a ski jump with flared nostrils, which all family members called "the Barker nose." The father of six, Barker was there along with a handful of other guys, including former Smelterville chief of police Jack Reichert, who'd given up the badge for a girl and for a job welding underground. The smoke seemed translucent, and there was some speculation that Reichert's torch had touched off some timbers. Barker went down to the timber station at 4500 to see if the smoke was coming from there, but found nothing. He rang for the cage, but no one answered. There was no phone on 4500, so Barker walked across the station to squawk for the double-drum.

Ten

BILL MITCHELL, TWENTY-SIX, THE MINER WHO'D MOVED to the district for the love of a Smelterville girl, had a crooked grin and a five-o'clock shadow that appeared before noon. Prior to the morning of May 2, Mitchell and his fifty-year-old partner, Bob Waldvogel, had driven a raise fifty feet up above the 4400 level and were mining a block of ore that ran along a particularly good vein. Instead of using the far more common—and far less dangerous—cut-and-fill stoping method, Mitchell and Waldvogel were shrink-stoping. In cut-and-fill, a block of ore about six feet in height is drilled and blasted down across the full length of the stope. A slusher drags the blasted rock to a chute that supplies muck cars on the level below. As each cut is made, sandfill is poured into the stope up to the desired level, after which the next cut is mined. In shrink-stoping, however, ore is drilled and blasted down onto a muck pile that fills the entire stope. After each cut, only enough muck is sent through the chutes to provide enough room for the men to set up to drill and blast another cut. And over and over it goes. When all of the ore has been drilled and blasted, mining ceases and all of the ore-laden muck is drawn out of the stope through chutes at the haulage level until there is enough room to allow the miners to repeat drilling and blasting. When the ore has been mucked out, the stope is a vertical crack, maybe 5 feet wide, 50 feet long, and 150 feet high.

In ordinary stope mining, each day twenty or so muck cars were loaded for the station, dumped in the ore pocket, and hoisted out of the mine. With what Mitchell and Waldvogel were doing, they'd have tons and tons ready at once—an endless parade of muck cars that lasted for weeks, or even months. Since 4400's narrow walls were considered "good country"—not prone to collapse—the technique met with considerable success on that level. Miners, however, generally didn't like shrinking the stope because it delayed their gyppo money until the completion of the project.

Late Tuesday morning, a motorman used his cap lamp to signal Mitchell, who was pulling muck and dropping it into a car. The signal was the rapid shaking of his head from side to side, the beam bouncing in an obvious "no" fashion.

"Hey!" the motorman repeated. "Stop what you're doing and tell Bob to get your dinner buckets and let's get the hell out of here. The mine's on fire and we're evacuating." The motorman said he'd been telling the rest of the crew to get to the station.

"Hold it!" Mitchell called up to Waldvogel, who was slushing, and couldn't hear above the racket of the muck against the machine. Mitchell shook his lamp from side to side and Waldvogel stopped, though he plainly couldn't understand the fuss. Nothing indicated anything was burning. Their stope was at the tail end of the drift, where there was very little air movement other than what came from the compressed-air line. In fact, smoke from Mitchell's cigarette blew *out* of their stope.

A moment after the motorman's hurried warning, the partners left for the station, swinging their buckets and shaking their heads. More than the worry of a mine fire was the thought that they were not going to make any gyppo money that day. They'd have to settle for the day's pay—$24.

There goes our contract, Mitchell thought.

Bob Waldvogel was less concerned than Mitchell about his paycheck, an attitude that reflected how he lived his life. Waldvogel bounced from Lucky Friday to Bunker to Galena to Sunshine as though employment were some kind of scavenger hunt and he could never really find the prize. Mitchell was rock-solid. He had two daughters and a wife to consider. Waldvogel's personal life was a shambles and was going nowhere. He roomed at Pat's Boarding House in Kellogg and filled his free time in district bars. More than once he'd come to work with the smell of a drink on his breath. Though Waldvogel had been an employee of Sunshine off and on many times over, it was Mitchell who had seniority. He'd been there two years steady.

Both men tasted the smoke. It wasn't heavy, just the light scent of a campfire that had been doused with a bucket of water and then had smoldered for a while. Visibility was fine. They were curious about what had caught fire and where it had started.

"Boy," Mitchell said, "smells like something's burning on the 4600."

Waldvogel, a severe asthmatic, looked down the drift through smudged glasses. Smoke was an irritant to his lungs, but working in a mine meant he had to put up with it. He kept inhalers in his bucket, and puffed on them whenever burning oil or dust gave him fits. The pair reached an air door and pushed it open. A thick, billowing cloud rolled over them, and visibility nosedived to barely twenty-five or thirty feet. It was like a chimney fire with creosote burning and sending ashy, thick smoke from a rooftop. They couldn't be seen, but men could be heard hacking as hot smoke entered their lungs. Waldvogel and Mitchell picked up the pace. As they rounded a crook in the drift, they saw the shrouded blush of the station's fluorescent lights. The lights were diffuse through the smoke, giving the drift the appearance of a full moon on the foggiest night. They couldn't see individual lights, just the shape of brightness through darkened air.

For a fire down on 4600, Mitchell thought, *we're sure getting a lot of smoke up here.*

FOUR HUNDRED FEET BELOW WHERE MITCHELL AND WALD-vogel wrestled with the smoke, Ron Flory and Tom Wilkinson rode a motor about a mile down the drift to alert the other guys on their level. Since they were working on a main level, the men of 4800 had their own motors to haul muck to the station. Motors beat walking any day.

"We need to get our self-rescuers and wait for the cage," Flory called out.

Wilkinson didn't know anything about self-rescuers, but Flory had heard a little about them. He had been told once by a shift boss that if there was dense smoke—other than blasting smoke—men were to put on a self-rescuer and call for the cage. He knew the units were kept in a box by the station phone. That was the sum total of his training—and he was the best trained of the nine men on the station. The smoke was visible, but nothing they couldn't handle. The men talked for a while and put on the breathing units.

A miner called for the cage again, and the hoistman promised it would be down to get them as soon as possible. Smoke was worse on the upper levels, he said, and they'd have to wait their turn. While this was going on, Flory started having trouble with the mouthpiece.

It was too hot to keep his lips around. It was as if he'd put his mouth around a shard of dry ice. He tried a second unit, and then reached for a third. Others did the same. Some gave up and breathed *around* their mouthpieces.

"Why are these getting so goddamn hot?" Wilkinson asked.

No one knew. None of them had given the units a thought before that moment.

The smoke grew in density, and the men heard the cage fly through the shaft at least twice—skipping 4800. Each time, the man on the station phone reminded the hoistman that they were there.

"In case you forgot us," he said.

Their eyes irritated to the point of tears, they retreated to the motor barn, a large, blasted-out working and storage area where train batteries were recharged. Although clouded with smoke, the air seemed better there.

"When is the damn cage gonna get here so we can go out?" Wilkinson asked.

No one answered. No one had a clue.

Flory and Wilkinson talked about getting a beer at the Happy Landing once the smoke thinned out and they got out of there. Maybe Wilkinson's buddy Johnny Davis, who had refused to dump shift, could meet them there to celebrate his birthday. They'd be early, which was good considering the popularity of the miners' hangout. It wasn't the only place to drink in downtown Smelterville, but the Happy, with its live country-and-western bands, foaming-over-the-edge schooners, and rowdy miners, always guaranteed a good time. Flory and Wilkinson were regulars there.

Flory would usually party with Myrna, who'd drop Tiger off with her mother or sister in Kellogg. Sometimes Frances Wilkinson would come along, but Tom liked drinking far more than his home-body wife did. When his wife wasn't around to keep him in line, some saw Tom Wilkinson as trouble—but no more so than half the guys in the district who enjoyed cutting loose. Wilkinson had a short fuse and had seen his share of trouble. Flory had had his scrapes with the law, too, but of the two, he had the more amiable reputation. The men were partners in the mine, superficially friendly, but neither would count the other as his best friend. Flory was quiet and considered himself a decent listener. A muscular man with a shy boy's personality, he could puff himself up and pretend to be comfortable in his own skin. Wilkinson, by far the bolder of the pair, thrived on the idea that money was made to be spent and a good time was there for the taking. He wasn't alone in his thinking. Few miners cared about saving a dime. *Hell, I could be dead in a rockburst tomorrow, and why should my old lady get something out of that?*

THROUGHOUT THE DEPTHS OF THE MINE, SMOKE SPED through the vast ventilation system. It had become a stealthy tornado. Wherever it could find a place to expand, it did. It was fast enough that no man wearing twenty-some pounds of mining tools, batteries, gear, *and* sweat-filled rubber boots could outrun it.

Eleven

A s a general practice, the doors to Sunshine's milling operation were kept open to let fresh air into the stifling building that sat on the rocky mountainside, just west of the men's dry house. The state-of-the-art mill used crushing, grinding, flotation, and filtering techniques to concentrate silver, lead, and copper ores for shipping to smelters in Montana and Washington. The milling process turned the stony rubble hauled from Sunshine into the consistency of powdered sugar.

A little after noontime the mill crew smelled something burning, but a quick check showed their machinery in good order. Someone called out that smoke was coming out of Sunshine's ventilation shaft. A group went to look, but the wind had shifted and the smoke had dissipated. The crew shut the doors and everyone returned to work.

On the first floor of the engineering building, stenographer

Richelle Pherigo, twenty-two, took over as relief switchboard opera-tor. Pherigo sat behind the small console and answered the mundane calls that came in at that hour—wives wanting to get messages to husbands and inquiries from men looking for the hiring office. Not long after she took her seat, an excited voice came from underground.

"Call down to Marvin at the North Shore! We need him and the rest back here, right away. Looks like we got a fire in the mine."

Marvin was Marvin Chase, the mine manager. He and the com-pany's top executives—including the New York owners—were addressing Sunshine shareholders forty miles away at the nicest place in the district, the North Shore Resort, overlooking Lake Coeur d'Alene—the aquatic jewel of the panhandle.

The mine itself had come off a good production year—though the company had lost more than a million dollars on paper due to write-offs and other vague financial hocus-pocus. Nevertheless, shareholders, large and small, assembled in a banquet room to look toward the future. There were fears that the company was running in the direction of bankruptcy, pulling money from operations and investing in ill-conceived ventures that only served to make the board of directors richer. Those fears were not unjustified. Turning a deaf ear to such subjects, executives announced plans for addi-tional ore exploration in the coming months, as well as the contin-uation of the record-breaking retrieval of the high-grade ore that made Sunshine legendary in the annals of mining. Things had been good for the mine in 1971, they said, and they were just about to get better.

The urgent message was a jolt, and Richelle Pherigo looked out-side. Smoke rose in the sky, dark and columnar, like the trail of a rocket. She dialed the resort and was connected to personnel direc-tor Jim Farris. She explained the importance of reaching Chase.

"He can't be disturbed," Farris said.

His response took Pherigo aback.

"Well, we got a fire here and he needs to call back to the mine," she said.

Farris promised to pass on the message, and Pherigo and the others expected an immediate call-back. But none came. The column of smoke became blacker and blacker, now shooting straight up, like one of those tall, black office buildings in some city far from the district. An agonizing half hour later, there still had been no response from the shareholders' meeting. From her front-row seat, Pherigo saw men swarming the yard. Shifters were breathing down her neck to get in touch with Chase or Al Walkup, the mine superintendent. Anyone who had some authority.

Sitting at her desk in accounts payable, clerk Linda Daugherty, twenty-four, could hear the buzz as the remaining office people continued in vain to reach Chase or Walkup. The way she understood it, the guys underground wanted to evacuate, but they wanted the go-ahead from the top.

No one, she thought, wanted to evacuate unless it was a real emergency. No one wanted to lose an afternoon's production.

SUNSHINE EMPLOYEES HAD NO GRIPE WITH MINE MANAGER Marvin Chase, but after years of abuse at the hands of the revolving door of managers, the office employees, who paid the bills and handled the voluminous paperwork of the state and federal governments, had been beaten down so many times that they were unsure and a little cowed. The previous manager, Tom McManus, a former linotype machine manufacturing plant manager, had been sent to Big Creek by the out-of-town owners. He quickly established himself as the manager from hell. Not only was McManus a tyrant and a mean-spirited eccentric, he didn't think staff people were worth a damn. All could easily be replaced. Engineers, he habitually ranted, were "a dime a dozen." He also remarked that he didn't see the value of a mine safety program. The effort stole profits from the bottom line.

Behind his back, McManus was called Black Mac, less for his taste in clothing—the shiny black suit that he always wore, his fly once fastened shut with a safety pin—than for his insistence that all lights be turned off unless absolutely necessary. Under the McManus regime, pens were locked in the safe and issued only by sign-out. A single pen was to be used until its ink was exhausted. When it ran dry, an employee took it to McManus's secretary and she tested it on a legal pad to ensure that it was dead before issuing a new one. Pity the poor clerk who discovered that someone had walked off with her pen. She'd be reduced to tears and left to beg for a new one. Black Mac thought the hiring office's water fountain was "wasting water" and ordered it disconnected. The tube lights in the office were so antiquated that when they were shut off at his insistence, they'd cease to function when turned on again. It got so bad that the electrician eventually moved into the office. In addition to humiliating the staff for personal sport, Black Mac could be unforgivably cruel. He once fired a clerk for taking the day off to attend her nephew's funeral. Another woman was given her walking papers because McManus consider her ample breasts a "distraction" to mine engineers and geologists.

Not until the fall of 1969, when they signed union cards, did the staff stand up to the little dictator. McManus refused to negotiate, and in February 1970 the emboldened office workers staged a strike. It lasted less than a day. The staff had feared the miners wouldn't be supportive. But miners coming for their shifts saw the office workers' signs and turned around. Talks with management, and a speedy resolution, took a sudden priority.

Six months later, when McManus was ousted, it was as if Dorothy had vanquished the Wicked Witch of the West. The McManus legacy was not how well he managed operations, but how frightened and damaged were the people who had cowered in his presence. Even with nice guy Marvin Chase in charge, the anxiety never went away. Fear lingered. When the events of May 2, 1972, began, no one thought he had the power to do a thing about it. No one wanted to lose his job by calling for an evacuation.

IT FELL ON THE SHOULDERS OF AN ACCOUNTANT TO GIVE IN to what was as risky as it was right—the official evacuation order from topside. He wasn't management, and he sat in an office that had once kept pens in the safe; the likes of such autonomy had seldom been seen. Few in the office were sure what was going on underground and what, if any, evacuation plan was already under way. Some assumed the source of the smoke was above 2700, a level well above where most of the men worked. They didn't think smoke could get down to 3100 without the men knowing well in advance.

Pherigo rang the North Shore for the third time. Superintendent Walkup answered, and she patched him through to a shifter. Walkup, a bear of a man with a foghorn voice, said he'd return to the mine right away. He was unruffled. All mines had little blazes. There was always more smoke than fire.

Twelve

AT HIS DESK ON THE SECOND FLOOR OF SUNSHINE'S warehouse, Bob Launhardt unlatched his dinner bucket and smoothed out a napkin. He set out a sandwich he'd made that morning and prepared to dig into the safety rules handbook, when his phone rang. Tom Harrah's voice shot through the line with a desperate urgency that at once propelled Launhardt to his feet.

"I want you in front of the warehouse. *Right now!*" Harrah said, abruptly hanging up.

Launhardt dropped the phone and hurried down the stairs. When he found Harrah, the shop foreman was sweating profusely and breathing heavily.

"We've got a fire in the mine," said Harrah, gulping air. "They want us to dump the stench and bring the helmets to 10-Shaft on

3100. You help our yard man get the helmets out of the safety office and into the mine."

Launhardt, caught completely off guard, said he'd release the stench. Stench was a warning system that hardrock mining operations used to alert underground personnel to evacuate. Historically, stench was a foul-smelling liquid made from garlic and other strong aromatics. Sunshine used ethyl mercaptan manufactured by Eastman Organic Chemicals, a product similar—though not as concentrated—as that used to odorize propane, butane, and other potentially deadly gases. The compound came in a glass ampoule that, when added to a compressor's air line, sent stomach-turning fumes through the mine. In the south end of the compressor room, Launhardt broke the glass and opened three green and three red valves to release the acrid vapors into the mine. The size, configuration, and depth of a hardrock mine made the electric-powered visual and auditory warning systems used in coal mines impractical. Sunshine employed stench instead of sirens because every part of the mine was serviced with compressed air.

"Helmet" was mining vernacular for a breathing apparatus used for underground rescue. The units kept in the safety office were somewhat similar to what firemen wore on their backs when entering a blazing building. But there was a key difference: those used by firemen were compressed-air units, like scuba gear; a mine rescue helmet used compressed oxygen in its cylinder. In essence, it was a re-breather. The air that its user expended circulated through the device and was processed by chemicals that removed the carbon dioxide by-product of respiration. A chamber in the breathing circuitry held a supply of cardoxide to absorb carbon dioxide. Without the cardoxide, carbon dioxide levels in a breathing unit would quickly reach toxic levels and the wearer would collapse and almost certainly die. The apparatus gave a man a maximum of two hours of rescue time—four times what a fireman had with the much heavier compressed air. Sunshine had ten helmets.

At no time in Launhardt's life did events melt and blur more than during the first few minutes after he released the stench. He could feel his heart pulsate against his rib cage. He returned to his office and dialed Central Mine Rescue's number in Wallace. But the director of the mobile unit that supplied rescue equipment and know-how to the mining companies of the Coeur d'Alenes was at lunch. Launhardt frantically called the Shoshone County Sheriff's Office and told the dispatcher that the rescue man and his familiar panel truck were needed at Sunshine.

ACROSS THE YARD IN THE JEWELL HOIST ROOM, LINO Castaneda kept his ear attached to the phone. American-born ("Sonora, Arizona, not Mexico!"), Castaneda had picked spuds in southern Idaho before finding his way to the district and steady, permanent employment at Sunshine. His half brother, Roberto Diaz, worked underground as a motorman. Castaneda, by and large easygoing, was seriously stressed as he listened in the morning of May 2.

He heard the hoistman on 10-Shaft's double-drum say he was about to faint.

"Will you hand me one of those breather deals? I'm feeling kind of groggy."

Castaneda hunched over a little where he stood, gripping the telephone receiver as if it weighed forty pounds. Every line that could be picked up throughout the workings of the mine had a man on it, pleading for help and offering whatever they could about the fire's location. Castaneda stood mute. When rock rabbit Larry Hawkins asked what was happening, the hoistman shook his free hand to tell him to shut up. That motion brought light to Castaneda's face. The hoistman's dark brown eyes had pooled with tears.

Hawkins left the hoist room and found Launhardt near the mine portal. The safety engineer's face was a study in anxiousness, but he spoke calmly. His reassuring tone suggested things were under control.

"I need someone to go underground with me," he said.

Hawkins held a restricted rescue card because his weight had ballooned. He reminded Launhardt that he was allowed on the helmet crew only in the event of a real emergency.

"This *is* an emergency," Launhardt said. "And I need you now."

The idea that there was an urgent situation somewhere in the mine was hard to grasp. Hawkins had just come out of the mine where everybody was kicking back, relaxing. They were fine. Nothing had been out of the ordinary. How could something so dire happen so quickly?

Before the call from Harrah, Launhardt had been most concerned about a shaft fire. Smaller electrical fires or waste fires in the mine could be extinguished with relative ease. Shaft fires, however, were far more lethal. Sunshine's primary fire safety measures revolved around a series of air doors that automatically shut when sensors detected carbon monoxide, thus stopping airflow that would feed a fire. In addition, deluge rings holding hundreds of gallons of water had been planted atop the Jewell Shaft to dump a cascade of water on any shaft blaze there. But that wasn't happening today. The fire wasn't a shaft fire.

A boiling plume had erupted from Sunshine Tunnel, an air outtake vent on the mountainside above the mine yard. It looked lethal. Now, carrying a flame safety lamp, used to monitor oxygen levels, and a Draeger 1931 multigas detector to check for concentrations of carbon monoxide and carbon dioxide, Launhardt joined a group of men around Sunshine portal. For a moment he could not look beyond the men who had just made it out. Fear was imprinted on every face. He studied each one, looking for the men he knew best.

Some were there. Many more were absent. Launhardt had no idea how many miners were still underground, nor did he know exactly where they would be. He knew there was only one place to go: into the smoke.

12:10 P.M., MAY 2

5000 Level

TOM WATTS AND HIS PARTNER, JACK LOVESEE, WERE IN the middle of lunch at the timber station on 5000, just east of the No. 7 raise. Usually by that time of day they'd be done and headed back to the stope to set off their rounds before calling it quits. Lovesee was still nursing his coffee. He offered his partner a cup, which Watts drank down in a few gulps.

"Where are you going?" Lovesee asked. "Back to work?"

Watts was impatient. "Well, it's about time, isn't it?"

"Hell, it's only ten after twelve."

Watts hesitated a moment and started down the drift and back to work. He picked up his earplugs and gloves from the water line, where he'd hung them. Lovesee caught his partner's attention and pointed down the drift.

"What the devil is that?"

"It's smoky in the drift," Lovesee said.

Watts thought someone must have blasted, but Lovesee wasn't easily convinced. He hadn't heard any explosion, and the smoke didn't look like powder smoke.

"I mean to go find out what's going on," he said.

Lovesee left for the station and Watts resumed drilling, the roar of the compressed-air drill's steel against rock, shutting out the world. A moment later he saw a light bobbing back and forth.

It was his partner, Lovesee.

"Smells like a fire!"

Watts put down the jackleg, and the two disappeared down the drift toward 10-Shaft. The smoke grew heavier and seemed infused with a heavy, acidic odor. It smelled like a burning plastic ventilation line, like the fire that had burned at the Star Mine not long ago. They thought it was likely electrical in nature, but whatever its origin, the odor was unlike anything either man had ever smelled—thick, plastic, acid.

On the station, a miner repeatedly belled for the cage. Others just called out from the dark.

"Come on, get us out of here!"

Watts asked Bob McCoy if he knew what was going on. McCoy indicated he'd called the blue room and was told by a foreman to sit tight, help was on the way. But if help was coming, the men wondered, why was it taking so damn long? Several men began to strip self-rescuers from their cellophane bags and began to read how they operated. Watts and others left the station for clearer air near the grizzly, a thick steel grate with eight-inch holes, mounted over a chute that fed muck cars waiting below. The grizzlyman pounded the rock to a size that would fit through the huge grate. It wasn't easy. Sunshine rock was hard. Sometimes hammers bounced off without so much as leaving a mark. The effort helped prevent the chute from clogging, and, to a lesser extent, ensured that ore was of a manageable size for milling. A grizzlyman's job was hard physical labor, the kind of work that faced prisoners with no hope for parole. No man liked working the grizzly.

Yet on 5000, just then, the grizzly was a little bit of heaven.

12:15 P.M., MAY 2

5000 Level

WHEN THE CONDITIONS ARE JUST RIGHT, A STORM CAN ROLL across a landscape without a sound. Clouds can fiercely and silently churn and turn the atmosphere into a Mylar shield stretched from the ground to the blackest sky. It can suddenly become so dark that it would be impossible to read a line of text, yet within the formation of the swelling storm there are tones of black, and amorphous shapes of varying darkness. The black shield can seem alive, like the sea on a moonless night. The smoke coming at the twenty-five men working on the 5000 level was like that when it rolled through the drift.

Delmar Kitchen and his partner, Darol Anderson, were fifty-one feet above the floor of the drift in a timbered raise, preparing it for mining. Water lines and air hoses snaked up from track level. They liked to keep the water flowing nonstop; it minimized the dust and cooled the air. Shifters didn't like the practice, so they'd come through the mine complaining that water was backing up and the pumps couldn't keep up with it. Whiz-bangs hooked to a compressed-air line were never turned off. Not by Kitchen, anyway. It was too hot to work without compressed air blowing air into their stopes.

Of the Kitchen boys, Delmar, with his black hair swept back so that he looked like a subterranean Elvis, was the softest of a pretty sturdy bunch. His twin, Dwight, and their older brother, Dewellyn, were the kind who thought it wasn't a good night around town if there wasn't a fistfight in Happy Landing's parking lot. Delmar had always hated going out with his brothers for that very reason. The fact that nine times out of ten his brothers would come out on top in an altercation offered minimal consolation. The single time Dwight didn't prevail ended his life. He was murdered in a bar in northern Idaho.

Kitchen and Anderson finished their meal and left the station for their working area up above the drift. Just as they picked up where they had left off, a motorman alerted them about the fire. Anderson acknowledged some smoke down the drift. But Kitchen, up in the raise, couldn't see any, and was perturbed about having to stop. He didn't think a little smoke was any big deal, but he climbed down anyway. When the pair got to the drift, a thickening layer of smoke met them like a wall.

In a minute's time, Delmar Kitchen went from the raise, with its whiz-bang and clear air, to a faint wisp of smoke, to a tornado that sucked him deep inside. He couldn't see Anderson as he staggered forward, gagging and unsure where he was going. Somehow he found an open air door, behind which was a fan, and just as quickly as he moved inside, the smoke thinned. Visibility improved to about five or ten feet. He found a water line, and doused his face and mouth. Thankfully, Anderson had been right behind him. The water brought instant relief. Kitchen thought maybe the water had delivered oxygen to his body. The air behind them was choked with smoke. There was nowhere else to go but forward. It was the only way out.

They followed the mine rails and traced the line of overhead lights, each lone bulb wrapped in a protective wire cage, a row of illuminated beehives. Farther down was the faintest outline of the station, buried under a mantle of smoke. It reminded Kitchen of another station fire, less than a year before, when a pump had burned up and sent ashy smoke through the mine. It had been hard to breathe, but the mine wasn't evacuated. Men returned to their working areas and waited until the ventilation system sucked out the smoke.

This, Kitchen knew, was far worse. There was much more smoke and it wasn't going anywhere.

ON THE WAY OUT TO THE JEWELL, JACK HARRIS AND KEITH Breazeal came upon a leaking air door on a cross-drift to old country intersecting with 3100. A sheet of smoke seeped under the door, arcing and blending with fresh air. The pair found a broken shovel and moved quickly to seal the door. They joked about the fine job they did with the crummy shovel. A few yards farther down was another failing air door. It was framed with rotten timbers shot through with a helter-skelter lattice of holes. Harris scratched his head. This one was beyond patching. They'd need fifty yards of burlap and a stack of lumber. He knew his Big Creek neighbor Gene Johnson could use more time to evacuate, but he and Breazeal were stymied. By the time it got really bad, Harris figured, all the men would be out anyhow.

Thirteen

CAGE TENDER KENNY WILBUR FROZE. ON 3700 BY THE Jewell, foreman Harvey Dionne and shifter Paul Johnson—no relation to foreman Gene—were on the phone with the surface and lower levels, talking out what could be done to get more men out. Their voices were sharp and loud, echoing off the rock walls before fading into the heart of the mine. Tributaries of sweat ran down Dionne's suddenly very haggard face. *Something big was happening.* Dionne couldn't decipher word for word all that was being said as men throughout the mine tried to talk over each other. The only voice that cut through the chatter belonged to Bob Scanlan. The hoistman on 10-Shaft said they were sending men up right then.

Dionne passed the phone to Johnson so he could try making sense of the overlapping dialog. Dionne needed a moment. From what he'd seen when he peered over the bulkhead and from what he knew about Sunshine's ventilation system, the fire was in all probability burning somewhere above 4800. Smoke-contaminated air could be leaking to the lower levels through the old workings that cut every which way through the mine. Some had been sealed off in the most rudimentary fashion.

"You know," he said to Wilbur, "we should pull off them laggings over 12-Shaft to get some fresh air to 4800."

Wilbur nodded. Despite its name, at forty-eight inches across, 12-Shaft was really only a borehole. In time, the company intended to widen it and build another shaft to take some of the burden off 10-Shaft. Its location was good. It was within a thousand feet west of the Jewell. When 12-Shaft was timbered out, it would provide access to a substantial new ore body to the east. It would also serve as a ventilation conduit and an additional escape manway.

At one time, mine management had considered extending the Jewell down to 4800, but the plan had been abandoned because the Jewell double-drum was already at capacity. The chippy could go deeper, to 4000, but it was only a service hoist for men and equipment. The company needed to get muck out. A new borehole was the only solution on which management, geologists, and engineers could agree. Dionne led the project, which had been completed only a week before. To keep wayward debris from falling through the 1,100-foot drop and injuring someone, Dionne's crew had sealed the opening with an improvised cover.

Wilbur took a self-rescuer and vanished down the drift. The air was reasonably clear, with only a few wispy patches of hazy smoke. In minutes he'd gone from the confines of a drift to an enormous room with three stories of overhead space and foot-wide belts of steel fastened to walls with five-foot rock bolts. Wilbur wanted to get the lagging cover off and get out fast. He grabbed frantically at the cover, but a piece of wood refused to budge. It was caught on the craggy rim of the hole, a mouth ready to swallow. Wilbur, a compact man only five feet four inches tall, yanked again, *hard*, and teetered at the edge. He started to slip. His lamp swung wildly, swiping the ribs of the drift with a spray of light. He was going down. He stiffened his arms and pushed back with everything he had; and just as quickly as he lost it, he regained his balance.

Holy smokes, that was close, he thought. *Oh, take it easy.*

It flashed through his mind that if he'd fallen, there'd be nothing left of him. And with all the confusion in the burning mine, there'd be no one to know what had happened to him.

He looked down the rough circumference of the borehole into perfect gloom. A warm breath from the enormous emptiness of the mine blew over his face, and was sucked into the chasm. Kenny Wilbur hoped someone down there could get the fresh air.

12:15 P.M., MAY 2
3100 Level

LAUNHARDT AND HAWKINS WERE BELLED DOWN TO 3100, where they found the McCaa oxygen packs stacked and waiting for them. A group of miners who'd escaped their working areas stood around on the station, a few in obvious shock. Some hacked up mucus. Others still held their self-rescuers. A couple wanted to help.

"Where are you going with the helmets?" someone asked.

"I'm taking them back to 10-Shaft," Launhardt said.

"I'm going with you."

The voice belonged to veteran shaft man Jim Zingler. Nipper Don Beehner, who had been killing time with cage tender Kenny Wilbur when the fire was discovered, also volunteered. Both men had been trained in mine rescue and the use of the McCaa.

Launhardt still didn't know how four men would get all of those oxygen packs back to where Gene Johnson and the others were waiting. They were heavy, about forty-two pounds each. It would be beyond their endurance to carry all ten a mile to 10-Shaft. Launhardt had a lanky build, but he was strong, and with the concern and fear mixing in his bloodstream, he was ready to carry whatever he had to. Hawkins, Zingler, and Beehner were ready, too. Each wore a unit on his back and carried one in his arms, the extra weight pounding their rubber soles a half-inch into the muddy floor.

We're not going to make it, Launhardt thought, just as a headlight appeared.

"Look!" Hawkins said.

A motor pulling a couple of muck cars and a timber car, each packed with hacking and nauseated miners, edged toward the station. When it stopped and the men got off, Launhardt's crew loaded the helmets and took off. Hawkins ran the motor, with Beehner climbing onto the back end and Zingler on the timber truck. Launhardt took the lead in the front car. About a quarter of a mile out, he moved his head back and forth, streaking his light from over the blasted-out drift. Hawkins stopped the motor.

"Look," Launhardt said, "those guys told us the smoke was really bad past the timber station. Let's put on the apparatus here, where the air is still clear."

They checked their air hoses and face masks, ensuring that everything was snug and in order. The seal around a man's face was as important as a good oxygen hose; a leak could kill a man faster than getting no oxygen at all.

Hawkins put the motor into gear. None aboard could be sure what they would find, but each knew they could be the last chance for some to survive. The sooner they reached the men, the better their chances. But a moment later it was as if someone had shut off the lights. It was a wall of smoke, astonishingly thick; a solid darkness emptied onto the drift and consumed everything behind it. It appeared that the smoke was coming from a crosscut intersecting with the drift near 5-Shaft.

Launhardt signaled again and Hawkins stopped the motor.

"There's heavy smoke here," he called out through his face mask. He turned his attention to his flame safety lamp and gas detector. "I'll check it out." It was like nothing Launhardt had ever seen. It was nearly tarpaper black. Wood smoke, he knew, was often a brownish hue. *What's burning down here?*

12:16 P.M., MAY 2
4400 Level

THE NORTH COMPARTMENT OF 10-SHAFT'S DOUBLE DRUM stopped at 4400 and picked up nine men, including shaft repairman Robert Barker and welder Jack Reichert, the ex–police chief. A minute later it stopped on 3700. The cage's movements were recorded in the hoist room by a device called a tattletale. Like the jagged lines of a seismic scale, a needle marked a sheet of paper whenever the north or south compartment stopped or started. It also logged how long a cage paused on a particular level.

12:20 P.M., MAY 2
5000 Level

FORMER HOMESTAKE GOLD MINERS HOWARD MARKVE AND Bob Follette were working off 10-Shaft at 10 stope. Markve was up 125 feet over track level, drilling and preparing to blast, when Duane Stephens, nineteen, came and flashed his light. Markve climbed down to learn about the fire and the evacuation. He noticed some smoke, but remained unconcerned. He worked on repairing a bad jackleg for a few minutes before taking off and riding a bucket down on the timber slide to join Follette, who had already climbed down to track level.

Through the smoky haze, the motor's headlamp appeared deep yellow. The color was curious. Markve put the jackleg in need of repair on the back of the motor. The station was 1,500 feet down the drift.

Fourteen

TIMBERS DECAYED QUICKLY IN SUNSHINE'S HOT, MOIST environment, and crews were forever replacing disintegrating wood and hauling it off to abandoned stopes as gob, or filler. The day smoke poured through the mine, twelve-by-twelve timbers and steel plates as solid as the hull plating of a Navy frigate were in the midst of being bolted in place for a new station floor on 4400. Bill Mitchell brooded over the possibility that welders working on the job had inadvertently touched off a fire. As Mitchell waited on the station for the guys on the east side of the drift to arrive, he began to believe the fire was somewhere on their level. The smoke was so damn intense, its source couldn't be far. Could a hot bolt have fallen somewhere from the station? Other miners on 4400 searched, but failed to turn up anything. Sinuses were running and eyes were burning, yet the seventeen men clustered on the smoke-filled station stayed remarkably calm.

The wait seemed long, and the smoke sent nearly every man into a coughing fit—some to the point of retching.

Mitchell soaked his shirt in water and wrapped the sopping garment around his face. At the same time, his partner, Bob Waldvogel, was working his asthma inhaler with unmitigated ferocity. Mitchell, who had no respiratory problems, could barely fill his lungs without gagging. The deep puffs from the little cylinders Waldvogel clutched seemed to provide little relief. But it was hard to tell just how badly he was doing. It was taxing to see much of anything at all. When the double-drum cage finally stopped at the station, Mitchell, Waldvogel, and the rest lined up. Several men from another level were already packed into the rear.

"Oh, I forgot my dinner bucket!"

It was Waldvogel. He could be forgetful. He had even earned a nickname in younger days as a Bunker Hill drift miner. Miners there called him Dumb-dumb.

Mitchell understood the real significance of the declaration. Waldvogel wasn't fretting over leftovers. He needed his bucket because a moment before the cage came, he stashed his inhalers inside and set his bucket on the floor.

"No problem. I'll get it," Mitchell said, stepping from the cage and disappearing behind the black camouflage of smoke. Because he could hardly see, Mitchell crouched low on his knees and felt around where they had been waiting. He found his partner's dinner bucket and returned to the cage. By then the conveyance was full. Mitchell figured he'd catch up with Waldvogel on the train to the Jewell.

"Bob, I got your bucket," he called out. "See you on thirty-seven."

The cage disappeared, and a tear in the smoke curtain momentarily revealed that Mitchell and Ed "Speedy" Gonzalez were the only men left from the original group. Randy Peterson had joined them, having jumped off the cage with shaft boss Dusty Rhoads. As they stood in the rapidly swelling smoke, Rhoads outright rejected the suggestion that a hot bolt from his shaft crew had touched off a fire. *It wasn't goddamn possible.* No one could find the fire anyway. Only smoke. And it came fast. Cage tender Randy Peterson was the first to realize he was dying. It was as though the smoke had gone solid, lodged in his throat, and created a barrier that good air could not penetrate. Hacking up a cork of mucus could get him breathing, if only there was something to breathe. Peterson left the station for the compressed-air line that ran an air tugger, a conveyance used to load heavy timbers onto the cage. As quickly as he could, he knocked the nut loose that held the air line and released a breeze over his face. Seeing this, others followed his lead. The force of the blowing air peeled off the smoky layer and gave instant relief. It would have been even better had Peterson been able to suppress the heavy coughing that sought to clear his lungs. He was worried.

There ain't anyone coming back here, Peterson thought. If the cage didn't get there soon, he knew he was going to die. So would the others. The smoke had built to the point where it could be *felt* as much as seen and tasted.

Several minutes later, fill-in cager Greg Dionne appeared at the gate on 4600. A tall guy with a sturdy, sinewy build, Dionne was foreman Harvey Dionne's son. At twenty-three, Greg Dionne was a well-liked go-getter who could size up a fellow and pronounce him a best friend before a beer was half drained. He swung open the gate and removed the mouthpiece of his self-rescuer. He'd come just in time. They loaded and belled the cage to 4600.

12:22 P.M., MAY 2
4600 Level

WITH THE FOUR MEN FROM 4400—BILL MITCHELL, RANDY Peterson, Speedy Gonzalez, and Dusty Rhoads—on board, Dionne left the cage to answer a ringing phone while Peterson helped Dennis Clapp, Virgil Bebb, Charlie Casteel, and several others climb on. When Dionne returned, he belled them to 3100—*not* the station at 3700. Mitchell, who had once been a cager, knew the bell system and wondered what was up. The man train was on 3700. The men from his level had gone to 3700.

As the cage passed 3700, the men aboard saw a wall of smoke backlit by lights that normally flooded the station with daytime brightness. Some of the guys groaned when it dawned on them they wouldn't be stopping there. They were soaking wet from their own sweat. One complained that his coat was on 3700—and he needed it.

"Shit, it's cold in the Jewell," he said.

Around 3550, the cage sputtered and yo-yoed without warning. Bill Mitchell wondered if the hoistman had been smoked out, and had had to clutch out and stop the cage. It made no sense to stop it there for any other reason. The 3550 had been boarded up for years.

"There's no place for us to get off," someone called out from the back.

"What's he doing? What's he stopping here for?"

One man let out a kind of guttural scream, and Dionne tried to keep order. He was calm, and his reassurance felt genuine.

"He's clutching out one side," he said.

A moment later the cage heaved again, upward to 3100, where it stopped. Gene Johnson was there, sitting on a block of wood to the right of the station. Flanking the foreman was Byron Schulz and cager Roger Findley. Some saw Schulz as a goof-off—a kid who didn't take mining seriously. Schulz, twenty-one, was a cut-up. He'd make a joke, pull a prank, or just kick back a little longer than some thought he ought to. At Sunshine he'd done most of the jobs given to the green guys out of high school. He'd operated the mucking machine, done a little mining, acted as a helper, and run the cages—double-drum and chippy. Schulz was caging on the double-drum the morning of May 2, pulling muck from pockets on 4200 and 5600.

Shift boss Virgil Bebb distributed self-rescuers, but nobody was having much luck getting them to do the job. One miner rammed his against a coupling to activate the breather.

"I *want* to get this thing working," another said, as though the force of his will would make it operate.

Seeing this, Johnson got up, his movements slower than the usual quick deliberation he gave to everything. He yelled at the men to get moving and not stop for anything. He told Dusty Rhoads and Arnold Anderson to get down to 3400 and he'd give them the go-ahead to turn off a pair of 150-horsepower fans used to boost the ventilation system. It occurred to Johnson that the fans might be making things far worse—pushing bad air into the mine.

Only two—Mitchell and Peterson—knew the way out to the Jewell. Dennis Clapp had worked at Sunshine for a couple of years and had never before set foot on 3100. Speedy Gonzalez passed a wet T-shirt to Peterson to plaster over his mouth and nose until he could get his self-rescuer working. Peterson stared blankly at the cylinder with the nose pinchers, mouthpiece, and flimsy head straps. *This is a piece of crap. They are all pieces of crap.* He scuttled it to the floor. Peterson was jacked up and anxious to get out of the mine.

"Forget these fucking things! Let's go!"

The men below 3100 continued their frantic calls for a cage. Each was answered, but one thing wasn't disclosed. The trapped men thought they were talking to the 10-Shaft hoistman on 3100—the man who could get them out of there. Instead, the suggestion to crack open an air pipe and build barricades came from a foreman on the surface.

"Hang on, help is on the way," he said.

Castaneda stayed on the overloaded party line. As frenetic over-lapping voices taxed his comprehension, it hit him hard that miners in the deepest levels where smoke was not as severe were almost apologetic when asking for help.

"Yeah, I know you have a job to do," one coughed into the phone. "But I want you to know we're down here."

By then the hoist room on 3100 had been silent for what seemed like hours but was more a matter of seconds or minutes. Castaneda refused to think the worst—that the hoistman was dead. Maybe he'd passed out and another was on his way.

A moment later, Castaneda heard Dusty Rhoads's voice break the silence. From 3400, on the mission to turn off the fans, he said that Arnold Anderson had passed out. Gene Johnson answered, and the instructions he gave should have clued in everyone to how serious things had become.

"Don't wait," he told Rhoads. "You just better get out of there."

12:23 P.M., MAY 2
3100 Level

FEAR CAN PARALYZE. IT CAN MAKE A MAN COWER LIKE A kicked dog as he gives in to terror. Occasionally it leads men to actions they would never, ever disclose. Cowardice in battle is written about only by someone other than the man who ran. Terror can also jolt a man and transform him into something greater.

Cage tender Peterson was as anxious as he'd been in Vietnam, when mortars hurtled right at him in streaks of white, only to hit another soldier, sending fireworks and chunky blood raining down. As he led men through the drift, his eyes burned and his lungs convulsed as though they were skirmishing inside his tightening chest— as if there was no room to hold all his vital organs. Peterson had suffered from asthma since childhood, a mild form that precluded running as a sport or pastime. At that terrible moment, his asthma made sifting oxygen from the black air nearly impossible. The only thing that kept the twenty-three-year-old from giving in to the smoke that was waging war against his respiratory system was that he believed if he didn't lead them out, they'd all die. He didn't think of his family, of any regrets he had or what he wished he'd done in the event that his own life would end right there. His only concern was the other lives on the line three thousand feet underground.

Just a little longer, he thought. *If I can only hold on a little longer. These are my guys.*

Things were deteriorating with a suddenness that scared the hell out of the men on 5000. Smoke turned opaque. Men were gagging, and nobody knew how to work the self-rescuers, which had been locked in a bright orange cabinet on the station wall. Darol Anderson, the timberman working with Delmar Kitchen, raced to the box, busted it open, and, despite the smoke, somehow read the instructions. The plunger that activated the unit by breaking a protective seal, however, proved formidable. Anderson used his wrench to smash open the seal.

Anderson scooped up self-rescuers and passed them out. Markve was so unfamiliar with the units that when the canister cover fell onto the track, he took his lamp off to look for it. He thought that the protective cover was the self-rescue unit itself.

Kitchen kept his teeth clamped on his mouthpiece and helped others smack their self-rescuers into working.

The men on 5000 were blind. It was so dark, one man pressed his palm into the shaft to feel the steel gate of the cage—in case it was there and no one could see it. The smoke moved in a circle, following the airflow of the drift. It skirted over the grizzly, leaving the air there, approximately forty feet from the station, halfway clear.

Men huddled in the grizzly, sunken below track level, and let a whiz-bang discharge fresh air over them.

"Come over here! At least we have a little air," one called over to the station, where the smoke continued to build. None went over. They were paralyzed.

Fifteen

WHEN THE CAGE CAME, IT WAS SO SUDDEN AND FULL that Delmar Kitchen didn't make it in time to get a spot on board, though he was right behind his partner, Darol Anderson, who had. It was impossible to see exactly how many were on board, but it appeared to be about ten men. Another couple could be shoehorned inside, if not for the muck pile that consumed a back corner. Kitchen stood on the station and worried about his father, Elmer, and his brother, Dewellyn. He hoped they were already out of the mine.

Cager Greg Dionne held a rag over his mouth and nose, and was making a move to bell the men up.

"You're going with me," Anderson yelled at Kitchen.

Kitchen took a couple of steps back. "I'll wait here. I'll catch the next one."

"I'm not leaving you. Jump. Jump aboard. *Now!*"

Anderson held out his arms and scooped up his partner. Another miner frantically pushed some muck to the side to try to improve Kitchen's footing, but the effort proved futile. Somehow, as Dionne belled the cage up, Anderson kept his arms around Kitchen. Kitchen flailed and grabbed for a railing. With no room for his heels, most of his weight remained on his toes. He caught a rail and hung on. The cage screamed up the shaft so fast that some thought it was going at muck speed. Even in the dimness of the cage, Kitchen could see that another miner was having trouble.

"Can I have a bite of that thing you got in your mouth?" he said.

Though it was risky, considering his precarious balancing act, Kitchen removed his mouthpiece and the other miner took a long drag. Seeing this, Anderson offered his self-rescuer to another young miner while he held his breath. At about the 3550 level, there was a sudden burst of fresh air. Good, cool, fresh air. It was as if they'd all been underwater and suddenly, when they'd thought they might drown, they broke through the surface.

"Thank God, we have some air!" a man called out. Relief was more powerful than fear. For a moment the men thought the worst was over. But in another flash, the smoke returned.

ACE RILEY WAS CONFUSED BY THE SOURCE OF SOME SMOKE. At first he thought the pig, or jackleg's oil reservoir, was throwing too much oil, but his partner, Joe Armijo, disagreed and the two even argued for a moment what it could be. Armijo, thirty-eight, was more than a partner; he and Riley were drinking and hunting buddies. The son of Mexican immigrants, Armijo was both tough and stubborn. He had reason to be. Beyond the rigors of a tramp miner's life, moving from the Coeur d'Alenes down to a gold mine in Nicaragua and back, he had an additional burden. His wife, Delores, was emotionally unstable. His home life was a living hell.

One time he told Riley about an incident that had occurred en route to a doctor.

"She jumped out of the car and ran to the police station. Said I was kidnapping her. They damn near arrested me."

Riley counted his own lucky stars. *No man should put up with that*, he thought.

When warned about the fire Tuesday afternoon, Riley was somewhat indifferent. There'd been other fires, and using past experience as a gauge, he figured they'd sit around the station and yak until all the hubbub and smoke cleared. Gyppos didn't have a minute to waste. Every moment was spent working to make money. Coffee breaks and jawing over lunch at the station was for the day's-pay guys. Even when an Idaho mine inspector came through and wanted to talk, a typical gyppo would turn a deaf ear and get back to work. Short of cutting off his air supply, no real gyppo would stop to talk to anyone. Keep blasting, breaking rock, and planning the next round—all the way to the bank. If they had saved, which most didn't, their bank accounts would be flush. In the best of times, up into the early 1970s, the best gyppo miner made upwards of $50,000 a year.

Ace Riley gathered up his cigarettes and looked down the drift. He was overwhelmed by how thick the smoke had grown. It had a strange golden or yellowish cast and smelled a little of sulfur. It was more extreme than anything he'd ever seen underground. When he and Armijo got to the station, someone directed them to respirators stored off the station by the waste dump. Riley's mind was so fogged from the carbon monoxide that at first he thought the nose clip was the part that delivered good air. And like the rest of the men, he struggled to push down the button so that the unit could perform its lifesaving task. He beat it against the corner of a wooden box. He put in the mouthpiece and drew a breath. Nearly instantly, he felt better. He found himself thinking, *This ain't so bad. I could go on all day like this if I had to.* He didn't know that the BM-1447 self-rescuers were only good for about a half hour.

Not everyone was doing quite so well. Norman Fee, the son of Kellogg High School teacher Elizabeth Fee, braced himself on the station's concrete and steel-plate floor. Fee, twenty-seven, was one of those who could have pursued another career, and was in fact close to earning a college degree. He faced the shaft head-on as the column of smoke spilled a fetid, inky cloud into the drift. He wore a BM-1447 around his neck, but the mouthpiece dangled. Over the next few minutes, different miners picked it up from the floor and shoved it back into his mouth, but it never stayed put. Nearly delirious and weak from the poisoned air, Fee could only mutter that the mouthpiece was too hot to take. His eyes had rolled back, and whenever he looked upward, they were half-moons. The force of his guttural coughing seemed strong enough to turn his lungs inside out. On all fours, Norman Fee waited like a dying dog at the opening of the shaft, waiting for someone to come.

Riley dropped to his knees. Fee's self-rescuer had not been activated. That had to be the reason the grizzlyman was failing so rapidly. Riley yanked his wrench from his tool belt and beat the button on Fee's rescuer until he felt it pop. He slid the mouthpiece into Fee's mouth. Fee's eyes showed nothing if not increasing fear. Men had seen that look before—a diner choking on a steak in a restaurant, aware of everything around him but unable to get air into his lungs.

He spat it out. "It isn't doing any good," he said.

"Keep the goddamn thing in your mouth," Riley said, putting it back in with a less than gentle force. He meant business. The act alone should have been enough to shock a man into biting down on the mouthpiece, even a man with a mind consumed by fear. But Fee wouldn't have any of it.

While Riley continued to fight with Fee, the cage with Dionne and Schulz appeared at the station. Someone had got word to the hoistman on 3100 that Fee was in serious condition. The cage stopped on 4600—bypassing the men on 4800—to get him out of there as fast as possible.

Riley reached under Fee's arms and dragged him over to the gate. He wasn't going to leave him alone there, gagging. Fee was a convulsing heap on the deck of the cage. Bob Goff, an experienced miner who had just come from an Arizona copper mine only two weeks prior, was also having problems. Goff was only just able to stand. Riley pulled his coat up over his head, using it as a shield against the smoke, and called out for Armijo and the others to get on the cage. In the heat and smoke of the 5000, the men on the cage could only feel the shuffle and movement of others as they stepped aboard. They couldn't see much of anything.

Riley noticed that Greg Dionne's self-rescuer was a different model from what he and the others had. Instead of seeing a black rubber cover over something about two and a half inches tall, Riley saw a white cloth cover over a unit about four inches tall. At the top of the white cloth cover was a gray component about one inch high and with a stainless-steel exhalation valve mounted on the front. The mouthpiece, also gray, came from the back of the W-65 self-rescuer.

The cager said it came from the hoist room. Despite the chaos escalating all around them, their conversation remained remarkably casual.

"How's it working?" Riley asked.

"Pretty good."

"That's good."

And then, at 12:33:30, the cage lurched and began its ascent. Only whooshes of air and a noticeable drop in pressure signaled a station every two hundred feet. Station and track lights were completely sealed off by the heavy, moving partition of smoke. And though a million things were going through his mind as they shot up the shaft,

Howard Markve kept coming back to the most immediate of dangers. The doors to the cage were stuck open, and he could feel the wall plates of the shaft whizzing by his shoulder one right after another. If one was out of alignment and caught his shoulder, he knew he would die. Less than two minutes later, at 12:35:15, they were on 3100. Knowing it was 3100 and not the more familiar 3700, some men assumed they'd be going out the Silver Summit escape route. The Silver Summit mine connected with Sunshine on 3100, and was the only way out if the Jewell was in trouble.

Shaft foreman Gene Johnson waved them off. Tom Watts, who'd just made it from 5000, was confused.

"Gene," he said, "did you say the *Jewell Shaft?*"

"Yes, dammit, I said the Jewell Shaft!" Johnson gave him "the look"—a steely-eyed glance that said, *Are you sure you want to bother me again?* Even in the midst of confusion, the shaft foreman's personality stayed true.

The smoke consumed them one at a time. Watts wanted to help, but Johnson told him to get out. Watts offered the foreman his self-rescuer, believing that though the smoke was dense, he didn't need it as badly as did the men following him.

"No," Johnson snapped. "We have everything we need."

As they went west along the drift, Watts felt as if he had a mouthful of dry ice splinters—a hot-and-cold sensation like a peculiar frozen burn. He took out his rubber mouthpiece. Others did the same.

THE SECOND TIME THE CAGE CAME DOWN TO 4600, GREG Dionne was running it by himself. This time he carried a box of BM-1447s.

"Everybody takes one," he said. None huddled at the station knew the first thing about the self-rescuers, so Dionne calmly told them what they were and how they operated. His composure was reassuring. It was needed. Some were choking as they fiddled with the rescuers and tried to pay attention to what the young man was saying.

"See that little button on the front?" he asked through the smoke.

The men closest to him, those who could actually see where he was pointing, found it and acknowledged it.

"You push *that* button. It'll tear the canister seal loose and you can breathe through it."

Raise miner Terry Jerome clamped his teeth on the rubber mouthpiece and put on the nose clip—one of the few to use one. Smoke assaulted his eyes and he tried to breathe.

"Man, this dumb thing don't work," he said. "You can't get no air through it."

"Take your wrench and beat the damn button," Dionne said. "Make sure it tears the seal."

Jerome whapped it, heard the seal pop and tear, and in a second sweet air was filtered into his ravaged lungs.

"It might get hot," Dionne said. "That's okay. It means the thing is working. Whatever you do—don't take it out of your mouth."

The smoke thickened. Although they stood right next to Dionne, none of the men could see him. They listened to his every word. He was the only one who knew what to do.

"Okay," he said, "everybody get on."

On what? Jerome thought, unable to see a damn thing.

Dionne wrapped his arms around their shoulders and started guiding each man onto the cage. Jerome felt a flutter of fear in the slurry pit of his stomach. *God,* he thought, *I hope that cage is really there—or we're dead.*

The cage was a heaving bulge of men with thumping hearts. Roger Koisti, one of the last men on, spread his arms across the open gate and held on as Dionne belled them away. It was fast, and it needed to be. The smoke was turning the two-thousand-foot-deep shaft into a chimney flue. But at 4400 the smoke started to thin to some extent, and Terry Jerome saw just how much his partner Koisti had been hanging over the edge of the cage. A loose timber a couple of inches closer would have killed him. A minute or so later they made it to 3700, where Charlie Casteel waved them to the Jewell. The air was clear there. Everything looked good.

Sixteen

THE MEN IN THE EXTREME REACHES OF 5000 HAD NO inkling of the chaos overhead. Dewellyn Kitchen and Buz Bruhn were timbering a chute in a raise on the east side of 10-Shaft, in an area that longtime miners called "Good Hope Country." Thirty-nine-year-old Bruhn was using a saw powered by the compressed-air line when a motorman came up the raise.

"You better come out, Buz," the motorman said. "There's smoke out there on the station, and they want you guys out."

Bruhn conferred with Kitchen. They were so close to finishing shift that neither wanted to stop. A little while later an unusual odor wafted through the air.

"Kitch!" Bruhn hollered. "What's that smell?"

"I think that fan's getting hot back there," he said, looking in the direction of one of the big fans that pushed air through the drift.

"Okay."

But the odor was peculiar, an acrid scent that didn't really reek like burning oil, more like rotting garbage, heavy and wet. They continued lacing up the chute with timbers before climbing down the raise a few minutes later. The fetid odor intensified and could not be ignored.

"Hell, if we don't go, they'll send that kid back here to get us again," Bruhn said, rolling his heavily hooded eyes as he and his partner got on the motor and started off for the station. A few feet off the 15 raise, they found themselves against a black, vertical, undulating ocean. The edges of the smoke masked the drift in such a way that the underground space seemed endless and constricted at the same time. The two miners considered returning to their raise where the air had been clear, with the exception of the sharp, foul odor that appeared to come from the air line. Neither had recognized the odor as the stench warning Launhardt had released some thirty-five minutes before.

"If we don't go out, they'll send someone back here. Just put the motor on one point and let's go," Bruhn called out.

Kitchen set the motor at its slowest and steadiest speed. "One point" was not unlike locking a foot on the accelerator and keeping it at ten miles an hour. It was the operator's guarantee that they wouldn't jump the track. Doing that would certainly be problematic, leaving the men to walk through that wall of smoke. And neither man—no matter how tough—was up for that. As the smoke advanced and thickened, they pulled off their T-shirts, wet from sweat and water, and covered their faces.

They could scarcely see five feet when their motor crawled into the station. Closer in, through the shroud of smoke, they could see men scattered about. Some were by the shaft, a few more sat on benches, heads down, coughing their lungs out. Bruhn was drawn to the group on the benches. A few crouched down low, unnaturally so.

He couldn't determine whether they had fallen or had assumed that position to catch better air, below the smoke. Some breathed through self-rescuers. Most were hacking so hard they were nearly choking.

Another miner fought his way through the smoke to reach Bruhn, whom he knew had been a mechanic. The miner contended that a pump off the station had burned up and was the source of the smoke. Bruhn went over to check it out. He knelt down and parted the smoke with his hands and studied the pump. Everything, it seemed, was in working order.

Where is the damn smoke coming from? he asked himself.

In the meantime, Kitchen found a small cache of self-rescuers. He reached down and snagged a couple for Bruhn and himself, leaving only one remaining in the box. Bruhn tried to decipher the instructions, but the smoke was so irritating he could barely read a word through his vision-blurring tears. Anger overtook frustration. He wondered what idiot thought a man could read tiny instructions in a smoke-filled mine?

A miner who had been crouched nearby used his pipe wrench as a hammer and beat down on the release button. In that messy moment, when fear and confusion were escalating, Bruhn couldn't even thank the man, who disappeared back into the smoke.

"Come on, Kitch," he said, holding the black rubber mouthpiece away from his face, "let's get over by the shaft."

AFTERNOON, MAY 2
Big Creek Neighborhood

IT WAS BETTY JOHNSON'S DAY OFF FROM THE SILVERTON nursing home where she worked as an aide. That morning she'd curled up in bed while her husband, foreman Gene Johnson, dressed for work as the soft light of dawn ladled down the mountainsides. Sleeping in was a deal they'd struck when she'd returned to the workforce. It was a one-sided pact. On Gene Johnson's days off, he would rise at his usual time, however much Betty coaxed him to stay put. Johnson tried to comply with her wishes, but resting up just wasn't his way. He was always antsy about wasting a moment of the day. That morning he fixed a big breakfast for the kids and perked strong, oily coffee. Before leaving, he reached over and gave Betty a kiss. She rustled in her slumber. He might have said something, but any words vanished in the fog of sleepiness. The screen door shut and he was gone.

After lunch that Tuesday, Betty Johnson noticed a surge in traffic up Big Creek Road. A glance at the clock told her the timing wasn't right for shift change, but she disregarded the discrepancy. A little while later she looked out the window and saw a neighbor home early.

"You're supposed to be working," she called over. "Why aren't you at the mine?"

"Don't know how bad it is," he said, telling her of the fire, "but they cleared everybody out."

Gene Johnson's wife remained at ease. The very idea of a fire, certainly a serious one, in Sunshine seemed out of the realm of possibility. She waited at her kitchen table for her husband to come home.

Seventeen

HOWARD MARKVE CIRCLED THE STATION, NURSING A pain that shot through his legs like a steel spike. Although he'd experienced his share of injuries, nothing had ever hurt like his knees at that moment. He kept the self-rescuer in his mouth, and after each lap he checked to see how his partner Follette was holding up. Markve wondered if it would be smarter to get back to their working area and climb up 125 feet, where he knew the air was freshened by the piped-in atmosphere of the compressed-air line. He wasn't sure he had enough time to make it, and he didn't know whether Follette or any of the others could make it, either. In particular, he had serious doubts about Norman Fee.

"Let's get out of the smoke," he said, indicating where the men waited with blowing air from the whiz-bang. Follette pointed at cage tender Greg Dionne. He didn't speak, because he knew it would be dumb to spit out that mouthpiece. But he knew that if the cage was going to come to any place in the mine, it would come to where Dionne was standing—on *their* level. A few moments later the cage indeed returned, and the men on the station staggered on. Overcome by smoke at that point, Dionne appeared to be dizzy, and Schulz helped him aboard. Schulz was wearing a W-65, a self-rescuer with a heat exchanger that cooled the air coming off the hopcalite. The BM-1447 could heat up to 450 degrees Fahrenheit. It was like breathing air from an oven.

Follette wondered why the men across the drift just stayed put. He could see them through gauzy air. *Why don't they get over here?*

"I'm going to catch the next one," Joe Armijo said, backing away to the fresh air.

"You can squeeze in here," Markve called out, urging Ace Riley's partner to get on. Armijo refused. He was hacking badly and didn't think he could make it up the shaft just then.

"I'll get some air down at the grizzly," he said, retreating behind the thickening black curtain.

A young miner, a kid, appeared in the smoke and said that he was going to go with Armijo to get some air, too. This time Follette wouldn't hear of it.

"Get in!" he said.

The kid backed into the cage, and Follette swung his arms around him. There were at least fifteen or sixteen men crammed on the twelve-man cage. Follette hoped nobody would move behind him, or he'd fall down the shaft. He could see the other men across the station, still standing there. Markve planted his feet on the muck pile on the floor, and the cage took off. A hundred feet from 3100, a miracle of sorts materialized—a sudden rush, a band of fresh air. Markve took a deep breath. Never in his life had he tasted anything as sweet. Not honey on a spoon. Not the freshest milk poured from a bottle topped with a plug of cream. *Those things would be sour compared to this air,* he thought.

There was smoke on 3100, but nothing like they'd seen on 5000. Foreman Gene Johnson and shifters Virgil Bebb and Charlie Casteel yelled for the men coming from the cage to get out to the Jewell. Howard Markve went over to help Bob Goff, though he really didn't know what he could do. Goff needed a doctor. He was slumped against the rib; his body was swaying. Others were gagging and coughing. A few crumpled to the ground. Markve kept coughing, and every time he did, he let more smoke into his lungs. One of the bosses told Markve and Follette to leave Goff and get going.

"We'll take care of him," he said.

Markve trailed the others down the drift. He felt woozy. What was happening in the mine didn't seem real.

About that time a motor came into view, and the motorman called for the men to jump into the empty cars. Markve and Follette rode together. Three-fourths of the way to the Jewell, they hit another gust of sweet, fresh air. The motorman ordered everyone out of the cars, and returned to 10-Shaft. Follette helped steady Markve as they walked out. If the motorman hadn't come just when he did, Follette doubted that Markve would have made it out. He was convinced that some of those men left back at the station didn't have a fighting chance. He hoped the motorman would get to them in time. Bob Goff's twenty-nine-year-old wife had already lost one husband in the mines. It didn't seem fair that she'd have to suffer that again.

BUZ BRUHN, DEWELLYN KITCHEN, AND A FEW OTHERS STOOD by the shaft on 5000; the smoke seemed lighter in color, more or less white. In the midst of it all, Bruhn noticed a man standing by the grizzly with a cigarette hanging from his mouth. The miner was talking, smoking, and casually holding his self-rescuer as if it were a dinner bucket. On the station, miners talked about what under God's green earth could be burning?

And suddenly, Byron Schulz appeared.

"Get on," the young cager said.

"On *what?* What the hell are you talking about?"

"Get on the cage."

Tentatively, Bruhn stepped through the smoke. It was right there. Eight or nine guys were aboard, some in a bad way, while others seemed fine. Bruhn reached back for Kitchen and pulled him through the smoke. By then the cage was full; men held each other with viselike determination. No one was going to fall through the open doors. A few seconds later the cage disappeared up the shaft. Men closed their eyes to shut out the stinging cloud. There was nothing to see anyway; smoke blocked the pulsating lights that signaled the changing levels. Only decreasing air pressure and the give of the cables indicated they were moving. At the station, Gene Johnson commanded in the center of a black cloud, barking out directions. He punched his hands through the smoke in the direction of the old hoist room, about a hundred feet from the shaft. Some muck cars were lined up there behind a motor. Several men were already aboard, and others climbed in.

Buz Bruhn couldn't find Dewellyn Kitchen. The miner he had yanked aboard wasn't his partner after all. It was a tall, thin young guy with a mustache who'd just come back from Vietnam, some kid who had been in the mine no more than three or four days. One of the other guys from 5000 called over that Kitch had stopped to remove his false teeth so he could put them in his dinner bucket, something he did every day. Bruhn knew another cage would get back down to 5000 and pick up the rest of the crew. He'd meet his partner in the dry.

Bruhn's mouth was afire. The BM-1447 was a red-hot poker. He removed it for a few seconds of relief. His lips and tongue had been burned.

"Buz, the motor's there," Johnson said. "Go get on it."

"Can I give you a hand?"

Johnson shook his head. "Get on the motor and get out. *Now.*"

ONLY ONE MAN WAS ON THE STATION AT 3100 WHEN DELMAR Kitchen and the others stumbled in. It was Charlie Casteel. The twenty-nine-year-old shifter, a former Air Force airman second class, stood like an apparition next to the shaft. The beam of his lamp scratched at the thickened air before stabbing at Kitchen's raining eyes. Casteel did not hold a self-rescuer. Kitchen carried his, believing after the burst of cool air on 3550 that the device was not necessary. It took only a second to see that he was wrong.

"Get through that door!" Casteel shouted. But Kitchen remained inert. He didn't know what the boss was talking about. Up to that moment, he'd never set foot on that level. He was lost.

Casteel kicked his voice up more and worked his smoke-sore lungs. "Get through that door and don't look back. Just keep going!"

Though he was unsure of what he was doing, and the fire— wherever it was—had laid a veil of smoke obscuring everything, Delmar Kitchen plowed ahead as fast as possible. His lungs burned. He could see faint red lights, like burning embers of a campfire, and he knew to follow them. He pushed open an air door, and more smoke charged in. By then, Kitchen had given himself over to only one thing. He would not look back. He would save himself. He had three children and a wife, and the smoke was coming for him like some kind of unrelenting monster. His partner, Anderson, was a few steps behind, but if others were following, it was unknown to him. He traced the tracks and moved as fast as he could, clenching the self-rescuer in his mouth. He knew he didn't have much of a chance.

Throughout the mine, in pockets and stations where they waited, miners were trapped and unaware of the extent and the whereabouts of the fire. They didn't know that the 3700 level was in worse shape than the 3100. None could conceive of what was happening above wherever they were. Thousands of feet of rock separated them. Each crew was isolated, each man in some way alone.

12:46:30 P.M., MAY 2
5000 Level

THE SOUTH CAGE ARRIVED ON 5000 WITHOUT A CAGER. IT had been sent down to get shift boss Bob Anderson and miner Merle Hudson—and the other men who had missed it or had stayed put by the grizzly, taking in gulps of fresh air that became increasingly smoke-filled. No one got on this time. The cage hovered for fourteen minutes. Then it left the level for the last time.

3100 Level

A MILE IN NEARLY COMPLETE DARKNESS OFFERS NO REAL sense of time. Each step was at once timid and desperate. A man couldn't be sure where he was, but wasting time to figure it out wasn't possible. Delmar Kitchen never looked back. Not once. He'd been told to get his ass out of the station, and he meant to do just that. No matter what he encountered, he'd keep moving forward, holding the self-rescuer to his face and trying to see where he was going. A moment of relief was only that, a fleeting respite from eye-searing smoke. It appeared to thin and thicken in patches, as though it were a solid that coagulated along the ribs of the drift. The effect was cruel. Every time it cleared, there was the false hope that the worst was over. And then he was back in it again. Kitchen used a free hand to rub the smoke, sweat, and grimy tears from his eyes. He squeezed his eyes shut even as he continued his run in the dark. Relief came as the smoke dissipated a bit between 5-Shaft and 3-Shaft. But would it last? Would the smoke return as it had before? His legs trembled, and he wasn't certain how much farther he could go. He didn't understand why he felt so strange. Was it the smoke or shock?

Tom Watts fell in the muck. Though his body gave out, his brain processed an eerie and peculiar sight. He could see *under* the smoke; a layer of fresh air a foot high insulated the track rails. It was good air. Watts got up, and found the smoke growing thinner as the he traveled west down the drift. He stopped at the old timber station not far from 4-Shaft.

"I can't go much farther," Watts said, "without taking five."

At the station, men watched and waited for more of their buddies to arrive. A soft, hazy light of a motor pierced the smoke down drift, growing brighter and larger. The motor's cars were stuffed with men. Bob McCoy, in the last car, was in grim shape. The fifty-six-year-old had been on the cage up from 5000. He was propped up in a car with another miner, fighting to hold a self-rescuer in place.

Ace Riley's muscles pumped, pulling taut the fabric of his soaked T-shirt. He felt dizzy and weak. As he lifted himself from the muck car, he lost his balance and fell. Pain shot through his body, but he didn't cry out. He just lay there watching. It was like he was viewing a slow-motion replay from a TV football game. Miners moved with seemingly hurried motions, but at a protracted pace. Riley saw Launhardt and his crew running with backpacks, but they didn't seem to be getting anywhere. He scanned the drift. Men were all around, scattered like fallen leaves. A few were receiving oxygen from tanks brought from the machine shop. One fought off his rescuers, saying he didn't want a "damn mask" over his face.

"You're trying to kill me," he said, shoving a mechanic away.

Finally, at the station, Delmar Kitchen was even more confused, nearly disoriented. He couldn't understand why he had difficulty walking, even after a couple of mechanics gave him a blast of oxygen.

McCoy struck a match and took a drag off a cigarette. Without any apparent warning or reason, McCoy fell to the ground. Everyone was utterly dumbstruck. He'd just come from a smoke-filled drift and one puff of a cigarette knocked him to the ground? What caused that? They pulled McCoy to his feet and shook him, snapping him out of his stupor.

Out of the twenty-five men working on 5000, sixteen had made it to the Jewell.

BACK AT THE 3100 STATION, MEN CONTINUED COMING OFF the cage, gagging and gasping. Some held BM-1447s to their mouths, and others either hadn't been given one or had given up on the tuna-can-sized unit. Roger Findley steadied himself by the shaft. The nineteen-year-old counted the crew emerging from the curtain of smoke. Forty-nine men stumbled off the cage before the last cage zoomed to the station, returning empty. The cage was lowered another time, to the 5000, but once more returned without a soul. Findley was growing dizzy and doubted he could hang on much longer. His nose sent out streamers of mucus, and he could hardly see through the water in his eyes.

"I can't take the smoke no more," he called over to Gene Johnson. "I'm going to head out of here."

The foreman nodded. "We'll see you, Roger."

Findley picked up an oily rag and didn't look back, but he knew that ten or more men were still sitting around the station, coughing and waiting. One guy was eating his lunch. Very nearly overcome by fear and the burning-rubber-smelling smoke, the cager made it another 150 feet before he tumbled in the darkness. Reaching to pull himself up, he felt the form of a human body. Then another. *What the—?* He started moving again only to fall a second time. There were bodies of several men, maybe a dozen or more. He could hear several making gurgling sounds as life seeped away. Findley called out names, but none moved. He wasn't a big man, at only five feet five, but he was muscular and in good shape. Still, he couldn't lift those miners. He couldn't do a damn thing for any of them. At the junction of two drifts, Roger Findley grabbed a whiz-bang and directed its flow to a fallen miner's face. What else could he do? He went on.

12:53 P.M., MAY 2
5800 Level

AFTER MORE THAN A HALF HOUR OF BEING IDLE, THE NORTH compartment of 10-Shaft's double-drum moved once more with about ten men from 5800 and 5600 on board, bound for 3100. Among the group were Delmar Kitchen's father, Elmer; Bob Launhardt's buddy from the Talache gold mine, Duwain Crow; and a Mullan man named Doug Wiederrick.

One of the three would make the ultimate sacrifice.

Eighteen

S OMETHING HAD HAPPENED TO THE HOISTMAN AT 10-SHAFT ON
3100. Surface hoistman Lino Castaneda didn't know what the
problem might be, but he knew someone had to get down there and
run the hoist, or the men wouldn't be able to get out of the mine.
He dialed the Kellogg number of another Sunshine hoistman. That
was a bold move. No one was supposed to call in another employee
unless directed to by a shifter. In the culture of Sunshine Mine, no
one ever second-guessed a higher-up or did anything that cost the
company money without getting approval. Castaneda didn't care.
He'd pay the man out of his own pocket. But the phone just rang
and rang. *Come on, answer!* He thought of another hoistman, but that
guy lived in Coeur d'Alene. He couldn't get there in time.

1:03 P.M., MAY 2
4800 Level

ABOUT THE TIME THE TATTLETALE RECORDED ITS LAST movement, most of the men on 4800 had determined that their self-rescuers were useless and had ditched them. The air was reasonably clear where they had gathered by the battery barn. But looking at what was coming down the shaft, it seemed a good bet that the air around the station would soon be contaminated. No one conceded concern. Help would arrive soon. Someone suggested that opening a pair of air doors about fifty yards down the drift might drive away the smoke. The doors ran east-west across the drift and were used to channel airflow to the lower levels. For all that the miners on 4800 knew, the ventilation scheme was a house of cards, and one change could affect airflow a thousand feet above. It was a risk they had to take.

Partners Ron Flory and Tom Wilkinson took self-rescuers and went for the air doors. The first of the big wood-and-steel doors swung open without any trouble. But when Wilkinson pushed on the second door, it opened, only to slam shut again. It took strength to do it alone. He planted his feet, pressed his shoulder against the door, and shoved with everything he had. His self-rescuer fell from his mouth.

Nearly at that instant, Flory looked over. His eyes running from the acrid smoke, he strained to see his partner.

"Wilkinson's down in the piss ditch!" someone called out.

Flory spun around and yelled his name, but Wilkinson lay face-down in the narrow channel that carried runoff from the working areas. Flory cradled Wilkinson in his big bear arms. *Jesus, what's happened?* At 135 pounds, Wilkinson was slight, but his deadweight seemed ten times greater. Try as he might, Flory couldn't lift him high enough to get him over his shoulders. *Something's wrong. Lifting*

Tom shouldn't be this hard. Flory felt dizzy and called out for help. A couple of guys helped him carry Wilkinson back to the battery barn. He was out cold. Flory clenched his shoulders and shook him with increasing intensity.

"Tom! Tom!"

Flory had no idea why Wilkinson had suddenly fallen unconscious. Maybe a heart attack or something. He had been pushing on the air door and just dropped. No words, no "Hey, I'm feeling funny . . ." He just slumped. Wilkinson was a discarded marionette, slumped in the muck in a heap.

Flory's thumping heart propelled a surge of adrenaline through his heaving body. He looked at the other miners.

"I got to get him to better air," he said. "Gotta get him out of here."

THE LAST MEN ON 3100 WERE SPUTTERING WITH THEIR final breaths. Some had already stopped trying to fight the smoke. It was as if the air were infused with acid. Elmer Kitchen, who had been helping Byron Schulz run the cage that morning, was sprawled on the ground. Buz Bruhn's carpool buddy from Mullan, the decorated war hero Casey Pena, had plunged his head underwater in a trough in a wasted attempt to escape the merciless air. Duwain Crow, one of the toughest miners and motorcycle riders in Big Creek, was inert, lying across the track line. Blood surged from the stocky miner's mouth and nose.

Double-drum cage tender Schulz sucked hard on the rubber mouthpiece of his BM-1447. His eyes bulged and his heart pushed at his rib cage. He turned around and went to find Gene Johnson. If anyone knew what to do, Schulz felt, it was the indomitable mine foreman. He walked around like he owned the mine. New guys thought he actually did. It was Johnson who had given Schulz his first self-rescuer when the smoke started—and when there was time to hand them out. Schulz's light worked overtime as it passed its blade of light through the smoke and over dead men. It finally pinpointed Johnson. He was lying on the slab of the station; the big man with the military bearing had crumpled into a ball. He, too, appeared lifeless. Driven solely by adrenaline, Schulz went toward the hoist room, where he found Don Firkins, who'd escaped from 5400, buckled over on the concrete floor. Firkins, thirty-seven, was working desperately on a self-rescuer. His skin was nearly paper white, his black beard dripping in sweat and mucus. Schulz knew that Firkins had been safety trained. Why couldn't he get the self-rescuer working? Between convulsions, Firkins tried to speak, but his words were lost in the noise of other men fighting for their lives. Nothing anyone was saying made sense. It was gibberish mixed with grace notes of despair and anger. Schulz knelt and tried to talk to Firkins and other fallen men, but none seemed to understand a word he said. One by one, the men in the room fell silent. Besides Schulz, the last two standing were Bob Scanlan and Doug Wiederrick. Scanlan, thirty-five, stood by the hoist chair fighting to steady his six-foot-three-inch body. His ruddy complexion had gone pallid, and he started to shake. Then, very suddenly, he slumped over. Wiederrick, also thirty-five, was upright, but appeared dazed. It appeared he was desperately trying to get the cage to one of the lower levels, but in his confusion he was unable to do so.

"Doug, we got to get out of here," Schulz yelled, his voice raspy. "There's nothing more we can do!"

Schulz had doubts they could survive much longer. Everyone around them had passed out or was already dead. But Wiederrick, the last hoistman at 10-Shaft, was not completely in his mind. He didn't see the urgency. It was as though he didn't know all the men had fallen across the station like a toxic fish kill.

"We've got to get out of here!" Schulz repeated.

A brief semblance of lucidity came to Wiederrick's sweaty face, and he finally agreed to evacuate. The pair started toward the drift, but Wiederrick stopped.

"I'm calling topside," he said, returning to the hoist room.

Schulz clutched one of the three BM-1447s that he'd used while Wiederrick picked up the phone and said they were on the way out, and needed to know where they'd find fresh air.

"Oh my God," Wiederrick said. "We'll never make it. *I'll* never make it." Those words barely out of his mouth, he fell to the floor.

Schulz tried to feed Wiederrick a mouthpiece, but the hoistman spat it out like a baby refusing a pacifier. Schulz, now in tears, pleaded, but Wiederrick wanted no part of it. On Schulz's third try, Wiederrick defiantly batted the breathing unit across the concrete of the floor. Schulz fumbled in the smoke to retrieve it. *We're both going to die*, he thought. He begged Wiederrick once more, but the hoistman turned away.

He's giving up, Schulz thought. *Doug's giving up!*

Schulz stumbled over to the water hose where men washed off diggers to avoid muddying up the station at shift's end, tore off his shirt, and soaked it. Then he wrapped the dripping garment around the self-rescuer and his face. *Everyone is dead.* He could scarcely see. Tears surged in his eyes to impede the sting of the seamless, acrid black sheet. He tripped over a body. He couldn't tell who it was, but a white hat caught the fallout of his light. Shifters wore white hard-hats; crewmen wore yellow. *Virgil Bebb?* He got up, but after a few more hurried steps, Schulz toppled over another lifeless form. The young man's face was burning hot. His throat was constricted with coagulated mucus. This was like tear gas, he thought; it surely wasn't ordinary smoke.

AROUND 1:00 P.M., MAY 2

3100 Level

ROGER FINDLEY WAS FACING DEATH, AND THE SCARIEST part was that he knew it. He moved in a herky-jerky, meandering fashion as he tried to navigate the length of the drift. A wet rag stayed fused to his mouth and nose. With each attempted breath, he found himself coughing and thinking how he was going to get out of there somehow. Had the men he'd seen sprawled out on the drift or in the piss ditch thought the same thing? Just past an abandoned drift with a bundle of ten- and twelve-foot timbers, a pinhole of light from a miner's cap lamp pierced the blockade of smoke. A man had propped himself up against a timber, and was staring across the drift. When he saw it was a shift boss, Findley could have wept. He'd know what to do to get out of there.

"Hey," he called out, "what are you doing?"

The man was mute. Findley aimed his light directly into the man's face. His hazel eyes were an empty stare.

"Hey!" Findley tried again. A shudder of horror grappled with his overwrought emotions, chilling and escalating his own fear. The man was dead. Findley gulped for air, but there was nothing but rank-smelling smoke. He started to run. Another two hundred feet and he could go no farther. Though he hadn't been in church in years, the young man sat on a timber and started praying. He'd set religion aside in favor of partying and carousing in the district— territory well trod by miners. But now Roger Findley was back before God, asking for a second chance. He had made it so far, it was almost as if the Almighty owed him. There could be no greater cruelty than to steal a man's life when he'd fought so hard to live. He looked up to see the diffuse glow of a headlight and the firefly dots of three or more cap lamps. Someone was out there. It was a lovely dream as the lights drew closer. He got back on his feet and rocked his head back and forth. *I'm alive.*

Nineteen

THE RED LAMP ON THE BACKSIDE OF THE JEWELL PULSED like a heartbeat. The Sun Con Switch light warned everyone to get off the tracks because a motor was en route to the station. Harvey Dionne and Paul Johnson watched for the motor, but none came. Some haze hung low in the drift, but Dionne didn't consider it dense enough to be a real health risk. What had triggered the signal? He conferred with Johnson, who was back on the phone, and went to find out. It was quiet. No voices. No motors. Just the sound of his own labored breathing and his boots against the muck. About a hundred yards in, foreman Jim Bush emerged from the smoke. He staggered toward Dionne's light, and their beams dueled.

Bush's eyes were wild, and he all but fell into Dionne's arms.

"Bob's down!" he said, referring to his brother. His speech was oddly slurred, but there was no mistaking what he was saying.

149

Bush said he'd fought hard to bring him out, but he couldn't even drag him to safety. But he had more bad news. Wayne Blalack and Pat Hobson had tried to help with his brother, but they were also overcome. The men had collapsed about five hundred feet past 5-Shaft.

"They're all back there," he said, "three down back there."

Back on the station, Roberto Diaz, Richard Nickleby, and Ron Stansbury volunteered to help. With Dionne and Johnson leading the way, they took a motor down the drift. None wore a self-rescuer or even thought to bring one. The farther they went, the darker and thicker the smoke became. Time and space faded. None had any idea how far they'd gone when they hit something on the track, derailing the motor. Dionne jumped off and waved his lamp in the darkness. Was it a timber? His light followed a form on the track partially obscured by the front end of the motor. The foreman hurriedly traced the shape with movements of his lamp, but was unable to identify what it was until he saw the whole of it. It was Wayne Blalack. The thirty-five-year-old electrician had toppled onto the tracks and the motor had partially severed his leg. The father of two grade-school-aged kids was dead. Also down were Bob Bush and Patrick Hobson. There was no saving *any* of them. Fatigue, stress, and the effects of the smoke had tapped their strength. Each had keeled over in midstep. None had a self-rescuer.

"Let's get out of here," he said. The group tried to get the train back on its rails, but it was impossible. They started to walk, but with each step, Dionne grew weaker. He put all of his concentration into moving forward, away from the smoke. When he turned around at 5-Shaft to see how the others were doing, Diaz and Johnson were gone.

KENNY WILBUR RETURNED FROM THE BOREHOLE TO THE station to find Dionne and Johnson had vanished. In their place were an old Okie miner, an anxious motorman, and an electrician named Norman Ulrich. Another motorman took a rescue crew toward 10-Shaft.

"They ain't come back," Ulrich said.

Ulrich, who'd been left to monitor the station phone, handed the receiver to Wilbur.

"Two minutes ago the guys were all talking and all of a sudden, nothing."

Wilbur held it against his ear. *Nothing.* The cage tender wanted to believe that the lines had been cut by falling timber or maybe burned by the fire. But after listening more intently, he heard a muffled popping noise and it scared him. The lines were good.

"Anyone there?" he asked.

No answer.

Wilbur fixed his blue-green eyes in the direction of the drift, and the Okie shook his head.

"I've been in there. I ain't going back in that."

But something had to be done to get Harvey Dionne, the Bush brothers, and the other men back to the station, where they could breathe. It had been taking too long. Wilbur was hopped up. He was ready to do something—*anything*—to help the trapped men. He and Ulrich took a motor and went down the drift. Near 4-Shaft the smoke thickened to a boil, forming a more or less solid plug. It was as if the motor's headlight had been swallowed. Ulrich stopped and fished out a pair of self-rescuers that had likely been discarded by escaping miners. He put one in his mouth.

"This is great," he said, pulling it out. "Try it."

"That's okay. I'll get another one."

"No, you gotta try *this* one."

The thought of tasting that slimy mouthpiece made Wilbur nearly gag, but the electrician was so damn insistent. The cager acquiesced.

"Yeah, *great.*"

Ulrich stayed put, and Wilbur started walking. Visibility was so poor that he couldn't even see his feet. He stayed on the track line by sliding his boots at a blind man's pace. Fifty yards down the drift, an epiphany hit him. *What am I going to do when I get there? How can I pack a man out of here?* He returned to Ulrich, feeling completely defeated.

Ulrich dismissed the younger man's attempt at valor and announced he'd get the missing men himself.

"I don't think there's any sense in it," Wilbur said, but the headstrong electrician ignored him and retreated into the smoke. He stared at the black wall. In the nothingness of what was being accomplished, time raced.

How much longer should I wait? Should I go after him?

And when he could no longer put up with idleness, Wilbur started through the smoke a second time. He knew that what he was doing was pointless, maybe even stupid. He slowly edged about twenty yards when he saw a feather of light coming toward him, moving with the cadence of a man's hurried stride. Norm Ulrich had also given up.

A few minutes later, both men were on the cage to the surface with nothing to show for their heroics. Not long after, Wilbur saw Harvey Dionne out by the portal. But what happened to production foreman Bob Bush and shifter Paul Johnson? They'd gone into the drift and disappeared. Where were they?

MINE SUPERINTENDENT AL WALKUP DROVE HIS COMPANY car, a blue El Camino, over Fourth of July Pass to Big Creek as fast as the car/pickup crossbreed could go. He was new to Sunshine, having been hired in September 1971. At thirty-five, Walkup not only had a college degree from the Montana School of Mines at Butte, but he had done his share of mining, and had a genuine love for the underground. His dad was a miner, and he knew that whatever he'd do with his own life, it would be related to digging for ore. Walkup and his wife and son moved from Montana to Mullan and soon found that despite snowy winters that left the front windows of their house blocked of all sunlight, it was a pretty nice place to live.

Sunshine was head and shoulders above the others where Walkup had mined. He'd worked at some rinky-dink outfits in Montana where the owners didn't have a pot to piss in and where miners didn't know a pick from a shovel. Sunshine had financial resources. And despite the corporate backbiting, the company had mined more than 8 million ounces of silver in 1971. The plan for 1972 called for an astounding 10 million.

When he pulled into Big Creek, a turgid column of smoke was rising from the ventilation shaft, the likes of which Al Walkup had never seen. It filled the sky. He found his buddy, Jim Bush, in a small group near the shifter's shack. Bush had taken in a lot of smoke and was in a daze. He was also sweating profusely.

He's going to collapse any moment, Walkup thought. A couple of miners stood ready in case he fell. His words spilled out of his mouth.

"I tried to get Bob out, but I couldn't," Bush said. "There were bodies everywhere. Tried to drag him out."

Walkup felt tears welling up. Bob Bush had been his mentor.

"Some guys that went in for my brother didn't come out."

"Jesus."

The smoke was churning in the sky. No one had a plan. What could they do? The smoke had become an impenetrable barrier. Where did that leave them?

"Where are the others?" Walkup asked.

"Still down there," someone said.

And then the kicker.

"The hoist room is down on 10-Shaft. No one's answering."

The men faced the portal. Its concrete header spelled out JEWELL SHAFT in big block letters, making the entrance resemble some kind of underworld monument.

Twenty

1:05 P.M., MAY 2
3100 Level

THE APPROACHING CLOUD REMINDED SAFETY ENGINEER BOB Launhardt of a column spewing from the chimney stack of an old steam locomotive. It rose up black and thick, and rolled down the drift. He estimated visibility at five feet, though it was tricky to approximate. The heavy curtain kept heaving. Launhardt held a Wolfe flame safety lamp and a Draeger gas detector. Looking a bit like a tall, thin, brass seaman's lantern, the safety lamp indicated when oxygen was adequate underground. Launhardt noted that the flame slightly diminished in size, but there was still enough oxygen in the air to sustain life.

Next he prepared the Draeger to test for carbon monoxide. Developed by a nearly century-old German company, the Draeger detection tube had become an indispensable tool of mine safety, so much so that in the 1930s, mine rescue men were called "Draegermen" and were featured in the Superman comic book series. The Draeger came in two parts—a glass tube filled with chemical reagents and a small bellows to force air through the tube. The tube was etched incrementally from 1,000 to 3,000 parts per million (ppm) to measure the magnitude of the danger. Launhardt broke off the tip of the tube, put it into the chamber, and worked the bellows, passing about 50 cubic centimeters of mine air through the tube. Usually it took a minute or so for a dark stain to appear, thus giving a reading. Certainly it took a full air sample. Not this time. Launhardt stared at the tube, his light flashing against glass and smoke. With only one-fourth of the sample air through the chamber, the stain had gone beyond the manufacturer's calibrations. The tube went completely black. The mine was poisoned with more carbon monoxide than his instrumentation could record.

As Launhardt warned his crew of the air's ruthless toxicity, a light from a miner's lamp approached from down the drift.

A moment later, Launhardt fished through the smoke and grabbed a hand and pulled. It was Roger Findley, the cager who'd prayed for a second chance after running from the chaos of the station only to find a dead man propped up in the drift. Shaky and near collapse, but alive, Findley was wearing a BM-1447. Launhardt felt a small surge of hope. *More would come out.*

The young man was in shock, but he rattled off the names of dead men he'd seen back at the station. He also had a warning.

"Be careful with the motor," he said, "when you get back just before the crosscut. You'll run over those guys. They're laying all over the tracks."

Findley needed medical care, and Zingler asked Beehner to take him topside.

"No, you go ahead and take him out," Beehner said. "I'll go in with Larry and Bob."

"We'll head for 10-Shaft," Launhardt said, his rescue party now down to three. "But we'll take it slow."

Six hundred feet later, another light came down the drift. It zig-zagged and moved with the trajectory of a ricocheting Ping-Pong ball, side to side and up and down. To the unfamiliar, it might have resembled a flashlight carried by an exuberant kid or a sloppy drunk. Launhardt knew it was a cap lamp. And its erratic tempo meant trouble.

A frantic voice called out.

"They're all dead back there!"

It was Byron Schulz, the cager who'd escaped from the hoist room after Doug Weiderrick determined that he couldn't make it out alive and fell to the floor. Schulz stumbled at the motor, his wet shirt and W-65 self-rescuer hanging at his side. He was crying, and his sweaty face was red from his frenzied run in the dark. His deep-set eyes were a study in panic.

"They're gone! All of them," he said. "I need oxygen!"

Hawkins reversed the motor, pulling away from a particularly tight stretch of track, and Launhardt jumped from the car. Schulz's arms were flailing in desperation, and it seemed that he might grab at Launhardt's face mask. The air was reasonably clear there, but Hawkins decided to err on the side of caution and kept his mask in place. Launhardt did the same. Hawkins remained on the motor because, from the way Schulz was carrying on, it seemed a good bet they'd be returning to the Jewell.

"I need oxygen. Get me oxygen, please," Schulz said.

Launhardt told him that he'd be all right, but the words did little to soothe. He tried to hold Schulz's convulsing torso, like a baby that couldn't stop crying. The younger man struggled. He had been within a minute of dying, and fear had taken over reason.

Don Beehner got off the motor to help.

About that time, Hawkins's light cord caught on a timber, forcing the ray of his cap lamp askew. His stomach roiled and his heart rate escalated. *This looks very bad.* He glanced over his shoulder and saw

Beehner fiddling with the hose that ran from his McCaa pack, still not on his back but resting on the back of the motor.

"Let's get a helmet on him, so he can get some oxygen," Hawkins called out, his words muffled through his face mask.

Schulz was in that place halfway between passing out and being totally scared stiff. The self-rescuer plugged his mouth, stifling his words. His eyes were watery pools, with big dark pupils awash in fear. As Launhardt prepared a McCaa by clearing the hose and releasing the flow of oxygen, Don Beehner removed his own mask and held it over Schulz's face.

"Here," the nipper said, "breathe this. This is fresh air." After giving Schulz a shot of oxygen, Beehner returned the mask to his own face. He repeated the switch several times.

When Hawkins saw that Launhardt was ready, he pulled the BM-1447 from Schulz's mouth.

"You put the mask on his face," he said.

"They're all *dead* back there," Schulz repeated.

Launhardt tightened Schulz's head straps while Hawkins continued to brace him so he wouldn't fall. Launhardt told Schulz to be calm. He hoped that the Wardner kid wasn't in so much shock that he didn't understand that they were trying to save him.

"Breathe through the apparatus," the safety engineer said. "We'll get you out of there."

Launhardt turned around to tell Don Beehner things were under control, but he was gone.

1:05 P.M., MAY 2
Jewell Shaft Portal

FOREMAN HARVEY DIONNE ASKED IF ANYONE HAD SEEN HIS son. Many had, of course. Greg Dionne was the sole reason miner Bill Mitchell and others on his cage had escaped. Certainly, Harvey

Dionne had a job to do, but he was also a father, and his son was missing. The Dionnes had been one of at least a dozen pairs of fathers and sons underground Tuesday, including the Kitchens, Delbridges, and Follettes. Besides worrying about his boy, something else found room to lurk in the foreman's thoughts—the borehole on 3700. He wondered what had happened after Kenny Wilbur stripped the hole of its lagging stopper. *Did it work? Did it allow for good air to course down to 4800? And where was Greg?*

Twenty-one

Larry Hawkins's lamp, now hastily retargeted to his line of vision, illuminated the rib of the drift. Nothing. Where was Beehner? He lowered his gaze to track level and, with the rapid swipe of his light, saw Beehner's feet, legs, torso, and head. He was facedown in the piss ditch. Schulz was screaming again, and Launhardt was doing his damnedest to calm him. Hawkins knelt down and grabbed Beehner by the shoulders and rolled him over. He shifted his weight and pulled him upright; suction from mud threatened to pull off his boots. Hawkins knew there wasn't enough time to get a helmet on Beehner.

What am I gonna do? There's only one mask right here—and there's two of us.

Beehner felt heavy and startlingly lifeless. Hawkins returned the mask to his own face, breathing in quickly and deeply. He'd just come up from the bottom of the ocean, and this was the only oxygen he'd get. *This,* he thought, *could be my last breath.* He positioned the mask on Beehner's face. Blood had begun to fountain from Beehner's nose and mouth, splashing the inside of the face mask. Hawkins held his breath. *It'll be all right. We're gonna make it.* And then Beehner's body made a strange movement—a strong, then slightly fainter, twitch. A shudder, perhaps involuntary, possibly the man's last fight to live.

"Bob! Beehner's down," Hawkins called out. "Let's get the apparatuses off the timber truck and get him on it and get him out of here!"

Launhardt looked over, his terrified eyes filling his mask, as Hawkins wiped blood from his faceplate. The rock rabbit felt disoriented and nauseated. He suddenly became convinced something wasn't right with his own air supply. He thought he was rebreathing his own used air, but mixed with the deadly atmosphere of the drift. Panic took over. He struggled to lift Beehner onto the timber car, but he couldn't do it. He gave it everything he had, but he just couldn't do it.

"Bob, I have to go," he said, already moving away. "My machine isn't working right."

"Do you think you can make it?"

Hawkins thought he could. "Just go ahead and take care of Beehner and the kid. I think I can get to the fresh air back there."

With that, the rock rabbit hurried down the track, feverishly working the bypass valve of his McCaa self-rescuer.

LAUNHARDT BALANCED A FRIGHTENED BYRON SCHULZ ON A timber truck ahead of the motor, a precarious and dangerous spot. If Schulz thrashed and slipped off, the motor could slice him in two. Don Beehner was splayed out alongside the tracks, his body limp and damp. Launhardt squatted and hooked Beehner under his arms and lifted him chest high, but the sides of muck cars were wider at the top than at the bottom, making it awkward to get him inside. A cocktail of adrenaline and fear drove him, but Launhardt still couldn't gather the strength. He made at least three attempts.

This can't be happening, he thought.

Blood dripped from the nipper's mouth like red candle wax. *He must be dead,* Launhardt thought. He didn't feel for a pulse because he didn't think there was anything more he could do. Schulz needed out, or he'd die right there, too. Launhardt rolled Beehner away from the rails and started the motor for the station. Leaving Don Beehner alone in the drift was the worst moment of his life. He knew it even then.

WESTWARD DOWN THE DRIFT, HAWKINS FELL TO HIS KNEES. Which way to go? The sole source of light was the beam of his cap lamp. Everywhere he looked was another possible route to the Jewell. Tracks converged in a spaghetti of both rusty and polished steel bands. *Two men are dead. Probably a hell of a lot more. And I don't know which way to go to get out of here.* An answer came from the tracks themselves when burnished steel glinted off his lamp. Rust grew virtually overnight in a wet mine like Sunshine, so it was apparent to Hawkins that the parallel lines of the shiniest track had to be the way out. He moved as fast as he could, falling and getting up, the pack bouncing on his back reminding him with each blow how it had failed Don Beehner. He tried to tell himself his confusion was only his unfamiliarity with 3100. Yet as he hurried through the drift, he wondered if, like Don Beehner, he'd been poisoned by the air. Maybe he would die, too. He tried to rotate his bypass valve again, but nothing. His hands were sweaty, and his grip had weakened. He felt the valve give a little, but he still wasn't getting any air. Everything he'd learned in mine safety training came back in an avalanche, and he worked all the scenarios. Something, he thought, had to be wrong with his McCaa. Twenty more yards down drift, he came across Charlie

Casteel, standing along the rib of the drift. Relieved that he wasn't alone, Hawkins tapped Casteel's shoulder, but he didn't respond. It was more than the absence of even a flicker of life. Casteel was completely rigid.

Hawkins's terror was now off the meter. When had Casteel arrived there? How was it that they hadn't seen him when they passed by earlier? Launhardt and Schulz were probably dead, Casteel was dead, and if he made it out, he'd be the last one. Hawkins started to run.

But a hundred yards from Casteel's body, Hawkins came across something far more horrific—a crosscut into 3100. He hadn't a clue which drift went to the Jewell. This time the tracks offered no clues. Hawkins knew he'd reached the end. He'd never make it home to Ross Gulch and his high-school-sweetheart wife and their two boys.

Most who die in a mine perish in a quick gulp or a bloody splat that doesn't allow for much, if any, contemplation. Larry Hawkins was on the ground, thinking he was nearing the end. He did not reflect upon the moments of his life or on those he'd leave behind. Instead, the desire to survive took over. He pulled himself together when he heard the familiar sound of a motor. Adrenaline urged him to get back up and try one more goddamn time to get out of there. He fought for clarity. He wasn't sure where the sound was coming from. He turned around. A growing ray of light was coming from the direction of 10-Shaft. It was Bob Launhardt. Hawkins yelled for Launhardt to keep going, and he jumped onto the last muck car. Concerned that his apparatus could be snagged by a timber, Hawkins crouched down as low as he could. In doing so, his hat and lamp slipped. Now, unable to see, he braced his right hand against the car, and used his left to feel for the bypass valve. He worried that Launhardt might think he'd fallen off the car, so he grabbed for his lamp and held it to the edge of the car so the light was visible. He didn't want to stop for a second.

When the motor stopped at the station, Bob Launhardt tore off his face mask and went to help Schulz. Hawkins wanted to throw what he insisted was a goddamn piece of junk against the wall, but he stopped short.

"Bob," he called over. He held out the hose. "Look at this." His voice was a rasp. "It has a tear in it."

Launhardt really couldn't see anything. "My God," he said, anyway. "You're lucky you got out."

A couple of miners helped Hawkins walk across the station. The big man was drained of color and trembling, but he insisted that he was fine.

"Like hell you are," a miner said. "You need good air."

Launhardt stayed with Schulz. He put his own mask on the traumatized cage tender's face to give him an extra shot of oxygen. Schulz was petrified.

None would say so aloud, but everyone else was, too.

Twenty-two

NOTHING IS DIRTIER THAN A MINER'S DIGGERS. THE water, the heat, the oil from machinery, and sweat wick so much dirt into a man's Levi's or the weave of his T-shirt that no amount of detergent or bleach can remove it. In many homes across the district there were two distinct clothes piles—Dad's and the rest of the household's. Most men cleaned up with a shower and changed into street clothes before going home, but some didn't bother. Those fellows got into their cars and trucks and took that grime right with them. Myrna Flory had gathered up her husband's dirty clothes, planted herself in front of roiling coin-operated washers at the Pik Kwik in Kellogg, and thumbed through a magazine.

Early Tuesday afternoon, a keyed-up Garnita Keene spotted Ron Flory's blue '70 Charger parked in front of the laundry. She knew her sister, Myrna, had to be inside. Everyone in town knew that car and the man who drove it. "Ron Floorboards" some called him, because he drove with a foot pressed hard on the accelerator. Garnita hurried inside with the news of the fire at Sunshine. Myrna set the magazine aside and listened. She thought that a fire only meant that her husband would get home early. He'd grouse about being shut out of the mine, losing pay for something as silly as a little bit of smoke in a place that had no fuel, nothing to burn. The sisters chatted a minute and Myrna gave up on her remaining laundry and returned to the tiny house she shared with Ron and Tiger on Smelterville's Washington Street. A few minutes later she was on her way to have a look at what she fully expected was just a shack ablaze. She was among the first to arrive, and a quick inspection of the metal-sided structures of the compound made it immediately obvious that none were on fire. Instead, a column of smoke poured from a stack planted into the outcropping above the portal. Myrna pulled a cigarette from her purse, lit up, and waited. More women, some with young children in tow, lined up and joined her. No one expected more than a little inconvenience and maybe even some excitement.

When Garnita arrived and found her sister in the mine yard, her thoughts were on Billy Allen, her boyfriend with the sexy grin. She knew he'd missed work on Monday, and she hoped he'd dumped shift again. She didn't want to ask anyone if he'd been down on 5200 that morning. Allen was still married, after all, and Garnita didn't want word to get back to his wife and children that some woman was up at the mine bawling about the man who belonged to them.

1:30 P.M., MAY 2
4800 Level

IMPOSSIBLY, *INCREDIBLY*, THE SMOKE CONTINUED TO BUILD way down on 4800. But still no cage. Tom Wilkinson was out cold. Flory had seen that look on his passed-out partner's face before, but only after one beer too many. Plenty of district men had seen the gummy floor of the Big Creek Store up close. Most had probably *tasted* it. Flory, his eyes burning to the point of tears, didn't see how Wilkinson would have a chance if he didn't get some fresh air, and fast. Sweat dripped from his goatee, and Flory's heart thumped inside his chest like a door knocker, each beat reminding him of his own fright. *Something had to be done.* Flory knew there was clear air down by the borehole. By then, motorman Dick Bewley, forty, was unsteady and also needed fresh air. Flory put Wilkinson on the top of his motor while Bewley crawled onto the other. Down the drift, the smoky veneer cleared. Flory flashed his cap light and they stopped. He and Bewley carried Wilkinson near a cross-drift where the air was clear.

Flory bent closer and called out Wilkinson's name and patted his face. Wilkinson looked small and weak, a little boy with stubble on a dirty face. Had Tom had a heart attack? Had he passed out because of some illness? Or was it the smoke? And if it was, Flory wondered almost out loud, why hadn't it knocked him out as well? He gripped Wilkinson's shoulders and lifted, trying to snap his partner out of it. He set his self-rescuer aside.

"Can you hear me, Tom?" Flory pleaded, while motorman Bewley looked on between fits of his own coughing. It was undoubtedly the man's worst nightmare. On his Sunshine job application, he'd written that he'd quit Bunker Hill "to get away from the gas and smoke."

Wilkinson finally stirred, then coughed. He looked up from under his muck-caked caterpillar eyebrows, and the world had somehow flipped around. Or maybe, somehow, he'd been spun around to the point of disorientation. What had been on his left side now seemed on his right. Down was up, and up was down. He shut his eyes to impede his confusion, to reset his bearings. He had no recollection of his collapse, and no idea that his partner had lugged him to safety.

Flory rested a hand on his buddy's shoulder. He felt relieved. It probably wasn't a heart attack. Guys didn't just wake up from one of those.

"You're all right," he said.

Wilkinson nodded.

Though he was feeling sick himself, Bewley removed his own mouthpiece and offered it to Wilkinson while Flory climbed on the motor and started for the station. As he drew near it was immediately evident that things had deteriorated. The crew, knotted in a cluster, still expected help from the upper levels, but their hopes were fading. The first call topside had brought promises but no action. The next call, however, had been extremely unsettling. The line crackled, but nobody answered. Sunshine was a big mine, but as far as the men on the 4800 really knew, theirs was the only level in trouble. Speaking was nearly impossible, and their vision was increasingly impaired, but calm heads somehow prevailed. Since they had two motors, the men decided to leave one at the station with a note indicating that they had found good air down the drift toward the borehole. The rescuers could use the waiting motor to go back and retrieve the crew. No one could see any other options. Climbing out was out of the question. Smoke was everywhere.

Flory returned to the pocket and shared the plan with Wilkinson and Bewley. By then his legs were shaky and he felt light-headed, like the morning after too much drinking and not enough sleep. The three of them waited, talking about what was happening in the levels above. At first no one mentioned it, but all knew something was amiss. Maybe the motor was down or someone else had fallen sick? The crew should have written the note and made it back by then. Bewley said he felt better, and volunteered to check it out. He'd be gone a few minutes. As the motor pulled away, the smoke reappeared and vanished, bringing with it darkness, then light. It was as if someone had pulled a curtain open and shut.

But a few minutes turned into ten, then twenty.

Flory paced in the half-darkness. "Man, this is taking too long," he said. Staying there seemed stupid; he decided to go down the drift to see what was happening. Wilkinson said he was feeling more like himself and wanted to go, but Flory didn't see a need for it.

"I'll go down and see what's up," he said. "You stay here."

About two hundred yards down the drift, Flory caught sight of the headlight of the first motor; the other was cloaked in smoke. Something was wrong, and Flory strained to see more. It looked as though Dick Bewley had flopped backwards on top of the motor, his head hanging off the side of the little train. Flory called out, but he didn't answer. In the direction of the battery barn, the veil of smoke had lifted a little. He could see the other motor's light stabbing at the air.

Jesus Christ.

It looked as though the motorman had fallen first, causing the train to stop suddenly, jerking the men around and hurling their bodies off the front end. They were bunched up on top of each other, tangled and stationary. Fingers had clawed at the muck. Cap lamps pointed every which way. Flory froze. *A few minutes ago, all of those guys were fine. They were on the way for help. They were going to come back to get us when the cage came.*

Flory returned to Wilkinson, adrenaline running through his veins like water through a fire hose.

"Tom, they're just laying all over," he said. "Like pickup sticks." He spoke in fragments, broken by a short pause and then more words. It was more than just an indication of his fear. His childhood stutter reemerged.

"They've passed out. We got to go back and do something. Hell," he sputtered, "even *Dick* passed out on the track there."

The news rocked Wilkinson. Bewley hadn't been gone all that long. A few minutes. Ten at most. And he was down on the track? It didn't seem possible. Flory led Wilkinson back to Bewley's body. Neither knew CPR, but Wilkinson had seen someone pound on a man's chest on a TV rescue show. The two men took turns pressing on the motorman's chest, shaking him, slapping his face, *anything* to get him to wake up.

"Come on, you can do it," Flory repeated as he pressed the heel of his hand on Bewley's chest.

"Ron, that's no good," Wilkinson finally said. "He's dead. You gotta stop."

Flory couldn't. Adrenaline had taken over.

"He's dead," Wilkinson repeated. *"Stop it!"*

Dick Bewley's eyes were thin white crescents; his eyelids eclipsed his irises. The motorman's face was red and his body was limp and clammy. They took his limp arms and dragged him away from the motor, his boots cutting parallel furrows in the sodden muck. His eyes were open in a dead stare. Flory was nearly in shock. He couldn't believe those men had died. *The air must have some poison in it*, he thought.

The partners returned to their air pocket, their personal safety zone. Flory didn't say a word about it, but he was scared that the rest of the crew on their level was dead.

"What the fuck are we going to do?" he asked.

Wilkinson, who now realized how close he'd come to dying, could only echo his partner's thoughts.

"How the hell are we going to get out of here?" he asked.

BACK ON THE SURFACE, AT THE LANDING OF THE STAIRWAY to the dry, Sunshine carpenters had built a warren of cubbyholes to hold miners' dinner buckets while they went upstairs to shower after shift. That day it was nearly empty. Most of the crew, at least the first cage load from his level, should have been out by then. They had a head start and, being on 3700, had the advantage of the man train to take them that mile to the Jewell. Bill Mitchell noticed only three other buckets. He put Waldvogel's bucket away and went up the stairs. He plugged in his lamp battery, hung his diggers on his basket hanger, and pulled the chain to send it up to the ceiling. Only two nozzles on the multihead shower pillar were running. The men showering all wondered the same thing. Where was everyone? One of the guys showering was from 4600, and said he'd seen a couple of cages go up ahead of his crew.

"Where are all those men?"

Mitchell knew that the shaft crew had evacuated, too.

"They should be out by now," he said.

"Yeah, that's what I was thinking. What's the deal?"

"Maybe they got hung up on 3700."

One guy speculated that there'd been a wreck.

"Pretty smoky down there, maybe two motors hit head-on."

By then some miners from 4800 had arrived, but still none of the crew who had been on Waldvogel's cage. Mitchell dressed and went to the office to call his wife to say he was going to stay at the mine to help with the rescue. Mitchell saw a salary man at the portal and asked if he could put his diggers on and go back down.

"I can run the cage," he said.

The offer was declined, but Mitchell decided to stay near the portal anyway. Waldvogel needed his inhalers when he got out. Judging by all the smoke coming out of there, he'd need them in a bad way.

ESCORTED FROM THE MINE BY ONE OF LAUNHARDT'S HELMET crew, Roger Findley found his way to the Sunshine personnel office. He was in shock, but he wanted to let his wife know he was alive. He also had another, far greater, concern. His older brother, Lyle, a thirty-year-old father of two boys and a girl, hadn't made it out. He was seen last on 5200.

"Does he have a chance?" Betty Larsen asked when he told her.

"No way," Findley coughed out. As far as he knew, he had been the last one out of the mine. "And I wouldn't have made it if they hadn't thrown me on an ore car."

Larsen sat quietly while Findley was on the phone with his wife. She wanted to cry. The nineteen-year-old miner's words pierced her heart.

I can't imagine how she feels, she thought. *How would a woman feel if that was her husband calling?*

Twenty-three

SAFETY ENGINEER LAUNHARDT TRIED TO COLLECT HIS frayed wits. The station was wall-to-wall men; each looked down the drift, wondering what would come next. *Who* might be coming next? None were prepared to do anything. Many were without hard-hats and lamps. None had any breathing devices. All they could do was talk about what they *should* do. Some came down from the ware-house and the carpenter's shop, and some from the mill. Many prob-ably hadn't been underground in months. Some had never entered the mine before.

Launhardt checked the detector tube on the Draeger. It gave a positive reading for a slight amount of carbon monoxide. All at once, the usually reserved and laconic man found a boom in his voice.

"You guys get the hell out of here and back up the shaft, now! We *all* have to go up now. We're going to have a repair crew start at the surface and go in on each level. Need to seal where air's leaking."

ON THE SURFACE BY THE JEWELL, CLEAR AIR BLEW OVER HIS sweaty face, chilling Kenny Wilbur like the abrupt gush of a slammed freezer. A cluster of men swarmed around. All had the same questions. They wanted to know what he'd seen underground. Any sign of a partner? A best buddy? A brother? Wilbur could offer nothing to console them. It was so smoky down there, he couldn't be sure who he'd really seen.

Over at the shifter's shack, the bosses, hoping that it would lessen smoke in the drift, wanted someone to go down to open air doors just off the Jewell Shaft on 3700.

"I'll go back down," Wilbur said, without really thinking. As he saw it, he was obligated to go to 3700, since there was no cager there. It was his job. Another cager joined him for the quick trip. In a few minutes they'd wedged open the doors. The station was eerily quiet. On the way up, they stopped on 3100. Wilbur noticed the cars and the McCaas that Launhardt and his rescue team had left behind. They had probably done whatever they could and were out of the mine. A moment later, Wilbur was topside.

By the portal, Byron Schulz stirred from unconsciousness. The reprieve from his nightmare was over. Voices faded in and out. He could barely recall a moment after the frantic seconds of yelling when Don Beehner fell in the piss ditch. But he could not shut out what he'd experienced back at the 3100 station; each horrific image was etched in gruesome detail. Someone gave him a lungful of oxygen and loaded him into an ambulance.

EARLY AFTERNOON, MAY 2

Men's Dry House

NO ONE KNEW WHO WAS STILL UNDERGROUND. THE MINE'S timekeeper attempted to track who had exited the Jewell, but the effort was wasted. Some who made it out returned underground to help with the rescue. The best record of who *started* shift that morning was in each of the shifters' logbooks—slim, pocket-sized steno pads they carried in their hip pockets. All of those were still deep in the mine, because only a few shifters had made it out.

With the exodus from the mine, the scene in the men's dry should have been chaotic. Instead, an unprecedented stillness held the cavernous room. Buz Bruhn was soaping up in the shower when partners Markve and Follette got there. Markve was still hacking and looked pale. Bruhn looked over and gave his head a shake.

"Say," he said, "I'll tell you right now, Sunshine's gonna fool around today and kill somebody!"

Randy Peterson's cage load of guys, his company of men, showered in silence. Steam edged the ceiling, and water pooled over the slow-moving drains. As he dressed in his street clothes, Peterson processed a checklist of those he'd seen on the cage. With one exception, all had made it topside. He hadn't seen Dusty Rhoads, the fifty-seven-year-old mechanic who worked more for the fun of it than for the money.

Sometime around 2:00 p.m., Peterson returned to the portal, where he found men hovering over two supine miners strapped in rescue baskets. Someone administered oxygen, but it didn't seem to be working.

"Open it up!" a mechanic called out to a miner by the oxygen tank. *"Open it up!"*

Two men carried Bob McCoy, the man who'd lit up a smoke and fallen, to the shifter's shack. His face was crimson, but his skin was icy. They stripped off his wet clothes and wrapped him in a blanket. He also needed medical attention. Metallurgical accountant George Gieser expected more trouble to emerge from the mine, so he phoned the community ambulance service. He also told employees to stick around if they drove a station wagon or camper; they might be needed to transport men to the hospital. Central Mine Rescue, whom Launhardt had sent for, had set up four first-aid stations. Each had oxygen units to take care of the deluge of choking miners.

Peterson encountered Floyd Strand, the electrical foreman.

"Where's Dusty?" he asked.

"He's still on the 3400," the foreman said. "And we've lost communication with 10-Shaft."

A MAN MAKES HIS OWN CHOICES, AND THOSE DECISIONS SET the stage for whatever happens in his life. Bob Follette had never wanted his son, Bill, to go underground at Sunshine or any other district mine. It was supposed to be temporary, a way to earn some money to finish his college education. Some of the men underground had been there out of necessity; they had families to feed. But Bill, twenty-three, didn't fall into that category. He was married, a college kid who was bound to teach and coach basketball at some little high school in north Idaho. He had less than a year to finish his degree, but the lure of the money that came from mining sent him on a detour. Hunting, fishing, and playing around on one of the district's dazzling blue lakes was too compelling for a young outdoorsman. His father understood. Some of the best moments of his own life had been spent with his sons, hunting in the Bitterroots. The Follettes came home once with one deer lashed to the front and another to the back of their VW bug. They ate venison for a year.

The image of his son, as he'd seen him that Tuesday morning, stayed with Follette. The thin six-footer had been fighting a cold. His skin was chalky and his eyes rheumy.

"You don't look so good," the father had said as they waited for the cage. "I wish you wouldn't go down today."

"Oh, I'll make it all right," the young man had answered. He knew that his partner, Louis Goos, couldn't get a decent guy to fill in. A partner's missed shift could knock a hole in their entire week.

Bob Follette was stoic when he called home. He doubted his boy would come out alive, but he didn't say so to his wife.

2:45 P.M., MAY 2
3700 Level, Jewell Station

WITH 3100 A VERITABLE DEATH CHAMBER, BOB LAUNHARDT knew that the only other route to 10-Shaft was by 3700. Three new volunteers suited up. One, a squirrelly fellow who shaved about every two weeks, Stanley "Talky" Taylor, was a volunteer fireman in Wallace. Taylor, twenty-six, knew fires took on lives of their own, crawling through houses and sneaking into bedrooms, filling them with smoke while kids and family pets hid under beds. He knew smoke could hang in layers and filter through the thin spaces between doorjambs. But conditions on 3700 were totally foreign. The smoke was thicker and darker than a nest of burning tires, and its oily plume literally churned through the workings of the mine. Taylor was astonished. *What could be burning that would make a smoke like that?*

Launhardt's team advanced on the seldom-used 5-Shaft. Launhardt checked for carbon monoxide. The shaft was lethal; no one could survive without respiratory protection. That wasn't the worst of it. Launhardt studied the airflow and, even in the heat of the mine, felt a chill on the back of his neck. The drift's intake airflow was carrying the black smoke eastward toward 10-Shaft. The poisoned air was pushing back to where the men were waiting for help.

When the mine's safety engineer and the group came across the lifeless forms of fallen men, they knew there was nothing they could do for the men down deep, barricaded in drifts and waiting. They retreated from the mine.

Launhardt did his best to maintain focus, but the madness of the situation kept coming back to him. *Rock doesn't burn.* Sure, every man, woman, and child old enough to spend a silver dollar knew that basic truth. That made hardrock mining eminently safer than, say, coal mining. Coal, after all, was mined because it was a *fuel.* Launhardt, Chase, Walkup, and the others all knew that. But they also knew something else. There was a silent forest underground, too. Hundreds of thousands, if not millions, of board feet of wood had been used to shore up the mined-out areas—the old country, as miners called it—for decades. Rock bolts and steel mats had reduced the amount of wood brought underground by far, but in decades past the mine had been filled with timbers.

Launhardt thought back on the Draeger and how it went black in an instant. How could that be so? And if timbers and gob had somehow ignited in the dank recesses of the mine, how was it possible that the enormity that was Sunshine underground be filled so quickly with so much carbon monoxide? *It couldn't be a wood fire,* Launhardt thought. A wood fire underground in a wet mine couldn't rage like the one that was sucking the life out of this mine. *What was burning?*

MINER ACE RILEY SHOWERED AND DRESSED AS QUICKLY AS he could and went looking for Joe Armijo. Riley called out his partner's name, but no response came. At the shifter's shack, he saw men huddled in conference. Among the group were safety engineer Bob Launhardt, a shaken Jim Bush, and graveyard shift foreman Ray Rudd.

Riley asked if rescue crews were making progress.

"There's nothing more we can do," Bush said.

Riley's blood heated up. "Get your goddamn ass down there and get that man," he said, referring to Armijo. Launhardt was white. Bush, who'd just lost his forty-five-year-old brother, was in worse shape.

Riley didn't care about any of that. Not just then. "It's your fucking job!" he said to Bush.

The foreman didn't blink, but it was Launhardt who spoke up.

"We need to start building a seal," he said, "level by level." He told Rudd that they should start on the 500 level and work down to seal off drifts connecting with the Jewell. He was concerned about old crosscuts and corroded bulkheads—anyplace where seepage probably occurred.

The two-hour life of the self-contained breathing apparatus only allowed for about forty minutes into a rescue before a man needed to return to fresh air. With 10-Shaft more than a mile from the Jewell, it meant the fresh-air base starting at the Jewell would need to be moved forward, closer to the shaft. Launhardt insisted they start moving methodically down the drift, sealing leaks as they went. It would be slow going, but it was the only safe way to get to the men trapped in the mine.

Rudd didn't buy any of it. Until a few moments ago, all he'd known was that he'd been called out of bed and told to get his ass over to the mine. A veteran shifter with helmet training, his neck veins plumped like night-crawlers on a rain-soaked pavement.

"We're not going to do that," he said, his voice rising. "Were going back to look for people!"

He didn't say so, but Rudd blamed Launhardt for nearly killing Larry Hawkins, who, married to his niece, was family. Launhardt, Rudd thought, had made a huge error in judgment. Hawkins and Beehner didn't have training. And that's Launhardt's fault. Launhardt took those guys down there. It was a mistake. And a goddamn big one.

The ill-fated rescue effort on 3100 had cost one and almost two lives.

❖

AN HOUR AWAY IN SPOKANE, WORD SHOT THROUGH THE small bureau of the United Press International that a fire was burning in a Kellogg silver mine. Reporter Jerry McGinn immediately claimed the story. Though only twenty-six, the flame-haired and mustached McGinn had a better grasp on the culture of north Idaho's mining district than most reporters. He'd been covering the valley since he was a student stringer. He'd learned that the best places to call for sports scores were the district's hook houses. The madam would hold the phone to her breast and call out for the scores.

In fact, if there was anything other than silver, zinc, and lead that put the Coeur d'Alene Mining District on the map, it was the whorehouses that had catered to the men of mining and lumber camps for decades. Kellogg had shuttered the houses in 1966, but some entrepreneurial women still worked above a couple of the downtown bars. Wallace prostitutes, however, serviced a steady clientele in 1972 in the Oasis, the Lux, the U&I, or the other houses that served all-American helpings of sex. The Horseshoe Bar, below the Oasis in downtown Wallace, was a favorite waiting spot for dads who'd brought their teenage sons. They'd check in their boys with the madam and wait with a whiskey shot or two. "Brought my son up to initiate him. His birthday's this week." The son would call for his dad from the doorway, a boy not old enough to come inside for a drink, but ready to go home with a good story to tell.

If the hooker-with-a-heart-of-gold cliché had any genuine basis, it was in Delores Arnold, a Wallace madam with a powder-puff-coiffed white poodle and a practice of giving back to the community in tangible ways. Gutsy and enterprising kids always made a beeline to Arnold for school fund-raisers. But beyond band uniforms, a police cruiser, and scads of other things she gave openly, she also provided a service that local cops felt benefited the district in much bigger ways. The transient workforce of miners and loggers needed a sexual release. Arnold's girls were the tonic. Every sheriff's deputy thought so. Wallace-born movie star Lana Turner was the district's prodigal daughter, but Madam Delores Arnold was its beloved and eccentric aunt.

Besides Nevada, no other part of the country had whorehouses as visible and accepted as Wallace's. Their existence wasn't the last vestige of the Old West, because in the district, the Old West still thrived.

Reporter McGinn happily reported the quirky tales of Idaho eccentricity, yet in all his pieces he wove in a thread of empathy. Mining district people were living and dying by the price of silver much the same way farmers lived and died by the weather. McGinn knew that they had good times and bad times, and that the worst and best could happen in the same week. And no matter how rough some had it, they'd left something worse to migrate to the district.

McGinn drove east from Spokane. Miners' lives were wrapped up in uncertainty because that was the nature of the business. *You go down there and risk your life, and if you live long enough, you get paid. If there isn't a strike, if there isn't a rockburst or a drop in the metals market or if your wife doesn't leave you, you just might be able to pay your bills that week,* McGinn thought.

The fire was just another obstacle for people always hoping for the best.

Twenty-four

THE NIGHT BEFORE HIS FIRST DAY AT BUNKER HILL, IN the spring of 1964, college student Harry Cougher opted to camp overnight in his car rather than give up the bucks for one of Kellogg's famous rent-by-the-week rat-hole motel rooms. The smelter's seething black stacks dwarfed the town and smudged the mountains that dropped straight, and all at once, to the valley floor. If it was no longer the richest mine, Bunker Hill was certainly the district's biggest operation. Cougher stayed up half the night as heavy equipment lumbered along and workers dropped heavy kettles of processed ore, one after another. Working at Bunker Hill was more than just a summer job. His professor at the University of Idaho had set it up, saying Cougher had better get his butt over to Kellogg to see what he was going to do with a mining engineer's degree.

The first day at Uncle Bunk's, Cougher donned a white hardhat, letting every old hand know he was a trainee—the lowest rung. While Cougher could curse with the best of them in a bar or underground, his better-than-a-gyppo's vocabulary and profes- sional aspirations gave him away. He sat next to an old-timer for that intimidating first ride down the mine's incline shaft. The old miner's dinner bucket sat squarely in his lap, and his eyes were fixed straight ahead. Cougher did the same. They were the only two people in the world as the cage went into darkness and low- hanging timbers whizzed overhead.

If he can do it, I can do it, Cougher thought.

Eight years later, Cougher was Uncle Bunk's chief planning engineer—one of the youngest ever. He was in a meeting when the mine manager brought news of big trouble at Sunshine.

"A *helluva* fire," the manager said. "There's black smoke rolling out of Sunshine Tunnel."

Cougher was among a handful of Bunker managers who had com- pleted extensive "hotshot" training on breathing apparatuses supe- rior to Sunshine's equipment. There was a reason Uncle Bunk invested in advanced instruction. Other mines had bad country, with falling rock and rockbursts; still more regularly sent miners to the hospital for heatstroke. Bunker Hill had fires—about one a year. Old timbers and an antiquated electrical system that occasionally shorted out were the main culprits. Slushers were notorious for sparking, too. And at least once the shaft caught fire.

The Bunker Hill manager put the brakes on sending anyone to the rival mine.

"Let's wait until they call us."

The wait was brief, and Cougher and several others—an engi- neer, a geologist, and a maintenance foreman among them—packed up their gear for Big Creek.

2:10 P.M., MAY 2
Sunshine Mine Yard

ON HIS WAY TO GRAB A BEER BEFORE HEADING HOME, DENNIS Clapp, the skinny longhair who had escaped the mine after alerting Flory and Wilkinson, stood in the yard, mystified.

"Goddamn," he said, looking at the hoist's massive cables. "How come they ain't moving? Shouldn't they be getting those guys out of there?"

"Ain't nobody left alive down there," Ray Rudd answered, his face ashen and stony.

"Oh, come on," Clapp said.

"No, I don't think so."

"Oh shit." Clapp lingered a moment before leaving. It couldn't be that bad. There were too many still missing. Among them were Clapp's cousin and Ron Flory's best friend, Mark Russell, twenty-nine.

Rudd stayed where he was. All that he'd been in his life—baker, rancher, sawmill hand, miner—couldn't have prepared him for May 2. He'd been a district fixture since 1951, when he'd answered the call of a colossal banner stretched across the old highway: WANTED 500 MEN, BUNKER HILL & SOUTHERLAND. Nothing like this had ever happened before.

DOWN THE ROAD FROM THE SMOKING MINE, THE BIG CREEK Store seethed with mounting dread. The watering hole had become the nerve center for women from all over the district. Sunshine's switchboard operator told callers that she didn't know anything, and referred them to the store. The place was overflowing, and Big Creek Store owner George Dietz was in fine form. Dennis Clapp, having just been given a reality check about the seriousness of the blaze, asked to use the phone. He wanted to let his wife know he was all right.

Dietz flatly refused. "Emergencies only."

Clapp wanted to deck him. *Asshole*, he thought, *if this isn't an emergency, I don't know what is.*

Cager Randy Peterson was also among those who showed up at the bar. As cold beer streamed down his throat, Peterson overheard another miner say he'd seen Jim Bush lay down his dying brother Bob on 3700.

"Then the rest are all gone," Peterson said. "All that's out is all there'll be."

"You don't *know* that," said Dietz, acknowledging anxious faces around the bar.

Peterson looked over at the women. One was sandman Bud Alexander's wife, Celia. Mrs. Alexander's face was twisted in panic. Bud hadn't made it out. She tried to console herself that Peterson, a kid she'd watched grow up on the creek, didn't know what he was talking about. Others shot names through the air, but the twenty-three-year-old clamped down. It wasn't his place to tell some woman that only an hour ago he'd seen her husband buckled at the knees, hugging a T-shirt to his face. When a buddy pushed him for news about his own father, Peterson told a compassionate lie: "If he got back there in the fresh air and built a bulkhead, I think he'd be fine."

In reality, the Sunshine men drinking at the Big Creek Store were as trapped as their buddies underground. They weren't going anywhere until it was over—one way or another. All they could do was stare into the bottoms of their beer glasses as if answers could be found there. Women watched the door. With every new face in the doorway, silence fell and hearts jumped in unison.

Miners sequestered away from wives and girlfriends repeated the same questions over and over, as if truth could be found in the juiced mind of the fellow one barstool over. They wanted to know what their pals were facing underground, what they *had* faced already. Were guys stomping each other to death over a self-rescuer? Or were they helping each other out? What the hell had happened? And why? Sunshine's safety program came up frequently in their rants. Some held Bob Launhardt responsible for not teaching the crew how to use the self-rescuers. Many more blamed Sunshine management for not getting people out fast enough. Ace Riley was among the angry and bitter. By then he'd sifted through the day's events, and his distress had turned into resentment. He was sure the apparent delay in giving the evacuation order was a chief reason the fire had turned into a disaster.

"If they hadn't been looking for that fire," he said, "they'd have been out of there. The bigshot was in Coeur d'Alene, having that big meeting. All them bosses were scared to death they was gonna lose their jobs."

And just as the idea that something very bad, something very *newsworthy,* was occurring, members of the local press had already entrenched themselves in Sunshine's personnel and accounting offices. A Spokane TV station's fifty-pound film cameras jostled aside adding machines and Dictaphones as reporters and camera crews rearranged desks to their liking. No one could figure out how reporters had made it to Big Creek that fast.

IT WASN'T MUCH TO LOOK AT, A FLAT-ROOFED, LOW-RISE building of painted cinder blocks, but KWAL radio ("Silver Dollar Radio, 620 on your dial!") was Communications Central for the district. Just off the highway in Osburn, KWAL was not only the third-oldest station in the state, but the only one that disseminated the valley's news. Whatever was going on made it to the ears of sales manager Paul Robinson, thirty-two. Nothing, Robinson knew, escaped his listeners. Between the mélange of tears-'n'-beers country music, rock, and Golden Oldies tunes of his playlist, Robinson infused the airwaves with district news and high school sports.

When calls about the fire came, Robinson, a compact man with sparkling eyes under heavy black brows, was completely perplexed. He'd been underground at Lucky Friday, and considered it the world's largest steam bath. Sunshine, he'd heard, was the same way.

It would take a thousand gallons of gasoline to start a fire, he thought. *Water's everywhere down there. Dripping off rocks, timbers.*

Robinson made two phone calls: first to Sunshine, where he learned that no one knew much, except that the situation was serious and it was going to take some time to get the men out; and then to the Federal Communications Commission. Robinson asked for permission to stay on the air past the normal 11:00 p.m. signoff. FCC approval came straightaway.

Over in Wallace at the elementary school, the intercom had the timbre of a walkie-talkie. Fidgety kids grew still, however, when the announcer said the after-school basketball game was canceled.

"There's a problem at Sunshine Mine," the voice said. "Some of our coaches won't be able to make it today."

Players groaned. Matt Beehner slid into his seat, crestfallen. He was from a family of sports enthusiasts, and he loved hoops. What's more, his dad, Sunshine sanitation nipper Don Beehner, was going to be there to watch. Instead, Matt went home, got something to eat, and turned on the TV. Men with yellow hardhats and the turtleshell breathing apparatus on their backs moved around Sunshine's mine yard. They looked like a swarm of yellow-backed beetles moving around a hive. *This is weird,* he thought. The twelve-year-old ate his snack. His father would be home soon, and he'd have a great story to tell.

MIDAFTERNOON, MAY 2

Seattle

AS SHE HAD EVERY DAY ON HER WAY TO WORK DOWN SEATTLE'S Aurora Avenue with its row of kitschy motels, Janet Launhardt regarded the glory of snowcapped Mount Rainier. No matter how many times she'd seen the vanilla-sundae peak, it inspired breath-taking awe. Sadly, the days embracing that view were waning. As soon as school was out next month, she and the children would join Bob in Pinehurst.

Tuesday afternoon, a co-worker at the moving company where she was employed asked Janet if her husband worked at an Idaho mine.

"There's been an accident over there," she said. "It seems awfully bad."

Janet reached for the knob on a desk radio and turned up the volume. There were lots of mines in Idaho, she knew. A news bulletin provided the only really important details a moment later. It was at home, and it was Sunshine. She knew Bob spent part of his day underground, but she was unsure of his specific schedule. Janet spent the rest of the day a wreck, dialing for answers, but unable to get through to Sunshine. She searched for a reason why Bob hadn't called her. *He must be too busy.* It would be two days before they'd talk.

Twenty-five

ACCIDENTAL MINER JIM GORDON WAS RAISED TO BE A rancher, but a cheating wife and a motel business that went belly-up sent him and his three kids to a little house on Moon Gulch and a job at Sunshine Mine. Gordon found himself in the midst of men who were a tougher, rougher, and rowdier bunch than he'd ever known. He learned that if a man dropped a bar of soap in the shower, he'd best bend at the knees to retrieve it, or a guy would hump his backside for laughs. Gordon considered miners "uncouth"—a word choice that underscored the chasm between their worlds. But after he'd lived in the district awhile, something unexpected happened to him. Gordon found he was more like those men than different from them. In reality, *he* changed, and they remained the same. Miners shared a brotherhood, and Gordon learned that having a place in that fraternity assured if something ever went wrong, there'd be a fellow there to help out.

Standing in front of a Pinehurst auto repair shop, afternoon shift miner Jim Gordon glanced at his watch and scanned the roadway. His partner on 4800, Johnny Lang, was running a little late.

"No sense in going in today, Jim," a man called out from a passing car, just about the time Lang's truck reeled into view. "The mine's afire."

A quintessential miner, Johnny Lang loved speed, especially the hasty tempo of a day underground. With only six hours in the stope, there was hardly enough time to get everything done. Working at high speed was the only way to mine. From his first step into his stope, Lang was a blur. First he mucked out what the opposite crew had blasted. The muck pile was slushed down the chute to muck cars on the track below. Next, he and his partner would push forward, bolting the heading, drilling the next round, loading it, and shooting it, before calling it a day. Time flew on dragonfly wings.

Lang was also on the rescue crew, and he'd have to go to work whether the mine was on fire or not, whether it was open or closed. He assumed that whatever had been burning had been extinguished. In fact, on the drive to Big Creek, Lang remarked that he couldn't really think *what* could be burning that couldn't be snuffed out in about five minutes.

"Oh, man, what the hell's burning down there?" he asked a foreman, watching the monolith of smoke rising in the drift.

"Don't know for sure," the man said. "Timbers from those old, worked-out stopes, we think."

Lang and Gordon learned that Davy Mullin and Gordy Whatcott, their opposite shift partners, were among the dozens who hadn't made it out. The news hit Jim Gordon particularly hard. *They have to get those guys out. Those are good, decent men.* Whatcott, thirty-seven, was the kind of Mormon who drank an occasional beer and hung out with the guys. He and his wife were raising three boys and three girls. Mullin, thirty-four, was an Okie who stretched one-syllable words into two and walked with an ambling cadence that said "good ol' boy." He was the type who'd crawl up a raise dragging a jackleg *and* a thermos of coffee. Earning a little under $145 a week from Sunshine, Mullin and his wife were raising a combination of his, hers, and ours, which included nine-year-old twin girls with rhyming names.

A twist of fate had kept Lang from being among the trapped. Whatcott, who ordinarily worked the second shift, needed to take care of some personal business the first week of May. They traded shifts.

Meanwhile, Jewell hoistman Lino Castaneda finally left the hoist room. He tried to console himself with hope that his fifty-five-year-old half brother, Roberto Diaz, and the others had only passed out. Soon they'd be put on stretchers, tethered to oxygen tanks for the ride to the hospital. Castaneda knew Diaz had been in the group that went to save Bob Bush. None of them were brought out on stretchers. Not one.

If they are going to get anyone out, they will get Bob Bush. He's a boss. Roberto will come out because he'll be with Bush, Castaneda thought.

AFTERNOON, MAY 2
Downtown Wallace

THE AFTER-LUNCH HOURS DRAGGED AT WALLACE'S FIRST National Bank. Foreman Gene Johnson's daughter, Peggy Delange, twenty-one, was crunching numbers when a customer came in and gave the first report of the fire. She looked up at the clock. *Good. Dad's out by now. He's stuck doing paperwork, just like me.* She worried about her uncle and her brother-in-law, but was unsure what shift either of them worked. Yet as customers dispensed more news, a kind of urgency started to spiral. She began to doubt herself and what she actually did know. She had helped her father after school, and she knew his daily routine as well as he did. But each comment weighed on her, one stone at a time. Her boss told her to go up to the mine.

Even though grown and married, Peggy Delange considered her dad the most important man in her life. He always had been. As a girl, she would find herself lost in the inky images tattooed on his sturdy back, a pair of mermaids flanking a massive tall ship, waves, and sky swirling above and below. Her father's back was a storybook illustration of shapes and tiny thin lines, a Beatrix Potter illustration gone slightly mad. Peggy would study her father's back and his powerful arms as though they contained a mystery to be solved. In reality, Johnson's back told the story of his military career. He also had the names of his wife and his oldest daughter and son inscribed on his muscular arms. The middle kid, Peggy, so much wanted her name added to the graffiti that told the world where her dad had been, and who he loved.

"How come you don't have my name there?"

"You were an afterthought," he said, wrapping his words in a mischievous grin.

"I don't care," she said. "I want my name there, too!"

PEGGY DELANGE'S AUNT, JOANN BARKER, FELT HER OWN heart sink with worry Tuesday afternoon. Her husband, shaft repairman Robert Barker, was missing. JoAnn tried to minimize her anxiety with her continuation of a daily routine from which she seldom deviated. Robert wanted dinner on the table at five every day, not five-fifteen. He also wanted the TV off, and the kids at the table. She had always catered to him throughout their twenty-four-year marriage. During frigid Shoshone County winter months, she even started his truck in the morning so it would be warm for his drive to the mine. And the morning of May 2 she had served a sweet roll and coffee to Robert, still sprawled in bed in the bedroom of their cozy Kellogg home. He knew he was spoiled. Before leaving that morning, Robert kissed JoAnn and whispered a line from a Charley Pride song: "Kiss an angel good morning."

But Tuesday afternoon found JoAnn and the youngest of her six children around the radio. What they wanted to hear, of course, was good news. An interview with the president of the Northwest Mining Association provided the kind of hope they needed.

"If the men are at lower levels, they may be trapped by lack of transportation out, but it's hard to see where they would be physically harmed," he said.

The words barely eased her fears. JoAnn Barker knew how treacherous mining could be. When she was fourteen, her father was killed when his motor jumped the track at the Liberal King Mine and slammed him against the rock like a bug on a windshield. He bled for ten days and never regained consciousness. Her husband had also contended with a litany of injuries. Stripping collection plates at Uncle Bunk's zinc plant had left him with third-degree sulfuric acid burns from his hands to his elbows. Each night, JoAnn had applied a thick paste of baking soda to relieve his pain. Barker could have put on elbow-length protective gloves, but the Death Valley heat of the plant made such gear unbearable. Some workers even went shirtless at Bunker Hill.

AFTERNOON, MAY 2
Woodland Park

THE OLD HECLA MINING COMPANY WATCHMAN'S HOUSE WAS in need of repair when Don and Wava Beehner bought the white two-story in Woodland Park, just outside of Wallace. Fortunately, Don Beehner was quite handy with that sort of thing, as were his wife and, in time, their children. The first, a boy named for his father,

Donald Gene Beehner Jr., was born two weeks before Christmas in 1954. Two years later, Barbara Ann arrived; another two years brought Nora Jean. The last child came in 1960, a son they named Matthew. All would learn how to wield a paintbrush—green was their dad's favorite color, and much of what was painted reflected that hue—hammer a nail, and keep the garden patch turned over and planted.

When she first heard there was trouble at the mine, Wava Beehner knew Don was helmet-trained and was probably fighting the fire. But throughout the day, news and rumor were a dripping faucet. Everywhere she went, someone said something about it—all bad. Like any mother of four with a million things to do, Wava Beehner tried to focus. She spent the afternoon running errands and chasing after her kids. In Wallace, she came across a friend who also worked for Sunshine.

"Have you seen Don?" she asked.

"I seen him earlier. He's with the rescue guys."

"Do you think he's all right?"

"Oh, you'll hear from him. I'm sure he's doin' fine."

That satisfied her. Her husband would be in his element. He liked being in the center of someone else's storm. But as the day progressed, Wava Beehner could no longer ignore the fact that she really didn't know what was happening. When her sister-in-law offered to take her up to the mine, she was out the door with her purse. The sister-in-law knew a thing or two about mining tragedies. Her husband had been killed at Sunshine in 1964.

AFTERNOON, MAY 2
Cataldo

THE WESTERNMOST TOWN IN THE DISTRICT, CATALDO, WAS home to a ruggedly beautiful Jesuit mission built in the early 1840s.

The oldest building in Idaho—a structure of wood, wattle, daub, and "not a single nail"—the mission was a great white swan, lingering and watching over rolling hills. For the Catholics of the district, the Cataldo mission was a source of deserved pride.

Home from the Army barely over a week, Doug Dionne was visiting with his mother, Betty, in the family's tidy Cataldo home, when a radio news item cut their conversation. According to the report, a fire had trapped some men underground at Sunshine. Both knew Harvey and Greg were on shift and underground. Doug drove his mother to Big Creek, and when they arrived they found Harvey in the mine yard. He was grim-faced, saying that he'd narrowly escaped the smoke.

"But Greg's still down there," he said.

AFTERNOON, MAY 2

Shoshone Golf Course, Big Creek

TUESDAY HAD BEEN A NICE AFTERNOON ON THE LINKS JUST below Big Creek, marred only by an unusually hazy sky and the sound of the sirens as police cars whizzed passed Shoshone Golf Course. A skyscraper of a man with dark, flinty eyes, Art Brown was transitioning into the mine manager's job at Lucky Friday. The position was a mining man's dream. After spending the morning in the mine, mine managers returned to the sunlight of the surface for lunch. He did the books, reported to his boss, and if the sun was shining, he'd be out by 3:00 p.m., headed for the golf course or the fishing hole or, in some cases, to the district motel where his mistress waited. Mine managers didn't read the *Wall Street Journal* or fret over metal prices. All they had to do was get the muck to the mill every goddamn day.

Of course, things are never that easy. The back end of the process of getting ore to the milling plant was momentous. Say a mine extracted 800 tons of rock per day. That would mean hoist crews would be pulling 100 cages a day. For 100 cage loads, men had to fill 300 cars. To fill the cars, men all over the mine had to drill about 4,000 holes, and cross their fingers that at least 90 percent of them blasted. The entire process, from working area to milling plant, took five days. Mine managers looked for gaps in the production cycle and found ways to patch things up so that the steady flow of ore was never impeded.

When sirens wailed up Big Creek Road, Brown, a South African who'd immigrated to the United States through Canada five years before, thought Sunshine had had an accident. All mines did, but that afternoon the commotion that followed the first siren never let up.

Shit, he thought, *something's wrong up there.*

Someone told the golfers it was a serious fire, and Brown contemplated going to help, but he thought he'd be in the way. His telephone was ringing when he got home to Pinehurst. It was Gordon Miner, Hecla's aptly named executive vice president. Miner was a tall man with an oversized personality. His shoulders practically brushed the door frame whenever he entered a room. He was also well connected in the industry, having served on several government-sponsored mining panels. He said that he'd been reviewing safety records, and Brown's name came up as someone with helmet training.

"Get over to Sunshine," Miner said.

Managers from rival mines—Bunker, Crescent, Galena, and Lucky Friday—came with their sleeves rolled up, ready to assist. So many came that if smoke hadn't been hanging above Sunshine Tunnel like a painted-on tornado, it might have been a good time for some kind of impromptu convention. Within the group of dueling alpha males, however, were a dozen plans of attack and more than a good measure of disagreement. One look around, and Hecla's Gordon Miner questioned whether Marvin Chase was up to the task of helming the rescue effort. He might know the mining *business,* but he knew little about the workings of the mine. Chase was gathering data with Walkup's help, which only irritated the Hecla men. As stakeholders in Sunshine, they had a vested interest in what was unfolding. Not so much in the men, because it didn't seem that many could be in any real danger. Theirs was a business concern: *How long will the fire halt production?*

Twenty-six

2:40 P.M., MAY 2
Coeur D'Alene Mining District

Y MIDAFTERNOON, ANYONE WITH A CONNECTION TO A trapped man was en route to Big Creek. Women shoved aside housework and called babysitters. Cars dripping motor oil were abandoned on lifts. Bowling and dart teams were left shorthanded. Tom Wilkinson's wife, Frances, heard about the fire while grocery shopping. She went to their Kellogg home, thinking Tom would arrive shortly and they'd have dinner. When she realized he was still up at Sunshine, she packed three-year-old Tommy into their green Camaro. Daughter Eileen, twelve, just home from Sunnyside Elementary School, slid into the passenger seat. *Sunshine's just rock,* Frances told herself. *What's to burn, anyway?* She dropped the kids off with family in Kellogg and Silverton, and drove up to Big Creek Road. *And if there's a fire, how hard would it be to snuff it out?* What Tom

Wilkinson's wife didn't know was that a fire aboveground was easy to fight, because it was easy to see. A fire underground was another story. First it had to be found. And even then, sometimes the only course was just to let it burn itself out.

Over in a tidy house in Pinehurst, Lou Ella Firkins, thirty-three, spread out the fabric for a black dress she was making for a Jaycees convention that she and husband Don were planning on attending over the weekend. Lou Ella had kept the stereo on from morning to afternoon as she pinned the tissue paper pattern, cut the fabric, and put the pedal to the sewing machine. More than just a pleasant break from their busy Pinehurst household with five kids, the shindig at the Boise Rodeway Inn was the zenith of their annual calendar. Don was past president of the local Jaycees, an achievement of which the gyppo miner was justly proud. At almost six feet, Don Firkins was a confident and commanding presence wherever he went—topside or in the mine. It was Lou Ella's stepfather, shifter Virgil Bebb, who had referred his son-in-law to Sunshine's hiring office. Bob Launhardt, filling in for Bill Steele, accepted Firkins's application on June 20, 1967.

On Tuesday, May 2, she got up with him to get him coffee and fix his lunch—a tuna sandwich on bread that she baked herself. It was an early morning that almost wasn't to be. The night before, instead of stopping off at the Big Creek Store as was his habit, Don brought home two big bottles of beer and drank them in front of the TV, feet up on his lounge chair and a happy look on his face. He had talked Gene Johnson into letting him and his partner work that Monday and Tuesday. Foreman Johnson caught them cutting out of work early on Friday.

"He told us," Firkins explained, "we might as well take Monday and Tuesday off, too. I'll see if I can get him to change his mind."

Firkins left the house with a water jug, his dinner bucket, and a pack of Viceroys in a battered tin box.

When he didn't return on Monday morning, Lou Ella knew Don's persuasive personality had worked its magic.

Midafternoon on Tuesday, the Firkins kids began arriving home from school. Lou Ella looked up from her sewing and adjusted the volume on the stereo when her oldest daughter burst into the house and told her there was a fire at Sunshine. Lou Ella wasn't completely rattled by the news. Don made no bones about the dangers of the underground, but he always said fires were the least of potential perils. Rock didn't burn. Lou Ella went to the phone and called the Big Creek Store, but no one there had any news of her husband's whereabouts. Later she and a friend drove to the mine. It looked bad. Pulling into the parking lot, she caught a glimpse of the family's brown station wagon. Don hadn't made it out. A plume of smoke rose from the mountainside and formed a shelf over the mine yard. It could have passed for a light fog, if it hadn't smelled so bad.

If only Don hadn't been so damn convincing, he'd have been home with me.

JOANNE STROPE REICHERT SPENT THE AFTERNOON PLAYING country music records and puttering around the Big Creek house she shared with her common-law husband, Jack Reichert. For the first time, the pretty twenty-eight-year-old, with hazel eyes and her dishwater-blond hair ratted into a "bubble," felt settled. After a year and a half of living on the creek, they had finally set a wedding date—July 3. The road to marriage had been complicated. The pair had met in early 1968 when Jack was Smelterville's chief of police and she was coming off a bad marriage. Reichert had told her he, too, was unhappy in his marriage. He wanted something more. Reichert wasn't classically handsome; his eyes were pinpoints and his ears were fins. All the same, Strope fell hard. Sometimes she even walked ten miles along the railroad tracks from her Wallace apartment to Smelterville on the mere chance she'd be able to see him.

Reichert's wife eventually issued an ultimatum—either he

dropped Joanne or she'd divorce him and take their four kids away. What Mrs. Reichert didn't reckon on—what she couldn't possibly have calculated—was Joanne's remarkable perseverance. She was incapable of letting him go. In turn, Joanne hadn't considered the resilient pull of a determined wife. The next thing she knew, the entire Reichert family—including Jack—had moved to Edmonton, Alberta. Joanne swallowed the entire contents of a pill bottle. After word about her attempted suicide made its way to Reichert, he telephoned to say he still loved her and wanted her to come to Canada, where he was working as a welder in the oilfields. She went. The pair went from motel to motel, from so-so to rat-trap, until their funds dried up. They ate cold soup from the can and slept in his car. When cold weather exacerbated the pain of Reichert's varicose veins, he phoned pal Gene Johnson.

"Come back down," the Sunshine foreman said, "and I'll have something for you."

The couple moved to Big Creek in 1970 with only their clothing and a guitar. Joanne immediately started using Reichert's name. Jack's divorce, she believed, was only a formality. Life was good. When he strummed his guitar and played his favorite song, "Under the Double Eagle," she was swept away.

On the afternoon of May 2, Joanne drove the new Buick Skylark they'd bought off Nickerson's lot in Smelterville up to the mine. She had been oblivious to what had been happening up there. It surprised her when she ran into a traffic jam a hundred yards from the parking lot. She waited a moment and found an empty space and parked.

Sure are a lot of people waiting for the guys today, she thought.

She sat in the car, but none of the men came off shift. There were more people arriving in the parking lot, though. Lots more. It was strange. She asked a man waiting for his son what was going on.

"Fire in the mine," he said, indicating the smoky tower.

"Oh God, no," she said, really aware of the smoke for the first time.

Only a few weeks before, Joanne had been in the mine because Reichert wanted to show her where he worked. He helped her put on a hardhat and escorted her onto the cage, opening the gates as if they were on a date. She recalled how he'd switched off their lamps as they descended to 4400. It was so dark, and the motion of the cage was so disorienting, that Joanne didn't know whether she was standing, falling, upright, or upside down. But she wasn't frightened. Reichert made her feel safe.

LATE AFTERNOON, MAY 2
Sunshine Mine Yard

NO ONE KNEW FOR SURE WHO WAS TRAPPED IN THE MINE. Sunshine Mine manager Marvin Chase led a nervous discussion in front of the shifters' shack; his face was suddenly pale and haggard. Some men ignored reason and insisted that most of the miners had made it out, but Chase put the number at fifty or sixty missing. The figure troubled Kenny Wilbur.

"How come you keep saying *fifty* men?" Wilbur asked. "It's eighty or ninety, give or take a few."

Chase looked over at Wilbur. "How do you know that?"

"I'm the cage tender. *I know*. I loaded them up every morning and sent them out. About half made it out."

The mine manager went quiet. "Well," Chase finally said, "I'll look into it."

The mine bigshots should have a better idea where their men are. A man's life could depend on whether someone knew whether he was trapped or not, Wilbur thought.

Meanwhile, calls jammed Sunshine's switchboard. Family members could only be told that all mine personnel were focused on the rescue effort, and the switchboard operators could not confirm exactly *who* hadn't made it out. Sunshine was a gas-guzzling jalopy when it came to labor. The workforce was so erratic, so much in flux, that the mine kept more than five hundred on payroll. Three hundred were steady; the other two hundred were the ebb and flow of a workforce that seemed to turn over every two or three months. In the late sixties, when metal prices were good and manpower was relatively cheap, Sunshine kept men around as backup for workers who dumped shift. On May 2, 1972, 429 employees out of 522 worked on varying shifts.

Knowing exactly who was underground hadn't been a pressing concern of Sunshine management until then. Many mines used brass tags to keep track of men. A tag dangling on a rack indicated that a particular miner hadn't gone underground. Sunshine underground workers were assigned cap lamps and batteries, each numbered and stored at the end of the day in the lamp room to recharge overnight. A missing battery pack meant a man was underground. That system was seriously flawed—anybody could take another man's lamp. The only safety net was the pocket-sized notebooks shifters carried underground. But those books were still underground.

Accountant and twenty-five-year Sunshine employee George Gieser went to the men's dry to conduct a count. The big room was almost tranquil. Nobody was snapping towels. An unprecedented stillness filled the enormous space. Suspended from the ceiling were the first hints of who was missing—street clothes hanging in the hot, blowsy air. Hangers belonging to partners, sons, and fathers were frequently consecutively numbered—the missing came in pairs. Gieser put a pencil to his findings and came up with a number that fluctuated all day before settling at eighty-two. Kenny Wilbur knew even that number was wrong.

DON BEEHNER WAS DEAD, AND SAFETY ENGINEER BOB Launhardt was running on autopilot. He felt emotionally numb as he moved through the afternoon, coordinating with the rescue teams. His mind could not let go of the astonishing carbon monoxide (CO) readings that he'd recorded—or at least tried to—on 3100. The miners who had continued working, thinking the smoke was nothing more than an inconvenience, were likely doomed from the onset. Unlike many lethal gases, CO is tasteless, odorless, and colorless, devoid of any telltale characteristics that make its detection possible. It kills by inhibiting the blood's ability to carry oxygen. When CO is inhaled it combines with the oxygen-carrying hemoglobin of the blood to form carboxyhemoglobin. At that point, blood is unable to transport oxygen to the heart, brain, or any other organ, causing asphyxiation.

Because of its surreptitious nature, CO kills hundreds each year. In mild poisonings, a victim might recognize the symptoms of dizziness, headache, and nausea before it's too late. Launhardt knew it was even possible for men to survive several hours in concentrations of CO of 100 parts per million (ppm). A man taking in that much might not even know he was at risk. At 600 ppm, however, noticeable symptoms are felt in about an hour. Headache and drowsiness are the most common warning signs, and unfortunately these are often ignored. Many a victim has reached for aspirin, when an open window was the true remedy. In some instances, low-level CO poisoning causes involuntary retching. At 1,000 ppm, however, the effects become severe. Victims dry-heave and stumble like drunks at closing time. Once the level reaches 4,000 ppm, death is inevitable, usually in less than an hour. Only quick thinking, clean air, and a prayer can save someone suffering that degree of exposure.

Launhardt wondered how it was that the readings could be so high. *Why had no one any inkling?* That afternoon he heard a story relayed by graveyard-shift employees who said they'd smelled smoke at shift's end. Maybe there had been a warning, after all. Launhardt filed a note about the incident, and started a file that would grow by inches every day. He didn't know whether the report was significant or just the result of the power of suggestion and the need for the miners to offer up something in order to be helpful. He mulled over the scenario. Did the scent of smoke and the fact that miners reported headaches indicate the fire had been smoldering and releasing CO for some time? He looked in the direction of the shifters' shack. Several ambulances had lined up with back gates open. Stretchers and woolen blankets quilted the ground. All were waiting for men. By then he knew the fatality count was already high enough to be the worst disaster in the Coeur d'Alenes since 1936, when ten miners had perished at the Morning Mine. That mishap hadn't been a fire, but a mechanical failure that occurred when a flat hoist cable rope broke apart where it had been spliced together, a practice long since abandoned with the advent of wire-rope cables. By far the worst mining disasters occurred in coal mines. Industry estimates had it that since 1900 more than 90,000 coal miners worldwide had died on the job. A 1942 underground fire in Manchuria left more than 1,500 dead. The deadliest on American soil occurred in Monogah, West Virginia, when an underground fire killed 361 in 1907.

The most devastating metal-mine catastrophe had occurred near Butte, Montana, in 1917. The North Butte Mining Company's Granite Mountain Mine shaft caught fire when an assistant foreman's open-flame carbide light accidentally ignited oil- and paraffin-soaked insulation material on an electrical cable. That fire took the lives of at least 167 men.

AFTERNOON, MAY 2
Interstate 90, West of Kellogg

TWO YELLOW BUSES CARRYING THE KELLOGG WILDCATS track team were just outside of Coeur D'Alene, after losing a three-point squeaker against the Post Falls Trojans, when an Idaho State Police car, red light flashing and siren screaming, signaled them to the shoulder. Some kids thought one of the drivers was getting a speeding ticket—and that would have been cool.

"We need to get the kids back to Kellogg, back to the school," the cop said. "Don't send them home. The administration will make an announcement there."

"What's going on?" someone asked.

"There's been some serious trouble at Sunshine."

Twenty-seven

LIKE A POTENTIAL LOVER ON A BARSTOOL AT CLOSING time, Kellogg looked best, many thought, in the last hours of the day. The town's smelter stacks and grimy storefronts were always a little unforgiving in the light of a sunny day. But at night, Bunker Hill operations blazed through the gauzy air of the smelter. Pete Chase was ten when his father, Sunshine Mine manager Marvin Chase, brought him from Seattle to check out the place they'd call home. The boy was awestruck by nighttime Kellogg. The smelter was a big battleship buried into the hillside, and floating on a sea of smoke. Nothing, he thought, could be cooler than that.

Although fresh from Boeing in Seattle, where he'd spent a decade working as an engineer and support manager for the aerospace company's spare-parts division, Marvin Chase's interest in mining was hardly transitory. From rockhounding on the modest apple orchard in eastern Washington where he grew up to earning a degree in mining engineering, Chase had always been deeply interested in all facets of the industry. Over the years, he'd worked at zinc, silver, and lead mines. At the Atomic Energy Commission, he'd served as chief of ore reserves for the government's interests in uranium mines. Even so, to some around the district he was just "the Boeing man from Seattle."

Marvin Chase was quietly ambitious, a little different from most of the mine managers in the district. He didn't define himself solely by his position. He was a homebody who went to church and didn't cheat on his wife. Some of the men who ran district mines were flashy—players who picked up women while their wives stayed home in houses with wall-to-wall carpeting and wrought-iron patio furniture. After a day at Sunshine, Chase was content staying home with his family, playing with their Airedale, or working on his stamp collection.

Marvin and Viola Chase had six children—four girls followed by two sons. The age gap between siblings was such that the oldest were out on their own and it was a family of five and a dog that made the move to the district. Mary, an eccentric teenager who played the zither, was certainly like none of the other girls at Kellogg High. Rob and Pete rounded out the still-at-home brood. The children found themselves high on the pecking order. On their first day in church at St. Rita's, the priest introduced the family to the congregation. The boys were embarrassed by the misconception that came with their father's new job. Some kids thought that because Marvin Chase managed the mine, that meant he owned it. One boy asked if they had gold bricks or diamonds stashed somewhere in their big white house on Big Creek Road.

The district didn't have a trace of what Chase considered "fringies" such as there had been back in Seattle. No hippies, no college students waving cardboard signs. The Vietnam War was raging, and though the young men of the district were on the battle lines, the political turmoil that surrounded the war was nearly absent. It was like stepping back to the 1950s. It was hard for a newcomer to wrap his mind around it. Part of it was that there were indisputable connections among the district's people; many even shared family histories as marriages occurred and dissolved over time. But there was something at work that kept the fabric from being woven too tight. People came, went, and returned. That was certainly true among tramp miners, who zigzagged from one district to another. There was also quite a bit of migration among the upper echelon. All of the moving around made it simple to renew old bonds. Men connected at the Wallace or Kellogg Elks, executive wives at bridge clubs, kids at school.

More reserved than his older brother, Rob, seventh-grader Pete Chase had a difficult time adapting to Big Creek. Though a pack of teenagers lived on the creek, only one or two boys were his age. He was too young to tag along with the older boys—though they sometimes took him fishing up at the mine bridge. But the afternoon of May 2 had been the best day of his life. His class had its annual picnic along the frothy banks of the south fork of the Coeur D'Alene River, and for the first time in a long while, the Chase's youngest felt that he belonged to the group. When he heard there was a fire, he figured everything would be all right and never gave it a second thought. When Pete got home, he shot some baskets until his mother came outside. Her face was the picture of anxiety.

"Come inside," she said quietly. It was disrespectful to play a game with a tragedy taking place right up the road. "Some people have been killed up at the mine."

It was sunny and clear when Rob Chase got off the bus in front of the big white house. He had never seen so many vehicles headed up to the mine and parked along the road. Many were hastily double-parked. As the teenager made his way into the swell of onlookers, an afternoon shift worker yanked him aside.

"Bob Bush and some other miners are dead," he said.

Rob knew serious injury and death came with the extraction of ore. The phone rang late at night enough times in the big white house to make it understood that things occasionally went wrong underground. He went up the hill.

A young Sunshine worker still in his teens said 3100 was an inferno. Rob, completely stunned, stayed mute. He had no idea what to say.

If that's true, he thought, *how are we going to get those guys out?*

About that time, a man who had trained to be a priest, but had ended up at Sunshine, asked the mine manager's oldest son to help keep reporters out of the yard. He was stationed at the bridge over the creek.

"Just tell them no one's allowed in," the man said.

BUNKER HILL HOTSHOT HARRY COUGHER'S CREW WAS tapped for another attempt at 3100, following Launhardt's failed effort. Of the five on Cougher's team, only graveyard shifter Ray Rudd was a Sunshine employee. Rudd was a good choice. He made it his business to keep tabs on who was coming and going at *his* mine. Miners called him "Mother," which was as much shorthand for "motherfucker" as for his tendency to keep them in line. He'd trained half the crew, including Wayne Allen and Charlie Casteel. Rudd and former partner Duwain Crow also shared a bond—they'd survived a serious cave-in in 1961. Rudd had sustained broken ribs, shoulders, and vertebrae, requiring him to wear a body cast from armpits to waist for five months. Crow had been so shaken he had needed tranquilizers to get by.

Tethered together by a nylon link line, Cougher, Rudd, and crew worked their way down 3100; CO readings were deadly. Charlie Casteel was standing upright, stiff and lifeless, just where Hawkins had seen him. By Cougher's estimation, Casteel was only a hundred feet short of fresh air. Cougher puzzled over a self-rescuer, which he presumed was Casteel's. It was in the muck fifteen feet from his body, toward fresh air. *Why is it in front of him? Maybe it slipped from his hand as he was running toward fresh air. Or maybe he turned back for some reason.*

Moments later, deeper down the smoky drift, the crew discovered a clutch of bodies where men had collapsed where they stood. Rudd called out each man's name as he pointed wildly around the drift.

"That's Crow!" Rudd said through his mask. "That's Allen over there . . ."

The sight distressed the crew, though not one would have admitted as much. None wanted to say what weighed heaviest on their minds, that the others deeper in the mine could be doomed.

"Oh, to hell with it, pard," Rudd said, giving in to growing doubts. "Let's get the hell out of here. There's nobody alive."

Cougher wouldn't hear of it. His light swept over the faces of the crew. "They told us to go back to the station," he said, pushing forward. "We need to get back to the hoist room."

The link line went taut as they moved down the drift. They could hear the hoist's rectifier sounding the alarm that the hoist was having mechanical problems, or had gone down altogether. The noise droned, growing louder and louder, mocking hopes and reminding them with each step that there didn't appear to be a soul to answer the alarm.

Twenty-eight

AFTERNOON, MAY 2
Osburn

IN OSBURN, WHERE HOWARD AND SUSAN MARKVE LIVED not far from KWAL's blinking tower, the Osburn Club, with its worn-out jukeboxes and card tables, was a regular hangout for miners coming off shift at the Silver Summit or Sunshine. Markve stopped in on occasion, but not on Tuesday afternoon, though now, more than ever, he could have used a drink. His lungs hurt like hell and his limbs felt shaky. Susan, twenty-two, a beautiful woman with red hair and pale, flawless skin, had seldom seen her husband home so early. She'd *never* seen him in such a state. His face was blank. He was an automaton. When he said there was a fire at work, she assumed that it had been a brushfire on the mountain.

"No," he said, "underground."

She studied his face, but there was nothing, just the flat affect of a man in shock.

211

"Is it bad?" she asked.

He indicated so with a slight nod.

"Did Dad come up?"

This was Louis Goos, the fifty-one-year-old miner working with Markve's partner's son, Bill Follette, twenty-three.

Markve said he didn't know and asked her to brew a thermos of coffee. He was going back up to Sunshine.

A flicker of worry came over her face, and Susan Markve phoned a sister in Montana. In minutes all six Goos girls and their mother, Delores, were en route to the district. While she waited with her two babies, Susan answered call after call as women phoned to ask if *she* knew anything. She told them she only knew what her husband had told her, and what she had heard on KWAL.

Later, when Markve returned from the mine, Susan met him at the door.

"Well, did you see my dad?"

When he told her that he hadn't, Susan insisted she wanted to see for herself.

"There's nothing for you to do up there," he said. "You have to take care of the kids."

"I *need* to go up there," she said. "He's my dad."

Susan loved her dad, though he hadn't been the best father—not by a long shot. Louis Goos had been one of the better gyppos at Homestake gold mine in Lead, South Dakota, and he'd made a lot of money. He was an outgoing, take-no-shit, hard-drinking cuss who unfailingly put his own needs ahead of his family's. In mining towns, legends were built as much around drinking tales as around mining prowess. Goos benefited from all kinds of stories. One had him getting hammered in a Wallace bar. When a cop told him that he was too sloppy to drive home and needed to take a cab, Goos agreed. So he stole a taxi.

"You told me to take a taxi home" was his sheepish reply to the officer who caught up with him.

Whenever Goos drank, however, his mean streak worsened and his blue-green eyes, magnified by thick eyeglass, filled with rage. Susan, the fourth of his six girls, knew that whenever their daddy came home late at night, her mother, Delores, was in for trouble. In the years since her childhood, Susan would scour her memories for pleasant ones, but few stood out. Those that did were twisted. One time her mother had caught her looking for a high-heeled shoe in her parents' bedroom closet. Delores smacked her so hard with the other heel it drew blood. Seeing that, Louis blew up and lit into Delores, berating her for hitting their daughter. And though her head was hemorrhaging, Susan held on to that moment as a happy time. *My father really loves me*, she'd thought.

Years later, Susan set aside some of her anger; she even forgave her dad, but she couldn't sweep his drinking-related abuse under the rug. She confronted him once, and Goos denied that he'd ever laid a hand on anyone. There was no telling him how she'd prayed every night that God would intervene and save her mother from his balled-up fist. There was nothing to be gained in pushing the point, because the blameless look on his rugged face was so utterly convincing.

AFTERNOON, MAY 2
Hayden Lake, North of Coeur D'Alene

IT WAS AN INCOMPLETE JUMBLE OF BAD INFORMATION WHEN the news reached Delmar and Donna Kitchen's dream house, with its two bathrooms and two-car garage, in Hayden Lake. Someone said that it was Delmar who was ensnared in the drifts of the burning mine, and his brother and dad had escaped. Donna's mother came right over, and the two agreed that they'd focus on getting over to Sunshine, and not so much on what they'd find when they arrived. Donna, however, turned her worries to her sister-in-law, Margie, and how she would be able to cope if the situation at the mine was deadly.

"It would be better," Donna Kitchen said, "if Delmar died than Dewellyn."

Her mother was incredulous, and Donna tried to explain her remark. It wasn't that she wanted to trade her husband's life for her brother-in-law's; it was that she felt that if the worst happened, she'd be able to get by. Dewellyn's wife was more dependent on her man than Donna was. He'd made all the decisions. He had been her *life*. Donna felt she could draw on her own strengths and survive whatever God handed her.

Delmar was standing on the bridge when they found him in the crowded mine yard. His pale skin was whiter than paper. Donna ran for her husband, joyous at the sight of him, but also confused.

"Delmar," she said, "what are you doing out? They said you were trapped! They said your dad and brother went in after you."

Another man came running. It was an old classmate from Pine Creek. In a flash, he grabbed Kitchen and hugged him.

"I thought you was dead!" The man's eyes were floating in tears. "They told me you was dead."

"I'm okay," Kitchen said, before amending his words: "I'm alive."

But his dad and his brother and dozens of others hadn't been seen for hours.

TIME UNKNOWN, MAY 2
4800 Level

BREATHE AND REMAIN CALM. FLORY AND WILKINSON HUDDLED in the crosscut on the western end of 4800. The image of the dead men back down the drift was at once vivid and hazy. The swirling, rolling smoke made the drift otherworldly. Broad swipes of black against the dull sheen of blasted walls and the crisp, blue-gray ribbons of tetrahedrite would in themselves have been an awesome sight if that had been all they'd seen. But it was the unexpected and horrific spectacle of bodies splayed out over the tracks that they tried to comprehend. Men had simply slumped over—quietly, and, it appeared, suddenly. Maybe they hadn't even had time to fight whatever was killing them. Maybe they didn't know what had happened to the guy behind each of them and they fell like dominoes, one after another.

Flory had been the last to see the others alive. He'd had no idea if he'd make it, but he knew that the last moments of a man's life, his final words, were sometimes precious to survivors. *What can I say to their wives and children?* He didn't even know who half of them were. Neither did Wilkinson. They knew three of them as Gordy, Pat, and Dick. They might have shared a smoke with one or another of the men topside, but they didn't hang out at the Happy Landing, nor did they actually work together. They were familiar faces and nothing more. The newest of the bunch was a tall kid, Darrell Stephens, nineteen, just a year out of Wallace High. Flory wondered if it had been the boy's first day in the mine.

"I don't remember seeing him before," he said.

The men were unnerved, yet their fear remained unspoken. Wilkinson pinched a fat bunch of Copenhagen, and Flory pulled out a cigarette and lit up. Half the world was above them, ton upon ton of rock, water, and earth held up by God's will or the force of nature. They sat and speculated about what had happened above. Both were sure 4800 had suffered the greatest calamity.

"They'll be coming down here for us," Wilkinson said.

The toxic cloud tiptoed past seven dead men—Richard Allison, Richard Bewley, Davy Mullin, Hubert "Pat" Patrick, Darrell Stephens, and Gordy Whatcott. Each had a story. A child with a heart problem. A wife who had once been beaten by her husband's hand. A parolee looking for a second chance. Each had a future before that day, and some had a past for which they could no longer make amends.

Then the smoke stalled and rolled backward. It was both quiet and monstrous. Neither Ron Flory nor Tom Wilkinson could imagine what was causing it. And there was no way to find out. They were so far away from the outside world, the sky, the fresh air, and the men trying to reach them and the others. On 4800, Wilkinson and Flory were at a depth greater than the height of four of the country's tallest buildings—New York's Empire State and Chrysler Buildings, San Francisco's Transamerica Pyramid, and the soon-to-be-completed Sears Tower in Chicago—*combined.*

HARRY COUGHER'S CREW ADVANCED FARTHER TOWARD 10-Shaft, all holding hope that Sunshine miners were safely ensconced on the levels below, just waiting to get out. As they moved down 3100, it occurred to Cougher that the men might have barricaded themselves in the hoist room.

God, he thought, *what if there's a whole bunch of men back there and they try to steal my apparatus?*

On the station, the smoke parted a little, revealing an underground killing field. Their lights sweeping the muck, Cougher and his men just stood still for a moment. A couple of guys felt sick. Everywhere around them were bodies, faces staring upward. One man had hit the concrete floor and the steel of the train track with such force that blood leaked from his ears. Cougher wondered if he'd fallen hard enough to fracture his skull. But most men had just slumped and keeled over. They looked as though they had just gone to sleep, peacefully and without fear. One guy sat off alone in the corner of the station, pressed up tight against the timbers. He reminded Cougher of how they'd found Charlie Casteel.

Some men had died while drinking coffee; others had kicked back to drag on a cigarette in the middle of the smoke storm. *These guys weren't in a hurry to get out*, Ray Rudd thought. They might have made it if they'd taken the threat seriously. Rudd knew why the scene had been so serene, why there hadn't been panic. The men were mostly gyppos. Since they hadn't finished blasting for the day, they'd planted themselves on the station to wait it out. They had thought they'd go back to blow up some rock.

Cougher's eyes caught Rudd's. Next was the hoist room.

In the world of hardrock mining, a smart man would argue that there is no job more important to operations than running the hoist. Without a hoistman, nothing moved from level to level—not men, not supplies, and of course, not ore. Hot mines like Sunshine built air-conditioned compartments around the control area, making it the most comfortable place underground. Cougher's crew entered the hoist room. The last minutes played in each man's mind. It was almost as if they could hear what had happened. The coughing. The yelling. The promises that they'd be able to get out alive. The deadly smoke had entered through the ventilation system, and the men had fought with their lives to save the others below. Over by the console were fallen dominoes, the bodies of several men who had tried to take over the controls. As each had succumbed, another had shoved him out of the operator's chair. The last one to die was a heavyset fellow, stripped to the waist, wearing only his diggers and boots. His beefy chest was bright cherry red.

God, Cougher thought, *that poor kid had a heat rash before he died.*

Their air supply half-exhausted, the helmet crew returned toward daylight, heavy, life-giving oxygen packs loading their backs. Marvin Chase met them at the collar and warned them that reporters with TV cameras were facing the portal.

"Don't stop and talk to any of them," he said. His voice was a near whisper. "Go directly to the office in the maintenance shop. We'll talk there."

They gathered around a table, and Al Walkup set out a pad for notes.

"Well," Chase said, "what did you see? Did you recognize anyone?"

"No," Rudd said emphatically.

The response nearly knocked Harry Cougher out of his chair.

"Jesus Christ, Rudd, you *did*. You called out the names of those guys."

Rudd looked completely bewildered. He said he didn't know anybody who was down there.

Cougher mentioned Duwain Crow and Wayne Allen as two men Rudd had identified—names that meant nothing to Cougher because he'd never met them. Cougher was bewildered. He wondered if Ray Rudd was in shock.

4:00 P.M., MAY 2

Coeur D'Alene Mining District

THE CALL FOR HELP FROM KELLOGG, IDAHO, WAS HEARD ALL over the Northwest. Miners with helmet or rescue training and gear were en route from Kimberly, British Columbia, and Butte, Montana. The Butte bunch, a dozen strong, came from the Anaconda Mining Company. Though rivals, they were also brothers. So quickly did they get to Big Creek that some wives didn't even know their husbands had left Montana until after they called home. One Butte miner spoke with a Spokane reporter.

"You can quote me," he said, "as saying I think they're working damn well together. These guys from all over—who've never seen each other before—down there working right together, trying to get at those poor men."

But for all that was going on, the office at the end of the maintenance shop was noticeably quiet, as if no one knew what to say.

Johnny Austin, the fiftyish bulldog manager from Bunker Hill, cleared his throat and turned to Walkup and Chase.

"Can I make a suggestion?" he asked.

Hecla's Gordon Miner saw a crack in the door and pushed right through it.

"By God, it's about time!" he said. "I'm interested in anybody who's got a suggestion!" The forty-three-year-old with the steely blue eyes and no-bullshit attitude wedged himself between would-be power brokers at the head of the table. At six foot two, Miner's appearance was as imposing as his manner. Whenever Hecla's top man spoke, it was with complete self-confidence; he was clearly a man who put action first and apologized later. For that very reason, some learned to follow Miner's lead because they knew that there was no stopping him—with reason *or* force. Al Walkup knew Miner's reputation, but he'd never felt the brunt of his indomitable personality until May 2. He backed off.

Miner saw Sunshine's Walkup and Chase as indecisive. It didn't seem they could stick to any plan and, not surprisingly, they were easily pushed around. Miner, in particular, was quite aggressive. *That figures*, Art Brown thought. *Gordon Miner will run roughshod over anyone who's weak enough to let him.* Around the Hecla office, his autocratic ways had earned him the nickname "the Alone Arranger." Certainly he wasn't perfect, but Hecla's executive vice president was never short of ideas, and once he started moving forward, he never looked back.

Miner, in fact, had been through a potash mine fire in Utah. When they first realized fire was choking the life out of the mine there, some of the underground crew ran and some barricaded themselves in. The men who stayed put were the ones who survived. The Hecla chief hoped the trapped Sunshine miners were doing the same thing and were waiting for someone to get them out.

One thing troubled Gordon Miner above everything else, and he just couldn't shake it: the apparent delay in evacuating Sunshine. *You don't wait for a green light from the corporate types when they don't know anything anyway about that particular situation,* he thought.

Back in the command center, men unfurled schematics of the ventilation system and drift maps, circling the possible locations where they might find survivors. The room wasn't particularly large, about the size of an average dining room, with floor-to-ceiling drapes that made it seem more residential than professional. But it was packed. Advancing the fresh-air base through either 3100 or 3700 was proving slow going, with workers discovering that Sunshine's drifts were anything but airtight. Launhardt focused on Sunshine's connecting mine, the Silver Summit. From Sunshine's 3100, an eighty-five-foot ladderway joined the Silver Summit at its 3,000-foot level. The obscure route was Sunshine's designated emergency escapeway in the event the Jewell could not be used.

Coming from opposite directions, with the Sunshine effort west of 10-Shaft and the Silver Summit helmet crews to the east of the shaft, the rescue effort was a race in every way, with stakes no less than life and death. And above the constant discussion by men from all over—Sunshine, other district mines, the U.S. Bureau of Mines, the miners' union—was the ceaseless ringing of a bank of telephones. A big oak table was covered with so many underground maps that no wood showed. Some maps showed the suspected location of the fire; red markings indicated the belief that the fire had started in the abandoned stopes between 3400 and 3550, near the mined-out 09 crosscut or vein. The speed and fury of the smoke through the ventilation system pointed toward the failure of the bulkhead on 3400. The sixty-foot-long timber and polyurethane-foam-sealed bulkhead shuttered the 910 raise, which connected gob-filled workings to the 09 vein, a vein that hadn't seen a miner's jackleg since the mid-1940s. Harvey Dionne had seen the smoke boiling behind the eight-year-old bulkhead, just after all hell broke loose. Others reported that they had heard an explosion, which had been followed by billowing smoke darker than night.

Walls throughout the command center were papered with notes reporting air samples, contact information, and status of the crew. Cigarette smoke masked the ceiling. An enormous map of the mine with Mylar overlays, measuring ten by twenty feet, was spread over another table. Coffee was tepid, and sandwiches sent up by the Red Cross grew stale because no one thought to eat.

Lucky Friday's Art Brown volunteered to lead a ten-man team from the Silver Summit side of 3100, also known as the Sunshine Drift. Only a handful had any experience with McCaas; the rest were hastily trained on the spot. They were as ready as they could be.

DOWN FROM THE MINE OVER IN KELLOGG, BYRON SCHULZ sat up in his bed at West Shoshone Hospital and told reporters his harrowing story in a halting, raspy voice. There were some things the twenty-one-year-old just couldn't speak of just then, maybe never. At one point, tears interrupted the interview when Schulz blamed the company's safety program for the tragedy.

"There was no organization. Nobody knew what to do or how to do it," he said.

According to Schulz, the company had thwarted any attempts to improve safety, and any grievances related to safety were met with retaliation from the bosses. He himself had been given "bad time" for filing a safety complaint.

Schulz was the first to talk to the press and point the finger of blame at Sunshine's managers. He didn't know it then, but he had lit a fuse.

Twenty-nine

JUST AT THE CURVE THAT SWEPT UP TO THE MINE WAS THE last house in the Big Creek neighborhood. Not long after they married in 1956, Duwain and Lauralee Crow paid $3,000 for the sturdy little place. It was a sweet deal for both owner and seller. Their house payment was only $50, and Sunshine liked having its miners in debt and close at hand. Early on the morning of the fire, Mrs. Crow set out a big plastic jug and filled it halfway with water. From the freezer, she brought out six Campbell's Soup cans that she used as ice molds. She slipped the frozen cylinders from their tin skins and dropped them one by one into the oversized thermos. *Duwain gets thirsty down there,* she thought. *This ought to hold him until tonight.*

At the mine that afternoon, Launhardt instantly recognized her voice. Lauralee Crow got his attention by the machine shop. She stood behind the rope line. Lee, as her friends called her, was an attractive woman with long dark hair and fine features, though she could be tough as a miner. She was also a prankster. Her husband learned the hard way that he'd better think twice when he opened his dinner bucket. He liked to crack the shell of his hard-boiled egg on his head while sitting on the station. One time she'd tricked him with a raw egg, and all the gyppos around the station had a good laugh.

"Bob! Have you seen Duwain?" she called over.

Launhardt didn't ignore her, but he kept moving. Stopping and looking into her eyes would surely make him stammer out the truth. Duwain Crow was one of the confirmed dead. Launhardt thought he saw a couple of Duwain's children standing beside their mother. Lauralee Crow's dark hair hung lifelessly, and her winter-pale skin looked like frost.

"No, I haven't," Launhardt said stiffly. "Don't know anything yet."

"Oh," she said. "Let me know as soon as you can."

Launhardt nodded. But he couldn't tell her the Bunker Hill crew had found her husband's body in the muck on 3100. The body wasn't coming out until rescue crews made it to the lower levels. And that, Launhardt feared, might take some time.

WHEN SPOKANE-BASED UNITED PRESS INTERNATIONAL reporter Jerry McGinn arrived in Big Creek, he instantly saw trouble. Print and television reporters were already griping that Sunshine was trying to control the story. Sunshine bosses hated constant questions for which they had no answers. While all of the reporters understood the need for order in the midst of the unraveling disaster, only McGinn would take the access issue into his own hands. *They think this is under their control? It is beyond their control.*

Exiled with the other reporters across the bridge, McGinn scrutinized the scene. The miners' wives were stuck. Many didn't own telephones and lived in remote gulches around the district—where there were no neighbors to consult for the latest news. The only way to know what was happening was to stay huddled on folding chairs and wait. Certainly the women looked older than their years. The men might have enough money for a new truck every year, but they didn't see the value of regular visits to a dentist. McGinn liked the people because they were never given to pretense. To characterize them as salt of the earth was too easy. All sat there with cups of perked Hills Bros. coffee and waited. McGinn thought they deserved better. When a plane crashed, airlines were ready to release passenger names and casualty numbers from the first hours. Sunshine was holding the names for some cruel reason, he believed, and it angered him.

McGinn studied the grim faces of Sunshine's staff for a clue to their heartlessness. Instead, he saw fear. *These guys are petrified. They're in deep shit. The guys still underground are screwed,* he thought.

The reporter watched the goings-on around a table set out for Red Cross recruits. Two women were seated behind a folding table upon which had been neatly arranged name tags, brochures, and assorted flyers. McGinn picked up the sign-up sheet and wrote down his name. A few seconds later he put on Red Cross identification and was on the way to forbidden territory.

THE FOOTHILLS RISING FROM THE VALLEY FLOOR THAT RUN east to west through the district were dressed in a light shake of snow. While trees didn't have a sugar topping that late in the season, on May 2, 1972, a patchy carpet of white still tucked itself into the gaps between the conifers and the feathery spires of aspen that grew in fan-shaped groves. Susan Markve walked in the direction of the portal, staring at the scene as though she were looking at a painting, or maybe experiencing a dream. She had an odd feeling of complete detachment, as though whatever was going on at Sunshine was excluding her. She was watching it, but not participating. A Red

Cross worker asked if she wanted coffee. Susan looked lost, her pale skin now paper white.

"No," she said, not breaking her gaze from the portal. "I want my dad to come out of there."

Howard was in bed when she returned home after an hour of nothingness. She prodded him for more information, but he offered nothing more.

"I saw smoke," he said. "No fire, just smoke."

He didn't tell her just how black that smoke had been or how he had had to lower his cap lamp to within a foot of the track line to see it. Before restless sleep finally came late that night, Howard tried to reassure his wife. He said her dad would find an air pocket and bulkhead himself in. Louis Goos was taking it all in stride, deep in the mine in an air pocket that kept him safe.

He'll be okay, she thought. *He'll be getting out . . . tomorrow.*

Thirty

WHEN THE *KELLOGG EVENING NEWS* PUBLISHED ITS
Tuesday edition, it carried an article indicating that "some
eighty" miners were trapped in Sunshine. Things were not dire, the
paper reported, because the men could exit the mine through alternate routes. "It is believed that day shift workers will be able to get
out by this means, although it may be some time before they can get
out." About the time newspapers were landing on front steps across
the district, a kid who ran around with Gene and Betty Johnson's
son, Dennis, arrived at their Big Creek home. He caught his breath
at the front door while Betty answered. He was barely a man, but
he'd been working at Sunshine, following in the footsteps of most
district men.

"Gene here?"

Betty shook her head, and the kid's face went ashen. "Oh God," he said, "there are only two people I care about in that mine, and Gene is one of them."

She looked scared and, realizing that his words were the cause, he backpedaled.

"We hear Gene got out," he said, "and he was checking guys out. You've got nothing to worry about. I just wanted to make sure he was home."

"Not yet," she said, saying good-bye and closing the door. It sounded as if Gene had plenty going on up Big Creek Road. Mines had calamities of one kind or another very nearly every other day. Betty sat down and waited.

RAISED IN THE SHADOW OF THE BUNKER HILL SMELTER, Betty Jean Barker was the daughter of the night watchman and sometime worker in Uncle Bunk's blower house. She and her four siblings grew up in the district during the best of times. Boys always knew that when the time came, they had a job at one of the area's numerous mines or at Bunker's smelter. Most had new cars because summer jobs turned into full-time employment. Dances at Kellogg High and parties along the river went on without so much as a pause, even as boys were plucked out of the district for military service. Soldiers returned to certain employment and the girlfriends they'd left behind. In time, most of the men in Betty's life worked at Sunshine—her brothers and husband, and their son.

Frederick Gene Johnson and Betty Jean Barker were proof that opposites do indeed attract. He was a man who loved a good time, fast cars, and partying with his pals. She was a homebody, a shy, petite girl with enormous eyes that soaked up all the excitement around her. He was brash and she was reticent. He had tattoos and scars, and she wore sensible shoes. Johnson had altered his birth certificate to get into the Army so he could see the world; she took a job selling tickets at the Kellogg bus station so others could do the same. But in 1946, on that steep stretch of frost-heaved roadway that passes through Fourth of July Canyon, the two met. Betty Barker was returning home from Coeur d'Alene with her brother Robert when they came across Johnson and ended up racing him halfway home. At twenty-one, Johnson was only a few months older than Betty, but he was much more grown up. Not long after they met, he showed up at the bus station and started courting her. He wore long-sleeved shirts in the blistering heat of the summer to conceal the tattoos that were a roadmap of his tour in the military. He wanted Betty Barker to see who he was, rather than where he had been.

Gene Johnson, as the only son of Sunshine's boardinghouse cook, was a boy who never knew his father. Since his mother's job had her up at 3:00 a.m. to prepare for the changing shifts, she sent her son to a Catholic boarding school. Johnson loved his mother, but his lonely childhood had created a big hole that he only knew one way to fix— a family of his own.

Friends had warned the young woman that Johnson was too wild, but she ignored them. In her own quiet way, Betty Jean Barker set out to tame him. Some would later say she succeeded. They married, and in 1947 they moved into a little house on Sunshine Star Route, about a mile from the mine. Over the years they had five children: a son, Dennis, and four daughters, Linda, Peggy, Karen, and Brenda. The kids attended Elk Creek School, a three-story brick building near the base of the canyon. Because it was good business to keep miners and their wives settled in a community, the school benefited from the generosity of the owners of the mine. Mine officials knew that kids were the glue that kept some men from leaving for another mine.

But Johnson wasn't the type to plant his butt in a lawn chair with a beer and have five more cold ones lined up in the fridge. He almost always worked two jobs, even during some of his years as a contract miner. For a while, early in their marriage, Johnson worked opposite shifts at Bunker Hill and Sunshine, so that he could create the kind of life he had envisioned while growing up without siblings or a father, and with a mother who worked her fingers to the bone. The Johnsons always had new cars, boats, horses, and motorcycles. All of it, from the train sets circling the tallest imaginable Christmas tree to the toy racetrack in the basement, was fun stuff. Johnson was the biggest kid of all.

In turn, Betty wasn't shy about getting what she wanted. Her children could see how their mother manipulated their dad, but they also knew he didn't mind. It was almost a game. If Betty didn't get her way on some trivial matter, she'd give Gene the silent treatment. If he wanted to do something and she didn't, he'd pick a fight just to have the excuse to leave. Outsiders, who thought Johnson was a tough SOB and his wife was needy and weak, missed what those closest to the couple could see. He loved her. When Betty was facing surgery, Johnson called their daughter Peggy to the kitchen. The mountain of a man slumped at the table, bawling over the prospect of something going wrong. When the talk turned to his own mortality, he made her promise that if anything ever happened to him, she'd always take care of her mother.

Peggy agreed, but she was sure she'd never have to make good on the pledge. Her dad was invincible.

SUNSET, MAY 2
West Shoshone County Hospital

EVENING AND EARLY-MORNING HOURS IN WEST SHOSHONE'S emergency room were pretty much the same in all the years Keith Dahlberg served as its primary physician. When Bunker's swing shift let out, he'd see a flurry of women and children and some begrudging man who probably wished he hadn't gone straight to the Tip Top Bar. A couple of hours later, between 1:00 and 2:00 a.m., the bar swarm would arrive with injuries from a brawl. Around 3:00 a.m., the last distinct group would arrive at the ER, often rolled in on stretchers: teenagers who'd been out partying and maybe rolled a car somewhere along the river, too drunk to drive, but limber enough to survive the crash. Around 4:00 a.m., Dr. Dahlberg could finally relax. Even in the mining district, little happened at that hour.

In a town with more than twenty bars, fights in Kellogg on payday were numerous. Dahlberg had ER duty every Friday. He'd stitched up a lot of the same faces again and again. When he heard that Whitey's Bar had wrapped shag carpeting around its ceiling support columns, his sigh of relief was heard clear to the other side of town. The number of banged-up heads and busted teeth dropped precipitously.

Sadly, some workers never needed the company ambulance and its fast ride down the hill. One man Dahlberg saw had been run over by a mine car, and his head had been severed. Another miner took the one-way tumble down Bunker's incline shaft. When he was found at the bottom a mile later, his skin had been sanded down with grit so coarse it had wiped away all human features. He looked like a bloody salamander.

The West Shoshone staff braced for a deluge of burn and smoke-inhalation cases on May 2. Byron Schulz and Bob McCoy were the first of what they expected would be scores of miners. The medical staff heard that more than a hundred men were still trapped in Sunshine's smoky underground. The doctors pulled contingency plans from a gunmetal gray cabinet near the nurse's station. They knew that when miners started coming in, they had better be ready. Having been underground at the mine, Dr. Dahlberg realized how immense Sunshine was, and how difficult the rescue effort would be. There were endless drifts, and perpetual and wilting heat. Perspiration had rolled down from his underarms like water from a leaky shower head. With the added heat of a fire, the environment would be close to hell. *Just waiting down there could kill them,* he thought.

Things had quieted since Schulz's admission earlier in the day. Of all the things the cager related to the staff, nothing was more surprising than that the double-drum was only running the south side. Why had the north side sat idle? The fastest way to get the men out was to run both sides. Schultz had heard Gene Johnson give the order, but he didn't know the reasoning behind it. He also talked of going to a level and seeing men sitting with their faces in their hands. They were quiet, but alive. He'd made a second attempt to get them out, but it hadn't been in time.

"They were all dead," he said. "There was nothing I could do."

Dr. Dahlberg had finished his rounds and was leaving for home when Margaret Hanna accosted him near the ER entrance. She was the wife of Sunshine pump man Bill Hanna, forty-seven. Her husband was among those trapped on 3100. Her words sputtered from her lips, one bit at a time.

"I know . . . something's wrong. I'm worried . . . about him."

He reassured her and led her inside to write out a prescription for a sedative. She needed to get some rest.

Practicing medicine in the district meant dealing with sudden traumas and the stealthy illnesses of the workingmen of the woods and mines. Loggers arrived with bloody injuries, the kind that happen when steel collides with human flesh. Miners, of course, were seen because giant rocks had crushed their small bones. Zinc plant workers arrived with crusts of dried blood outlining nostrils from nosebleeds caused by the pervasive cloud of sulfuric acid in the refinery. Smelter employees came in with symptoms of lead poisoning—severe joint pains, and upset stomachs that no amount of seltzer could cure.

Sand, seemingly innocuous in itself, created an occupational hazard peculiar to hardrock mining, one that the new doctor hadn't read about anywhere in the annals of medicine. The fine-grained sand used to backfill mined-out stopes was a by-product of the milling process. Known as gall, it was tainted by chemicals and corrosives used to extract minerals from the ore. And, of course, it was everywhere underground. Miners called the result of sharp little particles working their way into the folds of their skin, especially around the crotch, being "galded." The gritty residue rubbed the flesh raw. It was inescapable, like wearing clothing made of sandpaper. For some, it had the sting of a dip in acid, cracking the skin around genitals or underarms to the point of bleeding. Others found gall an annoyance they could treat with the freezing jolt of a jock-itch spray. Many were galded around their brows or in their hair, too, the result of cap bands rubbing the skin. Redness and a dripping, oozing goo, like seepage from a bad burn, were the main indicators. Ridding themselves of irritating sand was one of the primary reasons men wasted no time getting to the showers after shift. Some went even further than merely soaping up to wash away the muck and sand from their bodies; they washed their diggers in the showers, too. The concrete floor sometimes resembled the silt of a braided stream.

And to each patient, the doctor suggested commonsense precautions.

"Wash your hands before you eat," he'd tell miners. "Change your clothes *at work*. Otherwise, you're taking lead dust home in your car."

Dr. Dahlberg understood the underlying reasons behind the inevitable rejection of his advice. The kind of men who took underground jobs were the kind who didn't listen to doctors, didn't wear seat belts, and gleefully tempted fate by taking chances.

Tuesday night, Dr. Dahlberg made up his mind. They could use a doctor up at the mine, and it might as well be him.

8:15 P.M., MAY 2
Sunshine Bridge

HIGH SCHOOL SENIOR ROB CHASE UNLATCHED THE GATE across the creek bridge. The first five bodies had been deposited in the back of a station wagon and the ambulances. They were Bob

Bush, forty-six; repairman Pat Hobson, fifty-seven; El Paso–born Roberto Diaz, fifty-five; shift boss Paul Johnson, forty-seven; and Wayne Blalack, thirty-five. Chase waved the vehicles through, very quietly and as unobtrusively as possible, though everyone knew their cargo. The teenager's eyes lit on two bodies shrouded by dark olive blankets as the ambulances rumbled over the bridge.

His cousin pointed at the largest. "That one's Bob Bush," he said.

Down Big Creek Road, Viola Chase and her youngest son stood outside and watched the ambulances drive quietly past, lights off, sirens mute.

There's probably a dead guy in the back of that, Pete thought.

Marvin had called Viola and said the fire was exceptionally serious. "From now on," Viola told Pete, "our lives will never be the same."

Thirty-one

THE CAR RADIO WAS PLAYING SOFTLY WHEN GOD SPOKE to Myrna Flory. Ron Flory's eighteen-year-old wife relaxed and loosened her grip on the steering wheel. The dark blue Charger moved on up the road toward the mine, and feathery conifers engulfed the windshield with a dark green blur. Somehow a message was telegraphed to her that her husband would be all right. *Don't pray for Ron anymore. He'll be all right. Use your prayers for the others.* She wasn't a particularly religious young woman. She'd had too much living to do to sit on a church pew. But at that moment, Myrna Flory was a believer. She parked the car, took a moment to steady herself from the revelation, and started across the parking lot. Her long brown hair, wet from a hasty shower, hung limp against her shoulders.

Within a few steps of the Big Creek Bridge, a man introduced himself as a reporter planning a book about the fire.

"They just found your husband dead," he said. "I'm sorry."

"No, they did not," she shot back, refusing to stop or give any more of a reaction. That's all he'd been after, anyway. She ran across the bridge to a mine supervisor and asked if he knew anything. The man, with a stony expression of shock, shook his head. She huddled with Mary Russell. Russell's husband, Mark, was Ron's best friend. Both women were convinced good news was coming.

WHERE THE COLUMN OF SMOKE FROM BIG HOLE MET THE night sky, there was a jagged tear in the atmosphere, angry and otherworldly. The mine vomited a dark cloud of such size that those watching had a hard time believing that, despite its vast size, it could hold that much smoke. And though it was some kind of war, with an army of rescuers itching to reach the battle zone to find survivors, another kind of skirmish was taking place between the families and the mine staff, and reporters with their billy-club-sized microphones and impertinent questions.

"If your husband's dead, what are you going to do?" a reporter asked a woman sitting on a bench.

The woman convulsed into a loud and unsettling spasm of sobs. The man scribbled something down, as though her response and not his insensitive question was the story.

"If your dad is in there and doesn't come out alive, what are you going to do?" another asked.

Angry words were exchanged between miners' kin and reporters. Marvin Chase wanted to put the focus on the rescue effort. He clung to the hope that those trapped were merely waiting for rescuers. Focusing on the worst possible outcome was counterproductive. He reminded reporters that compressed-air lines ran through the mine. They were chest-high and accessible just about everywhere a man could be. All miners carried pipe wrenches to tap into the air lines that ran whiz-bangs, drills, and other machinery that required a power source other than an electrical battery. Water could be accessed the same way. Underground, Chase insisted, the trapped men had ample access to air. As long as Sunshine's surface crew kept the flow going, he was sure they'd survive.

Bob Launhardt doubted the scenario's plausibility, but kept his mouth shut. He knew Sunshine's underground atmosphere was heavy with carbon monoxide, and that anybody who took a breath of it dropped dead. The only true hope, and a thin one at that, was that the trapped men had found a place with good air and then were able to build themselves an airtight barricade. It was a message that he wanted the rescue team—and reporters—to know.

"Someone could have gone up a raise and turned on the compressed air," Chase insisted. "Other men have done it at other mine fires. It can happen here, too."

The increasingly embattled mine manager went one better as the cyclone of reporters swirled around. Chase told them that air was being drawn out of the air lines. Implicit in that message was that men were drawing on the air line.

In truth, Marvin Chase knew better, but didn't know what else to say. He had been thrust into something terrible and unforeseen. He responded to all questions with a manufactured confidence that he thought would create hope, not despair.

RON FLORY'S MOTHER, BELLE, WENT TOWARD HER DAUGHTER-in-law with a sense of purpose that Myrna, chain-smoking and shivering by a smudge pot, knew on sight did not bode well. There was no greeting or outstretched arms. In fact, there never had been. Belle Flory was not shy about making her feelings known. She thought her "number-one son" could have done far better than Myrna Keene.

"I'll be handling my son's checking account," she said, her eyes fastened on Myrna's. "It's still in my name, you know."

Myrna stood there and said nothing. For a second the words didn't fully register.

"I'll handle everything that belonged to my son."

Myrna gave Ron's mother a cold stare.

"You *can't* write any checks," Mrs. Flory continued. "Everything is in my name—truck and car, too."

"No," Myrna said, finally finding her voice. "Ron's *my* husband and he's coming home." She was unsure of her rights, but she thought a wife would have some say in her husband's affairs. Why was his mother acting like he was dead, buried in an unmarked grave on 4800? Myrna wanted to believe that her big man would get out of the mine and carry her to the car, away from the mine and, most of all, away from his mother. God told her so.

THAT FIRST DAY SHE MET RON FLORY AT HIS TRAILER IN Osburn, Garnita Keene couldn't see what could draw her sister and the older miner together. He was quiet to the point of being almost noncommunicative. Myrna could jabber on like a magpie and flit about a room, soaking up attention and making people laugh with her sassy wit. Ron liked to stick around the house and quietly watch TV, or work on his truck. Myrna liked to go out to drink and party—though as a teen she'd confined herself mostly to riverside keggers. He was settled. She was a wild child. Yet, despite that, in time Garnita could see that there was chemistry between them. Instead of her dominating his life, Myrna settled, more or less, into his world.

"Want to go out for a beer?" she asked her sister not long after she met Flory.

"No, better not," Myrna replied, not unhappily. "Ron wants me to stick around here."

The reply shook Garnita a little. It was such a change, coming from a sister who never missed an opportunity to hang out. *It could be for the better,* she thought after mulling it over for a while. *Myrna needs to settle down some.*

Ron's younger brother, Robert, had doubts about the pair. He liked Myrna all right, but she came with a background and a baby. She needed a man who would take care of her, a man she could still control in a way that allowed her to keep her freedom. But when this pretty young woman said she wanted him, Robert watched his brother set aside a grown man's reservations and let himself fall for her. Myrna could be carefree, and Ron could be a devoted husband and made-to-order father.

EVENING, MAY 2
4800 Level

RON FLORY'S CAP LAMP WENT DARK. HE FOOLED WITH THE cable and the battery connection, but nothing happened. Tom Wilkinson's lamp was still viable, but for how much longer? Down the drift was an orange warning light used to alert the crew of approaching motors. It was no more than a twenty-five-watt bulb, but in the near absolute darkness of the drift it did a good job of illuminating the wall of smoke, burnishing it into an eerie golden brown. The motor's fixed headlight also spread a beam into the Safety Zone. That light was powered by three batteries, and remained steady, washing the black walls with an even spray of illumination. They had water—all they could drink—but they had no food. Even so, hunger wasn't as much of a concern as their dwindling supply of smokes. Flory, in particular, was a nervous smoker. Tapping a Pall-Mall Red from the pack, he saw that his cigarettes were nearly gone. No food, no smokes. The only thing worse would be no light. Wilkinson knew the battery on the motor wouldn't last forever. The lamp had already dimmed somewhat.

Wilkinson thought they should conserve the light.

"Let's try it without the motor," he said.

A miner's lamp is his most important link to survival. While shaft stations and underground shops throughout a mine are illuminated, often the beam from a cap lamp is the only thing between men and total darkness. Total darkness wasn't the same as night with eyes closed tight. A man holding a hand in front of his face in total darkness wouldn't know where it was, even when it was his own outstretched hand. A failed lamp meant it was time to sit and wait for help. Walking was suicide.

Flory shut off the headlight, and Wilkinson switched off his lamp. The world instantly went entirely black. Nothing can prepare a man for total darkness, how it rattles the mind to be blind when you know you can see. The darkness cinched tight around their necks and pressed against their chests. Their eyes spun in their sockets, searching for a pinprick of light, or even a shadow, to suggest a variation in the darkness. Their world had been immersed in a great, oppressive nothingness.

It bothered Flory more than Wilkinson, perhaps because he had no cap lamp to reach for if panic seized him. The mine felt suddenly claustrophobic, closing in on him in a way that made him feel the whole thing was crushing him in suffocating darkness.

"Jesus, this could be bad," he said, in an understatement typical of him.

Both men had heard stories of miners who had been trapped without working lamps. Some had started crawling, feeling their way along the ribs, trying to reach the curve that would lead them to some light. Throughout the Coeur d'Alenes there were tales of miners who had come across the mummified remains of hapless men whose carbide lamps had long ago fizzled to nothing, and who had crawled on their stomachs feeling for a way out, but their fingers had found nothing.

A half hour elapsed, and Wilkinson decided they'd had enough of the experiment.

"We got light now. Might as well use it while we got it."

He turned on his lamp, and Flory went to the motor.

EVENING, MAY 2
Sunshine Parking Lot

NOBODY WAS SAYING IT, BUT AS DARKNESS DESCENDED ON the mountainsides around the mine—its lights a beacon like never before—it was becoming increasingly unlikely that first aid would be needed. Sunshine employees cut burlap yardage into seven-foot sections to cradle and insulate the injured from the cold floor of the drift. As a precaution in the event a helmet crewman was injured, a first-aid station was set up in the old Jewell Shaft. The night's subfreezing temperature left the intermittent puddles in the parking lot shellacked with ice. People stood in groups linked by proximity that easily indicated who belonged together. Many had Red Cross–issued blankets wrapped around windbreakers and hooded sweatshirts. Some shivered despite the woolly wrapping. A young man and woman kept a perch on the ledge below the safety sign. The man wore cowboy boots, and his sideburns touched his jawline. The woman wore bell-bottoms with a faded checkered pattern. Hot vapors from her coffee curled around wan features. She might have been pretty ten hours before. Now she looked lost, her eyes hollow from the late hour.

Frances Wilkinson prayed in the parking lot. The smudge pots had turned her naturally curly brown hair—which she'd painstakingly straightened—to gunk. Her hands were ice cold, but she didn't care. Things were bad, but she wasn't sure just how bad. She prayed Tom would be safe, that he and Ron were together, looking out for each other. *Tom will be all right.* When a Red Cross worker offered her a name tag, she declined.

"I don't need one," she said. "My husband is going to walk out alive."

Later, Belle Flory went looking again for her son's young wife. When she found her, she pulled a bottle of sedatives from her purse.

"You might commit suicide," she said, giving her a single capsule.

Myrna was distraught, but she wasn't about to kill herself. She was sure her husband was alive. Even at eighteen, Myrna knew what love was, and how devotion could frequently be paired with gratitude. Ron had saved her in some ways, taking her from unwed motherhood to a complete family; he was a father to Tiger. He'd given her a fresh start.

Myrna swallowed the sedative and settled her thin frame into the backseat of her mother-in-law's car. She surrendered to the sleep that her body, though stoked with caffeine, needed as much as air.

Thirty-two

WAVA BEEHNER UNDERSTOOD THAT A NUMBER OF SUN-shine miners were in serious trouble, but thankfully, Don wasn't a miner. His silence, she reasoned, was because he was help-ing with the rescue. That was the explanation of why he hadn't come home, why he hadn't even called. She told the children everything would be fine in the morning. When the youngest, Matthew, drifted into slumber, he thought he'd see his dad at the breakfast table. His dad was the center of their family.

Don Beehner held on to every nickel and saw no need to spend money on anything he could get for free. Sometimes he took his sons to the mine yard to scavenge timbers for their woodstove. In the summer it was huckleberries that brought sons and daughters into the Idaho mountains with their father. He kept a close grip on house-hold funds. When the family prepared its weekly shopping list, he held veto power. When his wife and kids wanted a telephone, he balked, so Wava took a job cleaning the bowling alley to pay for one herself. Daughter Nora considered her dad tighter than bark on a tree. Any extras, like bikes, were purchased with Gold Strike trading stamps. Beehner's tightwad tendencies came from the usual place. Living in Lead, South Dakota, his dad had been a miner and a boozer, a combination that ensured instability and lean times.

Because he'd been poor and didn't want that for his family, Don Beehner always moonlighted. In the mid- to late 1960s, when Beehner was a motorman, he had Wava and the kids making ammonium nitrate for her uncle's explosives company in Wallace, Trojan Powder. Trojan supplied mines with blasting agents it manufactured from fertilizer. The Beehners worked afternoons and weekends in a string of old semi trailers set up to produce the explosives. It paid well, but it was very dangerous. Once, eight-year-old Matt got his hand caught in an auger and lost an index finger.

Around 1970, Beehner came up with his latest and best money-making idea yet. That was when he leased the historic Wallace Hotel, above the Wallace Corner where he tended bar five nights a week. The Corner was a schizophrenic place—a bar and soda fountain with a sort of convenience store housed in an obviously out-of-plumb 1890s brick building. On one side was a rack of car and porno magazines. One miner bought every skin magazine a man could flip through for a one-handed read—more than $100 each month. Beehner knew every face that came into the place. He knew whose check was good and who'd ask to carry a tab a bit longer.

Wava didn't want to leave Woodland Park to live in the hotel, but the kids thought it was cool to live downtown, and she didn't have much of a say in anything. The parents took the office bedroom, the girls had a room assigned to them, and the two boys slept in whichever rooms weren't being used that night. Matt liked it. What he didn't like—and neither did his mother—was all the work they had to do.

People constantly told Wava they adored her husband, and how much fun he was to be around. Living in the shadow of a man whom others adore is seldom easy. There was even a time, about a year before the fire, when Wava Beehner felt physically exhausted and emotionally abandoned. She not only managed the hotel books, but she also had to fix all the niggling problems that went with running the place. Don got to stand around, pour drinks, and be charming. Wava felt she needed to take a stand. Accompanied only by Matt, then eleven, she went on strike and returned to the little green house in Woodland Park.

A month later, Don Beehner did a little soul-searching and reunited his family.

"I'm glad you're back," he said. "But you've been living with me long enough to know I'm not going to apologize. We'll just change things," he said.

It was the only time Wava stood up to him. And if it was the only time she ever won a battle, it had been the right one to win. They'd never been happier.

10:50 P.M., MAY 2
Silver Summit Portal, Osburn

LUCKY FRIDAY'S ART BROWN, THE SOUTH AFRICAN WHO'D been golfing that afternoon, arrived at the Silver Summit portal with his helmet crew. Brown was ready to get going toward 10-Shaft to reach the Sunshine men. His team finished setting up its fresh-air base and was ready to roll, but the green light wasn't coming from the rescue command center. Two hours later, Brown's frustration turned to anger. *Why the fuck aren't Chase and Walkup giving us the signal to get down below to get the men out? Every minute counts.* As Brown viewed it, if there were guys down below, as he knew there had to be, then what needed to be done had to be accomplished in minutes and hours, not days. He could feel the urgency of the situation deep in his bones, but not a word had come from Sunshine's side.

"Come on, let's get on with it," he said. "Let's start establishing new fresh-air bases and get these men out of here."

But the word from Sunshine was to hold off. Finally, hours after they'd loaded up a supply of USBM-procured breathing apparatus, cases and cases of cardoxide, O_2 and CO indicators, and oxygen tanks for the miners trapped underground, the signal came.

"Go in."

But after they'd sealed off a bulkhead on the Silver Summit side, deadly carbon monoxide readings hadn't abated. Neither had Brown's patience. Seal off the drift and move on had been the plan. But it wasn't working.

"Jesus," he said, "if this stuff is coming up this raise, and we've sealed it off, it should clean this up."

One of his team examined Sunshine's map and shook his head.

"Well," Brown said, his voice muffled by the shield of his mask, "where the hell is it coming from?"

No one had a clue.

A half hour later the source was discovered—a raise omitted from the mine schematic was forcing more smoke and carbon monoxide into the Silver Summit drift.

With each small failure, precious moments elapsed. The maps were not only outdated, they were out of scale. Brown was frustrated and wasn't afraid to say so. He wondered why Sunshine management didn't get some men to help who knew the old workings of the mine. He immediately thought of Jim Bush. The Bush brothers practically ran the mine.

"If Bush were here," Brown said in a cultured accent that belied his miner's getup, "he'd say, shit, there's an old raise that goes up here. Not on the map. It goes off to the left and the end."

LATE EVENING, MAY 2
4800 Level, Safety Zone

FLORY AND WILKINSON HUNKERED DOWN AND WATCHED THE light of the motor bear down on nothingness. Water trickled through the piss ditch, its flow thick and white, resembling glacial runoff. No voices, no rumbling of muck cars across grit-covered tracks or the pounding sound of the grizzlyman sending fractured chunks of muck down the timber-lined chute to fill a car. And yet it wasn't silent. The sound of air, a slow, overheated dog's panting, passed through the drift. Sometimes they could even hear or feel the subtle movement of rock as the earth relieved its pent-up pressure, shifting its innards and sending out a shudder.

Sitting there wouldn't get them out. They got up from their lagging to scout around the drift toward the borehole to see what, if anything, could take them to the surface—either by their own efforts or by whatever the crew topside was doing to get them out. The walk was more than three thousand feet, but unlike the walk to the east and 10-Shaft, the air blew a little cooler on their sweaty and greasy faces. It felt right. It was the place to go for help. The other direction was smoky and lethal. Off to the side of the pocket by the borehole was a green canvas bag holding a field telephone, sitting there like a cherry on a dirt sundae. Flory grabbed it, only to find the line was quiet. He double-checked the cable. It looked good. It ran up from the phone up the borehole before disappearing.

"Hello? *Hello?*"

He tried to call again, but nothing.

"Phone's no good," Flory said.

The two looked up into the darkness, the light from Wilkinson's lamp barely making a difference. Flory grabbed the one-inch cable and tugged. He pulled harder, and it seemed solid. He suggested that they could climb up the cable and get to 3700.

Wilkinson thought it was about the dumbest idea he'd heard.

"You'll never make it," he said. "You can't climb out one thousand feet on a cable."

Flory yanked it again, testing the cable to see if it could bear his weight. Wilkinson reminded him that the borehole was full of loose rock.

Flory remained undeterred. "That's why I'll take a steel," he said.

"What happens if we get up there a hundred feet and the cable breaks?"

Of course, Flory knew they'd die. At least where they stood in the muck on 4800 they had beaten the odds. They were the only ones alive on their level. Flory let go of the cable, and the pair returned to the pocket. Maybe they could make it to 10-Shaft—and, provided the smoke wasn't bad there, one or both could climb up the manway that ran alongside the service way, and the two compartments for cages. The manway had ladders.

Again, Wilkinson's cooler head prevailed. He remembered something about the last time the two of them had been there.

"There were a lot of broken ladders, some missing, too."

Flory knew he was right about that.

Climbing out the stopes through the connecting raises was the only other possibility. Missing ladders weren't so much a concern there, but the toxic smoke was.

"The air might be trapped in dead-end stopes," Flory said, dismissing his own plan. "We'd get up there and get overcome."

As far as either knew, there weren't additional self-rescuers on 4800. And even if there were, neither was sure how effective they actually were. Flory had struggled with three of them, and Wilkinson's tongue smarted from being burned by one.

They had been trapped less than a day. It was nightfall topside, but underground the world was the same as it had been at noon. Down there, there was no sense of time.

IN SMELTERVILLE, BOB LAUNHARDT'S FATHER-IN-LAW, GRO-
cer Bill Noyen, logged the day's events in a diary, a practice he'd followed since childhood: "A major tragedy hit the district this morning
when fire broke out in Sunshine Mine. We understand Bob brought
out one guy and is being kept real busy in the rescue work, but so far
we've had no word from him."

BOOK TWO

Faith and Fear

Where the rain never falls and the sun never shines,
It's dark as a dungeon way down in the mines.

—MERLE TRAVIS, "DARK AS A DUNGEON"

Thirty-three

BOB LAUNHARDT PUT HIS HEAD ON THE PILLOW IN THE basement bedroom he'd been calling home since February. His eyes stayed open, though he fought to keep them shut. Half of the mine's day shift had made it out, leaving something in the neighborhood of eighty to ninety men trapped underground. Launhardt could trace most of Tuesday with nearly minute-by-minute precision, but other sequences were muddled by the swiftness of the unfolding disaster. His natural tendency was to keep the world ordered and neat. Everything had its place. Nothing was separate; everything was linked in some way—directly or tangentially. But he couldn't draw connections right then. There was too much to think about. Too much to worry about.

It was dawn and a little cloudy when Launhardt dressed to return to the mine. News directors and editors outside the district led with

FBI director J. Edgar Hoover's death, but to the people of Kellogg and Wallace and throughout the mining industry, there was only one story that really mattered. Launhardt churned through what he'd seen and what he'd heard had gone on underground. Schulz and Findley insisted self-rescuers had outright failed. Others reported that there hadn't been enough of them. What happened?

Sunshine stocked two types. The primary model in use since the 1960s was the BM-1447, dubbed by safety people a "half-hour" self-rescuer. For short durations, in relatively light smoke of the type caused by a burned-out ventilation fan, it was considered more than adequate. BM-1447s didn't act as rebreathers, which would allow a man to carry on with whatever he was doing until the smoke cleared. They were only intended to buy a man enough time to exit the mine or secure himself a place of refuge. The mechanics of the unit were simple. As smoky and gassy air passed through a hopcalite bed, it oxidized deadly carbon monoxide and converted it into harmless carbon dioxide. But the by-product of that lifesaving process was heat. Launhardt likened it to heat generated by a car's catalytic converter. Among the escapees on May 2 were men with second- and even third-degree burns on their lips and mouths.

The W-65, the "one-hour" self-rescuer, which had a heat exchanger, was a substantial improvement. Sunshine had three dozen of them. In a big mine like Sunshine—one in which it took almost an hour to get from the smooth concrete floor of the portal to the muck-encrusted working areas—a heat exchanger could make the difference between life and death.

Launhardt drove up to Big Creek, his eyes tired from the sleepless night but his body and brain jarringly alert. Cars were parked everywhere, and people were standing all over the yard. Closer to the portal, an encampment had grown. The waiting people occupied cots, huddled in blankets, and drank from Styrofoam cups embossed with the indentations of their own gnashing teeth. And whenever the sound of the double-drum reverberated, or when a weary eye detected movement, hopes were buoyed. *Someone's coming up. Someone's getting out.* So far, it had only been a cruel tease.

Additional USBM men had already descended by early morning, as had a contingent from the U.S. Department of the Interior, its managing agency. Stan Jarrett, sixty-nine, director for metal and nonmetal mine safety, was among the second wave of bureaucrats to be briefed by Al Walkup. He candidly told them Sunshine was lacking in trained men, equipment, and firefighting knowledge. Further, Walkup admitted they still didn't have a decent count of how many men were trapped. One number, however, he did know and kept secret—twenty-four were confirmed dead. Also present was Idaho's governor, Cecil Andrus, a balding man with a stripe of wavy hair combed straight back. Andrus wasn't like those political and media freeloaders who'd arrived with expense accounts and designs on getting something out of the unfolding catastrophe that they could use later—a good story or political clout. Andrus, who came with a small contingent of aides and government delegates, rightly understood the crucial role mining played in northern Idaho and in the American economy. A big fire, he knew, could devastate the district.

Meanwhile, Gordon Miner continued to exert his ever-increasing influence. Hecla's executive vice president felt the USBM men were out of their depth. He was certain that most had never seen the likes of what was happening at Sunshine. He told Jarrett that his men were in harm's way, and that if something weren't done, the disaster might claim some lives of rescue workers, too.

"Stan," Miner said, "I don't want them down there. They don't know this mine."

Jarrett protested, but Miner remained undeterred.

"We're in a crisis," he said, "and your guys don't *want* to be in any crisis."

There was no winning against Miner, and Jarrett probably knew that. They compromised. A USBM man would accompany each rescue team. The backseat role the USBM accepted was far different from the position it assumed at a coal-mine fire. Many saw that as an admission as much as a concession.

6:00 A.M., MAY 3
3700 Level

JOHNNY LANG HAD FADED BLUE EYES AND THE BROKEN NOSE of a boxer, which he proudly earned in his family-owned gym in the small town of Cut and Shoot, Texas. Lean and with a powerfully built upper body, Lang always enjoyed the one-on-one aspect of a fight, and to his disappointment, he didn't have the right stuff for a pugilistic career. He never went as far in the sport as a cousin, a heavyweight titleist who once fought Floyd Patterson. Lang still liked the challenge of pitting himself against another man, but in his mid-thirties his adversary was not another man, but the load of ore he intended to gyppo. Lang's biceps were still bundled up tight with muscles, and he could last a good round in the mines.

When he arrived to join the Bunker Hill hotshot helmet crew, he was told there'd be two five-man teams to explore the 3700 level—one group was primary, the other a backup. Lang, the sole Sunshine man of the group, waited while the first team emerged from the mine to replace oxygen canisters and inspect rubber tubing for wear. Burlap and wood were stacked on the timber truck, along with a supply of polyurethane foam insulation. The insulation came in two heavy canisters that, when sprayed together, created a foamy material that expanded into cracks and turned solid. Crews advanced as they foamed sections of the bulkheads or around air doors that shouldn't have leaked in the first place. The flow from compressed-air lines kicked the smoke back out of the mine.

Lang assumed he'd be in the next group, but the crew chief told him to stay put.

"Hey, wait a minute," he said. "I *want* to go in. What the hell good are we as a backup crew if we don't have any experience? We don't even know what's going on in there."

"We've worked together for a long time," the crew chief said. "We don't want anyone to panic in there."

Those were fighting words to the ex-boxer.

"Listen, *pard*," Lang said, twisting a term of familiarity into an epithet. "I don't panic! And I'm going with you on your next trip in."

Twenty minutes later the former boxer inched his way down the drift. It was tranquil. There was nothing to hear but the heaving of their own lungs and the sound of the McCaas as they delivered oxygen in a world without any. Roped together and feeling their way along the rails, rescue crewmen brought in plywood and polyurethane foam spray to seal around leaky air doors and bulkheads. With each crosscut sealed, Lang and crew pressed on, worrying that they might actually be creating a tomb for a man who had found refuge in a forgotten pocket of the drift. But just beyond the 08 Shop, they stopped. No one could see a damn thing. It was as though they were up against a heavy drapery that was pulled farther away just as they reached to open it. Lang removed his lamp from his hardhat and held it below his waist, sending a beam along the wet track line. Lang couldn't draw a reference point about exactly where they were. Maps were useless. The only frame of reference that seemed relevant was the location of track switches.

On the return to the Jewell, Lang watched a USBM man monitor air quality. Oxygen was less than 1 percent and carbon dioxide was at 19 percent. Carbon monoxide levels were still beyond the test range of detector tubes—the USBM recorded 20,000 ppm. Sunshine's underground atmosphere was unlike any recorded in the history of the bureau.

Topside, Lang sought out the doctor.

"How long could a guy live in that heavy stuff?" he asked.

The grim-faced physician shook his head and conceded that a man might be able take in two breaths.

"But you'd never know you took the second one," he added.

6:00 A.M., MAY 3
Cataldo

THE GLASS IN FRONT OF MYRNA FLORY'S FACE WAS STIPPLED with a jeweled spray of condensation. It took her a second to sort out where she was and what had happened. She was in her mother-in-law's car. Her eyes focused on the world lit by the dawn. It wasn't the mine yard. There were no Sunshine families surrounding her. The car was parked in front of her mother-in-law's house in Cataldo. Myrna went inside, her face red with anger.

"Why did you leave me in the car? Why did you take me away from the mine? You know I wanted to be there."

Ron's mother looked over her coffee mug and remained cool. Her mouth was a straight line, and her eyes hardly blinked.

"I'll take you back after breakfast," she said.

"*No.* No, you won't." Myrna's voice broke again with emotion. "You'll take me back right now." No one was going to push her around. "*Now!*"

She made two quick decisions right there. No pills. No more trusting her mother-in-law.

In Osburn, with no word on the fate of his father-in-law, Louis Goos, or of his partner Bob Follette's son, Bill, Howard Markve returned home from the doctor's office. He was sure the fire had burned out his lungs, but the doctor's diagnosis of respiratory trouble was "chemical bronchitis." He'd told Markve to get some fresh air. Larry Hawkins also saw a doctor who told him about the symptoms of CO poisoning. Hawkins began to wonder if those guys sleeping and "kicking back" on 4600 had already begun to succumb to the deadly gas. Everybody seemed bone-tired that morning. Was that a warning sign they'd missed? Had they already been poisoned?

Thirty-four

CHASE, LAUNHARDT, MINER, AND A DOZEN BUREAU OF Mines men took up residence in the second-floor rescue command center. It was a mix of men who were both united and at odds with one another: the locals versus the outsiders. Each needed the other's lapse, negligence, or incompetence to be the reason for the disaster. Crew leaders from Sunshine and Silver Summit rescue operations also joined in to share reports of progress—or lack of progress. Art Brown blew a gasket when the Sunshine team reported they'd been working in the opposite direction.

"What the hell are we doing?" He pointed at a mine schematic. "This is the end of your fresh-air base. From now on we need to go in the *same* direction."

They don't even know their own mine, Brown thought.

Engineers unfurled more schematics of Sunshine's ventilation

258

system—to fight the fire they had to know which way the airflow traveled. At Sunshine, fresh or intake air came in the same way the men did—through the Jewell. From there it traveled eastward the long, dark mile to 10-Shaft—primarily coming in on 3700, though some came in on 3100. The intake air dropped down 10-Shaft to the working levels. This wasn't a magic act or even God's work; air doors and booster fans pushed the fresh air on its way. Exhaust air traveled through vertical ventilation raises to 3400, the main exhaust airway of Sunshine. From 3400, air flowed west to No. 3 shaft, then on up to 1900 level. Once there, it went out through the old incline shaft old timers called the Big Hole. The 3100 and 3700 intake air moved easterly to 10-Shaft. And between those two intake airways was the 3400 exhaust airflow moving westerly. It was a battle of pressure and flow; the exhaust airway naturally sought the path of least resistance, like any force of nature. If, for whatever reason, the airflow was stymied, the bad air remained in the mine and recirculated.

Even before USBM investigators put a pencil to any hypothesis, Launhardt was concerned about the ventilation scheme's role in the disaster. From the accounts of those who'd escaped, he surmised that crews on 3700 had had about twenty minutes before the deadly smoke hit the drifts on 3100. Hoistman Don Wood, Launhardt believed, was in dire straits *before* miners on 3100 even knew they were at risk. Wood was dead before he could hoist anyone. Big as Sunshine was, with its hundreds of miles of workings, on May 2, Launhardt saw it as a very small space, one without retreat.

The fatal flaw of Sunshine's ventilation system was the location of the pair of 150-horsepower fans upstream from the 3400-09 ventilation bulkhead. After the bulkhead burned through, it released smoke, gases, and carbon monoxide that were pushed out by the 300 horsepower of the combined fans through the mined-out 09 vein. From there, the cloud must have made its way through a sequence of ladders to the 4000 level, and west to 5-Shaft. Once there, it moved upward to the main intake airway on 3700. Then the smoke stormed toward 10-Shaft and, from there, down to the production areas where most of the men were. The entire ventilation system had been short-circuited.

If we had only shut off the fans on 3400. That, Bob Launhardt knew, could have put an end to recirculation of toxic smoke. There had probably been enough time, too. Arnold Anderson and Dusty Rhoads were standing by, waiting for the order to pull the power. But the command never came, and both were presumed dead.

Most believed it was Gene Johnson who had the primary authority to shut them down. Certainly, Johnson had the greatest understanding of the ventilation scheme and how the electrically powered booster fans maintained pressure and moved air through the mine. He knew the route of the airflow because he double-checked each level weekly to ensure that the system on which they all depended was in working order. A small fall of rock or a damaged bulkhead could upset the flow. Beyond that, Johnson was without question the alpha male of Sunshine miners. Love him or hate him, all men respected him. Whatever Johnson said, there'd be no argument.

There was only one problem, and Chase considered it quietly. *Maybe Gene didn't know he was in charge that morning.* No one told him that he was. And everyone else was at the stockholders' meeting in Coeur d'Alene.

The office staff also wondered what had prevented getting the men out sooner. The difficulty in reaching Chase or Walkup at the shareholders' meeting certainly didn't expedite things. Some thought that Harvey Dionne should have gone ahead and made the evacuation call earlier, but had been paralyzed by the residual impact of the Tom McManus years. If a man made the wrong decision, and there wasn't a real danger, it could cost him his job.

"If nothing is wrong, who are they going to thank? You know who they're going to blame," Betty Larsen told a friend.

Something also puzzled the clerks, accountants, and engineers. Just how long had the fire smoldered? Larsen recalled an industrial claim submitted by a miner a day or two before, complaining of dizziness. Had that been a warning?

The personnel office stayed at capacity all morning as rescue workers lined up for physical exams, and reporters commandeered telephones and desks. Silvery-haired and in his mid-fifties, personnel director Jim Farris tried to maintain control of what had once been his sole domain. The former Wallace High School star quarterback was used to putting on a game face and getting the difficult things done. He needed to. He had the worst job in the industry. It would fall on Farris's shoulders to contact a family to say their husband or son had been injured or killed. Some saw him as the district's Angel of Death. Whenever he telephoned or stepped onto someone's front porch, hearts sank to the floor. He never brought good news.

Betty Larsen burrowed her way through the crowd and sat down at her desk, and Farris abruptly handed over a handwritten paper to type. The heading took her breath away:

MISSING MEN BELIEVED TO BE TRAPPED

A hundred names, and Larsen knew every one: a man from her church; a couple of pairs of brothers; shift bosses who had been there forever. As she typed, she could barely see for the tears in her eyes.

TESTOSTERONE AND HOT TEMPERATURES MADE SKIRMISHES and hand-to-hand combat common among Idaho miners. There'd also been sabotage, bombings, and vandalism when district mine owners and workingmen tried to settle union contracts. So when Stan Jarrett and the USBM first suggested the possibility of arson, most

Sunshine men saw it as loathsome opportunism; the USBM, they believed, had to come up with some reason to blame the miners for the fire, to blame anybody but itself.

While there were arson-related fires in other mines, Sunshine miners would never knowingly endanger the lives of their brothers. They'd dangle a man over the open shaft by his ankles as a prank, but they'd never actually try to *kill* him. Launhardt knew of one arson case in which a disgruntled miner had set a fire, but that was in Mexico's Delores Mine. The chimney effect of a fire in the shaft had accelerated the blaze into a firestorm. Thirty-five men had died.

Among Sunshine men who felt the fire was deliberately set was Marvin Chase. Sunshine's manager thought it could be a prank that had gone tragically awry. Miners did things like that, not to be malicious, but for fun. The timing of the fire was the reason for some of the suspicions. In the eyes of some miners, the bigwigs were off at their annual meeting, whooping it up at a resort in Coeur d'Alene. Why not embarrass management with a little fire? Chase could buy into the idea that a miner wanted to cause a little trouble by igniting a small fire. But quickly—and unthinkably—it went out of control and sent a toxic cloud throughout the mine.

Another plausible theory making the rounds had a mechanic welding a broken grizzly on 3400 near 4-Shaft, starting the fire when a spark flew into the old workings, where it smoldered. Another rumor had it that an old miner on 3400 had dropped a cigarette. Because the fans on that level blew like jet engines, a man had to seek refuge in the old workings to smoke or take a nap. That's what this old miner did on a routine basis. Some thought he'd found someplace and bedded down with a smoke.

Launhardt certainly cared about the cause of the fire, but what baffled him was the volcano-like eruption that had sent the smoke so quickly through the mine. He'd never heard of a fire like that. No one had.

RON FLORY AND TOM WILKINSON HUNKERED DOWN AND watched the smoke shimmy down the drift. It expanded and contracted like a living and breathing being. The toxic cloud had stolen the breath of seven miners on their level and carried on, rolling and boiling, taking and killing. Hunting for more. Wilkinson knew he and his partner were alive because of each other. Flory had saved his life by bringing him to fresh air. But Wilkinson had also saved Flory's life. Flory knew that if his partner hadn't fallen victim to the deadly air when he did—when others could see there was a problem and still take action to save his life—neither man would have lived.

Tom Wilkinson had been a canary.

Thirty-five

AFTERNOON, MAY 3
Portal

W ITH THE PRECISION OF A DRILL TEAM, MINERS HAUL-
ing six bodies on a trio of timber cars rounded the tracks to
the supply warehouse to the right of the portal. The procession was
as discreet as possible. Each body was cloaked by an Army blanket.
Marvin Chase wanted dignity and order to reign where he knew
emotions were raw.

"We don't want to see pictures of this in the paper tomorrow,
either," he said.

Onlookers could see that the timber trucks weren't ferrying rescue equipment. One of the swathed figures revealed a miner's hat.
Worn black rubber boots rimmed in yellow protruded from under
the twisted fabric. Rolled into the warehouse, illuminated by overhead lighting, the dead appeared as though each had been dipped in
a dark stain. The color surprised Keith Dahlberg, the Kellogg doctor

enlisted to pronounce them dead. He'd been taught that CO poisoning flushed a victim's skin with a Kool-Aid red hue. What tainted the skin of the dead was far darker, resembling the darkest tan overlaid with second-degree sunburns. Rigor mortis had turned their lifeless bodies mannequin-stiff. In a few hours the muscles would relax. One of the six was Bill Hanna, the husband of the woman he had consoled at the hospital. Don Beehner was also among that first group.

When the rumor of more fatalities became undisputed truth, it sent a wave of anguish that grew to a tsunami. And the news became even worse later that day. Chase, dressed in a cardigan with a striped tie, spoke to reporters while an office assistant distributed a news release that revealed rescue crews had counted more bodies. All had been discovered on 3100. The official total had finally been updated to twenty-four.

"We still have hope that the other men are alive," he said.

Chase said rescue crews would advance the fresh-air stations on 3100 later that day. In doing so, they'd be able to send men down 10-Shaft to the lower levels, where there was the best chance for survivors.

"If they stayed down where they were supposed to be working, at the 4800 level, they should be alive," he told the press.

Spokane reporter Jerry McGinn knew the fatality figure the mine was giving out was a lie. He told UPI the number of fatalities was *twenty-nine* and going higher. He put on his Red Cross armband and passed out blankets and commiserated with women waiting for their husbands. Many were near collapse, and McGinn offered whatever comfort a twenty-six-year-old reporter could provide. But he had a job to do, too. McGinn took a big chance and found a place to sit inside the shifter's shack. The shifter's shack was no more than its name implied—a metal building with windows punched out on each of its four sides. The shack's most important piece of equipment was a wall phone facing the portal. It was the primary link to the rescue teams.

McGinn tried to be invisible while he listened to everything relayed from underground. As he sat there, however, he became furious.

This is bullshit, McGinn thought. *The mine is screwing those people out there. Screwing them twice. First, their men are dead. Second, they are sitting there with hope for no reason.*

McGinn left for a bathroom stall, where he pulled out a streamer of toilet paper and began to write down everything he could remember. Later he phoned in his notes to the UPI desk in San Francisco, and the news service pushed out his story. McGinn continued to play both sides as an undercover reporter and a Red Cross worker brandishing blankets. The crowd had swelled to at least three hundred, maybe more. Some of the women had no family but their men trapped underground. And from their folding chairs facing the portal they were doing all they could to hold it together. He could see that for some the only connection to everything they had—love, finances, everything—was a life in peril underground. Whenever he could grab a phone—once even in the shifter's shack—McGinn read his toilet tissue report. All the while, the number of dead men climbed.

IN THE FORMER NIGHT WATCHMAN'S HOME IN WOODLAND Park, Wava Beehner waited for news. She hadn't heard from her husband nor had a call come from the mine. The kids had gone to school, and she stared at the telephone that Don had refused to pay for because it was too expensive. She wished it would ring and put an end to her useless speculation. *Since I haven't heard,* she thought, *he's okay.*

A hoistman's wife, a friend of the Beehners, knocked on the door. The woman's face was puffy and red, and she trembled when she spoke. Her words poured forth without a breath.

"Oh, Wava," she said, her arms outstretched. "I'm so sorry, Don's gone."

Wava was unsure she'd heard right. The look on her face made it clear.

"Both of our husbands are dead."

Wava ran to the phone and dialed the mine and said that a friend had just told her that her husband was dead.

The mine operator told her that she couldn't verify anything.

"You can't tell me? Is he or isn't he?"

"Can't say, either way," the operator said.

Wava wasn't sure what to think, what to believe. She wanted the hoistman's wife to be wrong. She had too much at stake. She had loved Don Beehner since her family moved to Wallace from Nevada. The winter of 1948 certainly hadn't showcased the charms of the district—certainly not to a Nevada girl who didn't own a winter coat. Snow was four feet deep that winter. Creamy drifts buried cars, and residents with outhouses were forced to dig tunnels through the snow to take care of business. At twelve, Wava didn't know it, but she had arrived home. A big part of that was because of a crush she developed on her brother's new friend, Donald Gene Beehner. He was so handsome standing in a haze of cigarette smoke—blue eyes and a lazy smile. He wore his jeans tight and his white T-shirt with sleeves rolled up to show off double-dipped biceps. To increase the girth of his legs, Beehner liked to run halfway around Wallace—backwards—wearing heavy logging boots. He was a denim-clad god. Like most kid sisters, Wava suffered in silence and waited. When the sandy-blond-haired Beehner was at the Chamberses' one evening, he turned to her as she dried dishes and melted her heart like a birthday candle.

"I'll probably end up marrying you," he said, looking into her lovely green eyes, "or someone like you."

In January 1954, Wava Chambers lied about her age and married the boy she'd wanted since the day they met. She was seventeen. He was nineteen and a Sunshine mucker. Their first years together were a succession of jobs with the mines, a paving company, or the railroad, interspersed with the births of two sons and two daughters. The Beehners were close, a family dedicated to sports and children's activities. Both parents bowled on leagues. Wava had a decent arm and pitched for a Wallace softball team. The kids played football, baseball, and basketball, and performed in the school band. Every Friday, the whole lot of them went for a swim at the Y. It was the life Wava had always imagined.

She was sure Don was alive, because no one from Sunshine had told her otherwise. The switchboard operator refused to confirm anything. Bob Launhardt, who had been friendly enough with Beehner over the years to know that his wife and kids deserved better, said nothing. He could find no words.

Thirty-six

AFTERNOON, MAY 3
Sunshine Mine Yard

MARVIN CHASE, WHO'D BEEN PUSHED INTO THE ROLE OF PR spokesman, needed some muscle. He had discarded his suit jacket and rolled up the sleeves of his white shirt, now soiled with grease and sweat. His pockets were filled with pens and a pair of sunglasses. He called Bunker Hill's president for help with crowd control. Lee Haynes, twenty-four, was the solution. The former computer programmer and apprentice mechanic was a Vietnam veteran, and the lieutenant for Wallace-based Company A, 321st Engineering Battalion.

"Lee, we've got a mess up here and I need help," Chase said, when the pair met in the yard. "We've got families who won't go home because of loved ones that we don't know a thing about."

Chase hoped the sight of men in uniform would help bring order, and maybe even a little comfort. He was hopeful the need would be short term.

"But no one knows how long this rescue will take."

Chase was also very concerned about the media. Distraught family members were saying that all the cameras and questions were adding to their mounting grief. Chase asked Haynes to separate the newspeople from the families.

It's us against them, Haynes thought.

Within a couple of hours, fourteen men—miners, loggers, but, most important, soldiers—were in green fatigues and ensconced by the creek. Motivating the bunch was easy. Haynes promised a beer at the end of the day. To get them to move faster, he promised two beers. The men of Company A were wound up. They could roll up some reporter and toss him in the creek like a beach ball, then celebrate at the Big Creek Store.

Chase limited access even more with a lie, saying that federal safety inspectors required them to keep the area clear. A reporter complained that the barrier kept him from material for an article.

"Look," Haynes said, clearly irritated, "you'll get information when we *tell* you. You won't be left out. But you'll stay right over here, and that's it."

This is a disaster, he thought, *not a contest over who gets the story.*

Haynes knew about being a hard-ass, because he was the son of one. His father, Toughie Haynes, had been one of those miners who gambled and drank away his Friday paycheck by Sunday morning. He made good money, but it was *his* money. His wife had to fight for school clothes for the kids, and when food ran out, she served oatmeal for Sunday dinner. When Lee needed eyeglasses, his father scoffed. He only relented when he lost his driver's license to a stack of DWIs and he needed his boy to drive him around.

Lee Haynes also kept his focus on one of the missing in particular. Richard Lynch had moved in with the Hayneses to finish his senior year at Kellogg when his folks moved to Post Falls. Haynes and Lynch had enlisted in the Army together. They were brothers in all ways but blood. Lynch was also connected to others of the swelling vigil. Peggy Delange, the Wallace bank employee who was waiting for her dad, foreman Gene Johnson, was his sister-in-law.

Roger Findley, the cager who had been rescued by Launhardt's crew, pulled himself together and reported to Silver Summit in Osburn to pack supplies. He wanted to do what he could to get his big brother, Lyle, out of the mine. But as the morning of the second day wore on, Findley discovered that no matter how much he wanted to go into the mine to go after Lyle, he just couldn't make himself do it. He didn't know it then, but he'd been underground for the last time.

Big Creek resident Jack Harris signed on to relay messages to surface crews bringing down foam and wood for bulkhead building. The shaft repairman worried about the viability of the plan to advance fresh air by bulkheading. Building temporary bulkheads with plastic-coated burlap, wood, and polyurethane foam was tedious, and Sunshine consumed the supplies like the bottomless pit that its workers knew it was. Sunshine and Silver Summit shared the same bad country: an underground passage with more cracks and splintered fissures than a dried-out pond. Harris doubted there could ever be enough foam to seal off all air leaks. He wondered how long it would take to reach the men trapped inside.

NORMAN FEE'S MOTHER, ELIZABETH, DROVE SEVENTY MILES an hour whether she was going five blocks or fifty miles. A stretched-out plume of cigarette smoke followed the high school Latin and Spanish teacher as she drove her son's blue convertible, a '67 ocean-blue Malibu, with the top down. She had a sense of humor and an undeniable air of eccentricity. She was Rosalind

Russell in *Auntie Mame* without the foot-long cigarette holder. Army reservist Lee Haynes saw Mrs. Fee maneuver through the crowd in the yard. He averted his eyes, fearing that direct contact would lead to conversation—a conversation he was unprepared to have. Her son, twenty-eight-year-old Norman Fee, was missing. Bill Mitchell and others from Fee's level had made it out, and their last sight of the grizzlyman hadn't been pretty.

Haynes had hated high school, but he'd loved Mrs. Fee. She'd even made Latin tolerable.

When his father, a school principal, had died the year before, it was Norman who'd stayed with his grieving mother. She was fragile, and his presence in her house on Third Street in Wallace was just what she needed. Mother and son took a monthlong tour of Europe in June the same year. It was, she told everybody, the best time of her life—after the saddest.

Elizabeth Fee caught up with Haynes.

"I don't want anyone else telling me about Norman," she said. "I don't want some cop or some preacher. I want you to tell me. I need to hear it from *you.*"

Lieutenant Haynes was in the back of the classroom, hiding his eyes and hoping the teacher wouldn't call on him.

"Mrs. Fee, what do I know about saying something like that?"

"I want *you* to tell me."

The woman who'd taught Haynes Latin by the sheer force of her quirky personality was going to get the worst news of her life—from *him.* He told Sunshine's personnel office of her request. It was logged on a card and stapled to Norman Fee's personnel file. Similar cards were made for all of the missing men.

Later, Rob Chase, the mine manager's seventeen-year-old son, also caught the schoolteacher's frightened stare from behind her cat's-eye glasses. Mrs. Fee was unraveling, and Chase hurried to her side. As she chain-smoked, she said that her worries were rooted in an incident in her childhood. Her father had been a mine manager in Montana.

"There was a bad fire there," she said, her voice beginning to break apart. "The hoist came up with the men on it all in flames. They were all burning."

The story horrified the teenager.

"Don't worry," he said. "That can't happen here. We'll get your son out," thinking, *God, how I hope that is true.*

Norman Fee's mother faced the portal. With each breath, a prayer.

AFTERNOON, MAY 3
Woodland Park

HOPE SELDOM WINS OVER TRUTH. ON WEDNESDAY, ONE OF the Beehner brothers drove Don's red-and-white VW bus from Big Creek and parked it by the house. He hauled out a pair of dirty diggers and some other clothes and carried them inside. Nothing else had made the family's tragedy seem more real than the return of the VW. Wava Beehner's parents came from their home in Moon Gulch. *It was true. Don was dead.* Her younger brother took the children out for a ride in his brand-new Dodge—allowing each one a chance behind the wheel. Even twelve-year-old Matt took a spin. It was the only thing their uncle could think of to take their minds off their shock—if only for a split second. Later, Wava joined her brother-in-law and wife for a drink. Don's handsome face held steady in her thoughts. She remembered how he'd run all over town in heavy boots to build himself up when he was a teenager, how he'd rabbit-holed money everywhere in the house. He was everybody's best friend. He was the only man she'd ever love. While cigarette smoke swirled in the barroom air, Wava Beehner cried until her throat ached.

TIME UNKNOWN, MAY 3
Safety Zone

RON FLORY AND TOM WILKINSON HADN'T EATEN ANYTHING since lunch on Tuesday, and according to Flory's watch, that was some thirty-five hours ago. Water from the water line filled them up, but only to a point. They were hungry and lethargic. They needed food. Both knew that there was only one place on 4800 where they could find any—their own dinner buckets. Safe in their air pocket, they didn't know how bad the air was down the drift at the station. Hunger and hope drove them to take the chance. Maybe they'd find a way to get out.

Not forgetting that Wilkinson had already lost consciousness once, they agreed that at the first sign of dizziness they'd pull back and give up. They removed their T-shirts, wetted them down, and covered their mouths and noses. Wilkinson's lamp was their source of light as they walked toward the station. As they drew closer, they could see the men. Most were in a bundle by the motors. One was alone on the station. The images were seared onto their brains, but to discern who was who was beyond either man's ability. The dead had swollen in the heat, their clothing stretched to splitting. Their faces were so distorted that Flory couldn't have identified them if he'd had a list of names from which to work. A rush of adrenaline propelling them, they grabbed their own buckets and hurried back to their pocket. Inside the buckets they had a few bites of a leftover sandwich and a cookie. The taste of food only made their hunger grow.

They sat in the dark, in their good air, acutely aware of what it felt like to be alone—how the sound of their own voices was all they'd heard since their seven co-workers dropped dead. Dying like that was wrong. It wasn't a miner's death. A miner usually died in an accident, sometimes the result of a chain reaction he'd started himself. Flory and Wilkinson had taken their chances, goddamn stupid and big chances, many times. Sometimes they might knock at a slab or delay timbering a little bit longer than was safe. One of their regular and most dangerous endeavors was to use the charge of their cap lamps to ignite powder when they had to chunk up a large rock that couldn't go down the chute. They'd put powder on it, run wire off it, climb up the stope, and set it off. No one watching for safety. Just the two men blowing up stuff. Once when Wilkinson was drilling, a three-ton slab had crashed down right behind him. Instead of stopping and surveying the scene for other problems on the back of the stope, he simply glanced over and kept on drilling.

NEAR MIDNIGHT, MAY 3
Kellogg

THE PHONE RANG IN SUNSHINE CLERK BETTY LARSEN'S Kellogg home late Wednesday. It was well past her bedtime. On the line was personnel director Jim Farris, and he sounded frazzled. He told Larsen to come in and comb through the files for physical characteristics that could be used in the identification process. She knew that some such data was there, because she'd recalled times when signing up a new hire she'd ask if they had any scars or tattoos. Every guy who'd ever mined had at least one scar. Some were quite memorable. One man had a jagged white-and-pink one from a stab wound to his stomach.

"From my wife," he said, somewhat embarrassed. "But I had it coming."

Larsen spent the early-morning hours with manila folders holding the bits and pieces of Sunshine careers: notes from shifters admonishing a man for dumping shift one too many times; write-ups about poor safety practices; judgments from the local credit companies that showed how miner after miner had gotten himself into a financial jam; and, of course, work histories that documented the trajectories of lives that went from mine to mine on the never-ending search for big bucks. The records, however, were not particularly helpful. A few files acknowledged a scar, a tattoo, a birthmark, or other distinguishing characteristics, but specifics were elusive. Not *where* and not *what*. Height and weight information was frequently omitted, too. The hiring-mill mentality of mining's best years had doctors examining new hires as quickly as possible. Half wouldn't work but a week or two anyway.

Families provided some missing details. Richard Bewley's family reported he had a tattoo that read "30–40" (they didn't know he'd had it surgically removed two years earlier); Louis Goos wore a ring made of Black Hills gold; Glen Rossiter was the only miner with a handlebar mustache; Ron Wilson was missing the ring finger on his left hand; and Mark Russell had beautiful curly blond hair. Darrell Stephens's family said the nineteen-year-old's left leg was an inch and half shorter than his right.

Tom Wilkinson's best friend, Johnny Davis, was one of the few who wore a "Butte hat," a hardhat with a visor like a baseball cap. District miners thought Butte-style hats were a joke. Water from overhead could trickle down a man's neck if he was wearing one of those dumb hats. Why Davis wore one, no one knew. He was a Mullan boy, for God's sake.

Thirty-six bodies had been counted by the end of the day, with only eleven identified. That left fifty-seven missing. Bob Launhardt told the rescue team that unless the men had found a place to dig in and keep out the smoke—and had done so quickly—there was little chance of survival. Curiously, he told his father-in-law another story. Bill Noyen wrote in his diary that night: "Bob . . . said the officials definitely believe there is a good chance they'll find most of the missing people alive."

Thirty-seven

THE DIVIDING WALL OF SMOKE ADJACENT TO THE SAFETY Zone on 4800 stirred. Thirty to forty feet from where Flory and Wilkinson had first sought refuge, along the rib of the main drift of the 4800, a crosscut led to a raise down to 5000. A dimming signal light hung on the opposite side of the junction. They collected some three-by-twelve-inch-by-six-foot lagging and made miner's bed boards, set against the ribs at a comfortable angle facing the crosscut. Wilkinson used his powder knife to slice a section from one of the enormous rolls of burlap used underground to stabilize sandfill by acting as a colander of sorts, after the slurry of water and sand had been piped into mined-out stopes. He and Flory doubled, then quadrupled the loose-woven fabric to fashion a makeshift mattress.

It appeared that the smoke poured down 10-Shaft, across 4800 station, and down the drift, before hesitating and then continuing its route into the crosscut. Both survivors knew that as long as the smoke kept moving away, they'd be safe. Neither man thought much about toxic gases that could be hanging at different depths down the drift. All they understood was that the smoke had killed the others on 4800.

The flow of fresh air coming from the borehole created an invisible barrier, pushing the bad air away. Neither knew it, of course, but it was Harvey Dionne's quick thinking and Kenny Wilbur's unbridled nerve that had uncorked the flow by removing the lagging cover on 3700.

"As long as the smoke stays where it's at, we'll be all right," Flory said.

Wilkinson hung a paper towel as an airflow indicator on a fan line across the drift. The paper stayed suspended at a thirty-degree angle toward the crosscut.

MORNING, MAY 4
Sunshine Rescue Command Center

BY THURSDAY MORNING, BOB LAUNHARDT'S INITIAL SUG-gestion of advancing the good air by sealing bulkheads and cross-drifts wasn't working. Despite the deluge of help from mines all over the country and Canada, Sunshine had more leaks than could be fixed. Launhardt was caught in the middle. He wanted the men to get to the lower levels, but if they didn't seal the leaks, they'd put themselves at great risk. Crews working from Silver Summit's 3100 level started a suction fan to draw the smoke away from the Jewell side, but it, too, failed to do the job. More sealing was needed. In the command center, someone suggested procuring a supply of inflatable rubber life rafts and using them as makeshift barriers to hasten the process. The idea was dismissed as impractical. Someone remembered how truckers used collapsible bags to protect their freight. In fact, the four-by-eight-foot oversized pillows had even been used to stop a backed-up sewer system from flooding a Minnesota town. A phone call later, a jet loaded with a supply was on its way from a Goodyear plant in Georgia to Fairchild Air Force Base near Spokane.

And although Launhardt couldn't really conceive of it at the time, trapped as he was in grief and concern for the missing, he was becoming a target of criticism, especially in the death of Don Beehner. Someone needed to be blamed. One moment reran in a fuzzy replay. It had happened so fast that the mine's safety engineer wasn't completely clear on just how it was that Don Beehner had ended up passing his helmet to Schulz. Launhardt had been on the opposite side of the track from Hawkins and Beehner. Hawkins was sort of working on his hands and knees while Launhardt leaned over to help Schulz. It was possible that Hawkins hadn't seen what Beehner was doing before it was too late. Ten seconds, maybe twenty, and he was in the piss ditch.

The scene haunted him. How could that happen? How could a trained man take such a foolish risk? Launhardt sought details about what Beehner had been doing before he'd joined the ad hoc rescue crew. He learned that Beehner had been on the 3700 when the fire broke out. He'd gone directly to 10-Shaft, where he'd assisted several men with their self-rescuers. On his way up the shaft to 3100, a miner had slumped in the cage, and Beehner had pulled his self-rescuer from his mouth.

"It will help you," Beehner had reportedly said, offering it to the woozy and scared miner.

Others reported that the sanitation nipper had left the cage, leaving his self-rescuer with the other man, and walked the smoky drift to the Jewell, where he'd eventually met with Launhardt's rescue crew. His entire system, quite possibly, had been full of carbon monoxide, leaving him impaired.

Every man in the command center knew Sunshine was on the defensive, much of it owing to Byron Schulz's accusatory hospital interview. Ralph Nader's people—coincidentally in Spokane at the time—fueled the controversy. Nader charged Sunshine with a general disregard for safety. An example that surfaced was a fire on April 22, 1971, when a power cable on 2700 had shorted and set ablaze some drift timber. Federal and state law required reporting *any* fire, but Sunshine had made no such notification. When state investigators learned of the fire, the evidence was gone. Even worse, the mine had not been evacuated. Instead, employees were put on standby while shifters searched for the source of the fire. Even the diehard company men had to concede the scenario was disturbingly similar to the events of May 2, 1972. But there was more. During that same incident, Launhardt's predecessor, Jim Atha, had refused the inspector's request to test Sunshine's stench system. Atha had insisted all was fine, but the inspector was skeptical. He didn't think the system worked at all.

Most who escaped the mine Tuesday didn't smell anything other than smoke. A few questioned whether Bob Launhardt had even released the stench in the first place.

In theory, the stench could have worked to alert the men underground because the odor in the damp, wet mine wouldn't dissipate easily. When John Brandon, Sunshine's superintendent in the early sixties, used to go underground, he'd light a cigar after getting off the cage on 3100. He never took a motor to 10-Shaft, because he wanted to smoke that cigar. It was a ten- to twelve-minute walk, and about the time he was five minutes from the blue room where all the mine bosses congregated, they'd catch a whiff of cigar smoke. "Brandon's coming. Back to work!" And off they'd scurry with logbooks and pencil stubs. Smoke didn't fade away; it hung in the air and was carried by the intake airflow down the drift to 10-Shaft. Just like stench injected into the compressed-air line, Brandon's cigar had been a warning system.

The problem with any stench warning system at Sunshine was the mine's vast size; it took about twenty-five minutes for stench to get from the surface to 10-Shaft. Launhardt doubted that even if the stench had been dumped when the first guy smelled smoke, the foul-smelling odor would have made its way to all the lower levels in time to get the men out. There was another drawback, too. One in twenty people is anosmic—unable to smell. In metal mining, where stench-warning systems were the sole means of alerting men of a fire, safety engineers like Launhardt always hoped that no two men paired in a stope shared that genetic quirk.

Launhardt never complained about the paperwork or the politics of a job he considered his calling. He worked while others yakked about ball scores or fishing trips. He worked through lunch. The girls in the office, in fact, chuckled over his dogged work ethic. He'd get to his desk and pull up his typewriter and bang out a report. As the company's safety engineer, he didn't have to press a single key; but Launhardt just preferred not to bother anyone for anything he could do himself. He also felt a need to continually prove himself to others—long after he had likely earned their respect. Much of that was caused by his failure to finish college, though he knew ten times more than half the engineers who used Sunshine as a rung up the ladder to better pay and greater prestige. He did whatever it took to get the job done, in hopes that there would be some recognition for whatever sacrifice he made. He sought to define himself by his work. Janet and the kids understood that, and adjusted their routine to accommodate him. If the TV was on or someone was playing the piano, or even in the middle of a Monopoly game, everything would stop when Dad's car stopped in the driveway. Janet would put an index finger to her lips and remind the kids to hush.

"You're father's had a stressful day," she'd say in her soft, compassionate voice. "Go read. Leave Dad alone."

Yet, by the third day of the fire, there was no place to retreat. The biggest rescue effort in mining history was under way, and Bob Launhardt was in the middle of it. And worst of all, he knew better than anyone else how deadly that smoke was. One breath and a man would drop to the floor. *How could the guys underground escape the poisoned air?*

STEELWORKERS LOCAL PRESIDENT LAVERN MELTON WALKED the same two hundred feet through the yard to the office and back again, nearly wearing a rut in the muddy ground. He was rightfully bitter that so many of his union brethren hadn't made it out on Tuesday. The Steelworkers had been the glue that held the crew together, and not just at contract time. It was true that some meetings were sparsely attended, but the workingmen of the underground knew that the union was there for a reason—though it wasn't the same one union leaders espoused whenever they could get in earshot of a reporter or mine management. The rank and file wanted better pay. The union leadership concurred, but it also sought improved working conditions for the last industry in which men still held power over machines.

Melton was old school in his unfettered distrust of management. When the fire erupted, he pointed the finger at the company.

"They knew this was going to happen," Melton muttered. "We *all* knew it."

Launhardt, who had once been president of the local, was dumbfounded by the remark. He thought Melton was cutting his own throat.

"Why would he say that?" Launhardt asked a friend. "He's saying that *he* knew. If he knew, why didn't he say something before?"

Derided by the company as a blowhard union rabble-rouser, Melton wanted tougher safety measures in place even before the last body was pulled from the mine. Melton's rhetoric became blood splashed into shark-infested waters. Ralph Nader insisted that mining companies and the government agencies were in cahoots—neither had the best interests of workingmen at heart. Data from the USBM supported Nader and Melton. Bureau statistics pegged Sunshine as one of the worst safety offenders in the country, with more than thirty-five safety violations noted during a November 1971 inspection. The statistics on injuries were even more damning. In 1970, Sunshine averaged 136.15 injuries per 1 million man-hours. The coal mining industry average was 22 per million. Workers were three times more likely to meet their end at Sunshine than at any other U.S. metal mine.

Launhardt defended Sunshine's safety training, procedures, and safety record to a bunch of reporters, but it went badly. He confirmed that Sunshine did not stage fire drills; he knew of not a single instance when Sunshine ever had. Only one mine in the entire district ever ran such a drill—the Star Mine. And that had been fourteen years ago. Such trials were impractical; it would take a man several hours to climb a series of ladders up 4,000 feet or more. *Besides,* Launhardt thought, *why would Sunshine run drills for something that until a few days ago had never seemed possible?*

Sunshine's evacuation plan was also targeted after Schulz and Riley complained that men didn't know their way out on 3100. Launhardt pointed out that signs were posted all along the Silver Summit escapeway; he'd put them up himself. And the mine, he said, did have an evacuation plan. Men were told to gather on their respective stations at 10-Shaft and wait for the cage. Carbon monoxide readings would automatically shut air doors, and men would be belled up to 3100 to exit via the Silver Summit escapeway. It didn't work that way on May 2 because smoke had filled the mine so quickly.

Launhardt pointed the finger back at the bureau when a reporter told him the government considered the mine unsafe.

"If they knew, and it was true," Launhardt said, "why didn't they shut us down?"

When his remarks were carried nationwide, they made Sunshine appear ill-prepared and oblivious to the danger of fire. But in hardrock mining, shaft fires were the primary fear. Not only were shafts lined with timber, but they were gathering places for smoking men and, when repairs were needed, workers wielding blowtorches. Those running hardrock mines of Sunshine's size took precautions to ensure that shaft fires could be snuffed out. The Jewell had three enormous deluge water rings, and 10-Shaft had one. When needed, a Niagara was unleashed by the hoistman. But neither shaft was burning.

The self-rescuers. The safety training. The escapeways. Each had to be answered. Federal law required two such escape routes, and Sunshine met that on a technical level, with the Jewell and the Silver Summit. But there had been a problem when the fire broke out. And it was major. The men on the lower levels were unable to use the cage to get to either of the escapeways. Launhardt ruminated over this alone. There was no waking anyone to share what he held inside or what he couldn't allow himself to say out loud.

To save the trapped miners in the deepest levels of the Sunshine, Launhardt knew helmet crews were going to have to move deeper down in the mine—down where, he and others hoped, there was a place of refuge from the toxic air. Down there in the smoldering darkness, someone had to be alive. Down on 3100, a helmet crewman stood at the shaft and looked downward. It was impossible to see what was going on down another thousand feet of smoke-clogged passage. For all anyone knew, the fire was raging down there. Someone came up with the idea of loading up the cage with cardboard boxes and other burnables and sending the load to 4000.

Slowly the cage was lowered into darkness. A few minutes later it returned. The boxes were not scorched, so there was no fire below. Next, a ringing phone was lowered to 5200, but no one picked it up. Were the men bulkheaded in and unable to get to it? Or were they dead?

MIDDAY, MAY 4

Osburn

KWAL'S FREQUENT BROADCASTS FOR FOOD, SUPPLIES, AND volunteers continued to bring overwhelming, and almost unwelcome, response. Mountains of sandwiches were growing stale, and blankets and cartons of smokes were piled up so high their sheer numbers invited both waste and pilfering. The Red Cross started to reduce the quantity of whatever was needed by the rescue crews and the families. If they wanted one hundred sandwiches, they asked for fifty.

People sometimes focus on the smallest things to relieve their pain. When a few at the mine began to grouse about KWAL's music, a pastor stepped in and gave the Wallace radio station some friendly advice.

"Play two country-westerns and a hymn. Alternate them."

Radio station manager Paul Robinson rearranged the station's playlist—no more of the mishmash of music they played to try to please everybody in the district. He gave the miners and their families what they needed.

Thirty-eight

IN THE YARD THE SUN SHONE WEAKLY THROUGH PARTING clouds and a haze of smoke when gyppo miner Buz Bruhn returned to help with the rescue. He was sure his partner, Dewellyn Kitchen, was tough enough to survive, and Bruhn wanted to go in after him. He even had a plan. He went to talk to foreman Jim Bush about the borehole from 3700 and how he saw that as the only place miners could get fresh air. He'd helped drive the drift on 4800, and he knew fresh air poured down like a cold shower. There were coolers on that level, a battery charger, and a water line—water, light, and oxygen—everything a man would need. Bruhn wanted to go down the narrow shaft, with a single caveat.

"I'll put a gun in my pocket," he said. "When I get down there, those bastards will probably try to take my rebreather away from me."

Later, when Bruhn was in the toilet across from the double-drum, he heard men outside talking. Someone was boasting that Sunshine was going to come out of the disaster smelling like a rose. Not only did insurance cover the financial losses associated with a closure, but Sunshine was likely to reap profits from an inevitable spike in the metals market when it reopened to higher prices caused by a silver shortage.

"This isn't going to hurt us at all," the voice said.

The remark, Bruhn learned, came from the lips of New York bigwig Irwin Underweiser, president of the Sunshine Mining Company. He was huddled with a bunch of lawyers and accountants. They were counting money, of course, not bodies. That comment, and others, was heard by reporters, and it made its way into the nation's newspapers.

"Try to buy back the lives lost with higher silver prices. How can they even think about those things when the entire valley is in mourning?" asked a rescue worker.

AFTERNOON, MAY 4
Woodland Park

WITH HER HUSBAND'S BODY AT THE FUNERAL HOME AND HIS service looming in two days, Wava Beehner was worried about everything—what Don would wear, what she'd wear, and of course, how she and the children would get by. She marked off items like a grocery list. There was no other way. Frugal though he was, Don Beehner appreciated a decent suit. Not long before the fire, he'd purchased a fine-looking dark blue wool suit—not too heavy, not too light. He'd only worn it a time or two. Because a new suit demanded new shoes, Mrs. Beehner picked out a pair of oxfords. She put the shoes in a paper bag, and carefully walked the suit on its hanger to the car for the funeral home. She caught herself worrying that the shoes would be too heavy on his feet and he might not like that. She began to cry over her foolishness.

When it was time to pick out her outfit, Wava and her sister pored over dresses and suits hanging crisply in Cam's, a Wallace dress shop tucked into an 1890s building off the main drag. After a search, Wava found one that flattered her washed-out complexion and auburn hair. The bodice had chocolate and white stripes; the rest was solid brown. It was a sensible and dignified spring dress, one that didn't shout *funeral* and could be worn again. Best of all, it was a size eleven. She'd dropped weight, more from not eating than from her perpetual dieting.

When Wava emerged from the dressing room, her sister let out a gasp.

"Boy," she said without thinking, "Don should see you now. You've really lost weight."

It was the kind of remark one wished could be reeled back in. Her sister meant no harm.

Later that day, Wava and her brother-in-law returned to the funeral home. Music played faintly, and people spoke in muted voices. Tears zigzagged down her cheeks as she stared down at her husband's body, lying in the casket, eyes shut and looking peaceful. But something felt wrong, and her grief snapped into anger. The mortician's cosmetologist had a heavy hand. *Don would never want this.* She opened her purse, pulled out her handkerchief, and started to wipe away the makeup.

Her brother-in-law was horrified. "You can't do that," he said.

"He wouldn't want that on him in life," she said. "Why would he have it now? I *will* take every speck of it off."

The makeup from her husband's forehead and eyelids turned her handkerchief dark as she gently wiped his face.

Don was a man's man, she thought. *He'll be buried like one.*

Afternoon, May 4
Sunshine Dry

It was as if God hadn't wanted anyone to survive. No one wanted to announce to the media that the rescue effort had been stalemated to the point where, if there were men bulkheaded in somewhere, the passage of time in the hot mine was likely to be fatal even if there was good air. Rescue crewmen found Sunshine's dry the only place they could go to escape the families and the incessant pressure. They sat on benches across from the showers, smoking in silence. The hope they saw in the women's eyes had become a source of embarrassment. They were doing all they could, but nothing was working.

Talky Taylor knew where he'd find Delmar Kitchen. Everyone did. Kitchen had been planted on a bench in the dry for three days. His face was stippled with dark whiskers against pallid skin, and his eyes were bloodshot. He wanted to be there when news came about his brother and father. They had last been seen on 3100 near 10-Shaft.

"Forget it, Delmar," Taylor said, approaching. "They're gone. That's it."

Kitchen didn't say anything. He just looked up.

"Both of them. You might as well go home."

On his way to his car, Kitchen was an easy mark for reporters. He told them he'd never had a fire drill in his two years at Sunshine. Escape routes were never taught, nor were BM-1447 self-rescuers adequate—even though he admitted one had likely saved his life.

Other underground workers felt that death and danger were part and parcel of their industry.

"Working in a mine is like flying in a jet airliner," one miner said. "You know some jets are going to crash, but you keep on flying anyway."

THROUGHOUT THE AFTERNOON, SOME FIFTY CHILDREN AT Kellogg's Sunnyside Elementary kept transistor radios down low and tuned to KWAL. Many had dads up at the mine. And if not a father, they had a brother, a favorite uncle, or a grandfather. With each news update, little fingers would reach for the volume knob.

Thirty-nine

BETTY JOHNSON LOVED HER KITCHEN. THE CABINETS WERE new and the walls had been paneled in a warm, honey-colored wood. Places that required paint were a cheery, daffodil yellow. A big picture window faced the road to the mine. She liked to sit with a cup of coffee and a magazine, looking out, waiting for her husband, Gene, to come home. Her brother, Robert Barker, also stopped by nearly every day. As she sat there with her son and daughters, facing the darkened road, those moments were amplified in her memory. The ringing of the kitchen phone ended the forced small talk and speculation around the big round table. Peggy Delange answered the call. It was Jim Farris, Sunshine's personnel director. She handed the receiver to her mother.

"Mrs. Johnson," Farris said, "we found Gene's body."

Betty's face drained of blood. Her free hand fluttered. Peggy knew instantly that her mother had just heard the unthinkable.

"No, you didn't!" Betty screamed into the phone. She slammed down the receiver hard enough to break it. Peggy started screaming, too. Her eyes wild with shock, Betty reached over and slapped her daughter as hard as she could.

"Shut up! He's not dead!"

Betty didn't want any of it to be true, because none of it could be. Farris was wrong. Her legs moved on their own accord and started for the door, taking her into the night and up the hill toward the mine. She felt like one of those wind-up toys that Gene and the kids had loved so much. She was moving and she had no control. No wind-up key. She started to cry. *Gene can't be dead. He can't be.* The screams were echoing from her on the inside, until she collapsed in Peggy's shaking arms.

That Thursday, four other telephones rang from one end of the district to the other. Hoistman Lino Castaneda was at his sister-in-law's tiny Mullan home and took the call from Farris. He'd already prepared Teresa Diaz, forty-three, for the news that her husband was dead. It was good that Castaneda was there. The Guadalajara-born Diaz's English was poor. The confirmation was brief and final: *Roberto esta muerto.*

That she had been notified by telephone angered Betty Johnson. *A person who hits somebody's dog will knock on a door to give his or her regrets to the owner. Why didn't they think enough of Gene to come tell us face to face? They owed him that much. How many times did that phone ring in the middle of the night or on a day off with a request that Gene get up to the mine?* Gene Johnson never complained about any of that. He just pulled on a pair of Levi's, got in his truck, and did whatever he was asked.

How come, she wondered, *those bastards at Sunshine paid him back by not sending someone down to see our children and me?*

If ever a seed of hatred could be planted in someone's heart, Jim Farris's call was it. Farris probably even knew he'd screwed up. He wrote that he had notified Johnson by telephone: "She thought this was [an] unkind way."

TIME UNKNOWN, MAY 4
4800 Level

UP THE ROAD, AND ALMOST A MILE UNDERGROUND, THE ONLY survivors of the 4800 level took turns sleeping, though neither could manage a half hour. Ron Flory and Tom Wilkinson removed their boots, cushioned their bed boards with more burlap, but nothing could make either man feel like sleep was a good idea. The poisoned air might make its way to the Safety Zone and they'd never wake up. Rescue crews finding them would only know that they had been the last on their level to die. Sometimes they'd wake each other up. Neither could stand being awake and alone with nothing but their thoughts circling around, piling doubt upon doubt.

One man always remained awake, watching the gray, hazy smoke as it was sucked into the cross-drift, behind the paper towel. At times it resembled the wispy sheet of cigarette smoke from a district pool hall. At other times the form appeared solid.

"As long as it keeps moving that way," Flory said, "we'll be okay."

The pair had faced danger together before. Not long before the fire, in fact, it was Wilkinson who'd been the rescuer. They had shot a round in a back stope, and Flory needed to go over the top of the muck pile to secure the eyebolt so they could slush it out. Flory crawled over the muck into a small pocket. It was stifling hot, an overheated brew of gases, powder smoke, and dust. He could barely breathe, but he inched forward. *Have to get the work done. Have to go another ten feet.* But a little deeper into the pocket, panic seized him. He was shutting down. He couldn't go another foot, forward or back.

"I can't make it!" he called out.

Hearing this, Wilkinson grabbed his pard's legs and pulled, dragging him over the muck pile and back to cooler air—about 90 degrees.

Flory was nearly unhinged. "If you hadn't got me," he said, "I don't know if I would have made it."

That drama was nothing, of course, compared with what they were facing on 4800. Off in the distance, somewhere far down the drift, Flory thought he heard the muffled sound of men talking. It sounded like Richard Allison, one of the miners working on their level on May 2. He knew for a fact that Allison was dead. How could be speaking?

"Did you hear that?" he asked.

Wilkinson sat up and listened. He also heard what he thought resembled voices. It wasn't clear enough to determine whether it was real or just his mind wanting to hear it. It seemed like the noise of a distant television.

"I don't know," he said.

Flory hit a pipe with his wrench; a sharp sound echoed down the drift. He was unsure what he'd actually heard, and doubted anyone could hear him. After wielding the wrench a few more times, he stopped.

The voices—the noises that *sounded* like voices—would come again. Sometimes the trapped partners would acknowledge when they both heard them. Other times it was better to let it pass. Maybe the other guy hadn't heard it at all.

All the while, the cruel, needle-sharp hunger ate at their insides. Both men knew there were other dinner buckets on and near the station. *There might only be scraps,* Wilkinson thought, *but a hungry man will eat just about anything.*

"There are dinner buckets at the station," Wilkinson said. "We ought to go get them."

NEAR MIDNIGHT, MAY 4
Osburn

KWAL's PAUL ROBINSON HAD TAKEN DOZENS OF CALLS FROM people offering to help. Some offered food, money, even the use of a car. *What more can we do? This isn't going away tomorrow.* All the media folks who had been camped out in motels throughout the valley and on the studio floor in sleeping bags had come to take from the people living through the disaster. They were after a story. Robinson knew that when the story was over—no matter the outcome—it would fade, the reporters would move on, and the valley would be left with a hole in its heart. He thought of a man in Salt Lake who had a night-owl show that reached nearly coast to coast. The man's shtick was to work a prayer circle, sell some cruises, and mix in some causes. The priorities were not necessarily in that order. Robinson cogitated on that. *Maybe this guy in Salt Lake will help.*

Robinson looked up the number and dialed. A woman at the Salt Lake station answered and listened intently as he explained what had been going on at the Sunshine.

"I can't promise anything," she said, "but I'll let him know."

It was an easy sell. A moment later, Robinson was on the air coast to coast. He wasn't selling soap, eggs, or tuna for the friendly folks at the IGA. But he was selling the story to a nationwide audience of insomniacs who either couldn't sleep or just saw more clearly in the dark. Saying the words was difficult for Robinson, and the genuine emotion in his voice surely struck a chord.

"We have a lot of kids up here," he said, "dozens who've lost their dads. We're trying to help the kids so they can go to college."

AND OVER IN SMELTERVILLE, AS THURSDAY CAME TO A close, Bill Noyen picked up his diary and wrote of his son-in-law, safety engineer Launhardt: "Bob was on Spokane's Q6 TV this evening and I thought he answered questions thrown at him in good shape. However, there is a lot of criticism of the safety program. But one has to know that Bob had just started and to the best of our knowledge was hired back to do something to improve the safety facilities at Sunshine. . . ."

Forty

FRIDAY STARTED WITH A TELEGRAM SENT BY PRESIDENT Nixon: "The tragic loss of life that resulted from the fire at Sunshine Mine profoundly touched the hearts of all Americans."

While the president sent his condolences, Idaho governor Cecil Andrus rightly picked up on the severity and the possible long-term effects of the deadly fire. Sunshine was shut down, hundreds of men were out of work, and, tragically, dozens of women had become widows. Governor Andrus dispatched a telegram to Nixon seeking federal disaster status for Shoshone County. Nixon immediately denied the request. While it was true that federal law didn't cover a catastrophe like Sunshine's with disaster aid, many hoped that the government would find a way to help the community get back on its feet. Governor Andrus pulled strings, and so did Idaho congressman James McClure, but no federal agency would offer up a dime of postdisaster funding.

"Sympathy and concern are fine, but they don't buy groceries," Andrus retorted.

That morning, a miner called a USBM safety hotline ostensibly set up for coal miners and said Sunshine's "respirators" were unusable. "The chemicals in them were so old that they were solid," he said. He was correct, and the USBM acknowledged it in an internal memo: "The bureau has on hand two or more self-rescuers brought up from underground since the fire that are rusted shut; one shows marks of attempts to open it, apparently inflicted by a wrench."

More than a half-dozen lawyers from the USBM had arrived in Kellogg, joining the Idaho attorney general, lawyers for Sunshine, and the United Steelworkers. Bob Launhardt made a count of attorneys and he stopped at thirty-two. He knew the focus was shifting from rescue to blame.

By tradition, the last day of the workweek was usually the best day; miners with fat wallets descended on the Big Creek Store or the Happy Landing or any of the other joints strewn throughout the district. But with forty-seven men still trapped in the lowest levels of the Sunshine, the entire district could not have felt further from a party mood. When Betty Larsen opened up the pay window and women started arriving for their husbands' paychecks, as they always did, dark circles ringed their bloodshot eyes, and hair that might have been done up on the best day of the week hung like oily strings. Larsen had been distributing payroll for three years and knew most of the wives by sight and name. An unfamiliar face came to the window and asked for a man's check. He was among the missing.

"We already gave it to his wife," she said.

I'm his wife. I'm his *legal* wife."

"Wait a minute," Larsen said, confused. "I don't know you. Who's the other lady?"

The woman became irritated, and her snotty tone let Larsen know it.

"She's common-law," she said. "I'm *legal.*"

The scene played out again as the past lives of several Sunshine miners caught up with them in Big Creek. As she glumly issued checks, Larsen tried to stay detached from the confusion and heartache. But three times her heart soared when men who had been presumed trapped and were on her list of the missing showed up for their pay. It gave her hope. The temperature warmed to 72 degrees, and Larsen watched a Red Cross worker out in the yard scoop ice cream. Maybe things would be all right.

THROUGHOUT THE DAY, MAY 5
Sunshine Rescue Command Center

IN MANY WAYS IT WAS A "HAIL MARY" PLAN, BUT THE TIME had come for that. The anxious faces across from the portal reminded rescuers that the hopes of the entire mining district rested with a rescue effort that was long on activity but short on results. Someone suggested using a terra capsule to go down the borehole from 3700 to 4800. Terra capsules, or torpedoes as they were also known, were sometimes used to ferry men from one level to the next when shaft construction wasn't complete. One had never been used in mine rescue, and the USBM quickly declared it too risky. Not only was Sunshine's borehole newly blasted, but it crossed through bad country, an unstable area prone to rockbursts. Running a cable-suspended capsule down a jagged shaft with two men on board was, some thought, foolhardy. Hadn't enough died already?

Chase, Walkup, and especially Hecla's Gordon Miner pushed for the capsule rescue idea. It was time for a bold idea, maybe even a gamble. Sunshine had two capsules, both about seven feet in height and wide enough to hold two men. One was cagelike, and the other looked like a water heater with a small door and baseball-sized holes punched in it for airflow. Crews were assigned to make repairs and any necessary modifications to ensure they'd make it down the chasm to the level that might be the best hope for finding survivors.

Stan Jarrett of the USBM, however, was firmly against the use of a capsule. He was concerned the device would get lodged in the ragged borehole and rescuers would be trapped. He also suggested that a capsule itself could block airflow to 4800, thus risking the lives of any survivors ensnared down there. Either the plan had to be abandoned or a capsule that could endure either worst-case scenario had to be fabricated. Hope won over reason. A borrowed hoist from a Spokane company was sent down to 3700 and the borehole. A Sunshine capsule was lowered as a test, but with only an inch or so of clearance, it was too tight for safe passage.

Gordon Miner, the Hecla chief, refused to be defeated by the setback. Miner wasn't shy about calling in markers. He had served on a government mining commission and knew the Atomic Energy Commission used capsules at its test site near Mercury, Nevada, whenever the agency conducted underground nuclear weapons testing. Miner knew the two-man AEC capsules were smaller than Sunshine's—one man rode on the shoulders of the other. Not only were they already outfitted with communications equipment, but AEC capsules also had escape hatches. Miner told Jarrett to get on with the AEC request or he'd do it himself.

It wasn't a suggestion, but an order.

Across from command central at the portal, clergymen asked families to wear ID tags. That way, they promised, instead of calling out the name of a dead man, they could tap a family member on the shoulder. It could all be done quietly and without the rolling wave of fear that swept everyone into an emotional frenzy. Every name in the district associated with mining was consigned to tags or placards: Delbridge, Stephens, Russell, Byington, and more.

Nearby, Jewell cage tender Kenny Wilbur kept his eyes on the breathing apparatus spread out on a plywood sheet supported by a couple of sawhorses borrowed from the mine's carpentry shop. He saw a man approach with a piece of heavy white paper clenched in his fist. Written in black was the name GREG DIONNE. The man wanted to know if there was news of his brother. Wilbur looked up, but couldn't speak. He just stared. His mouth froze as though paralyzed. He knew if he said anything, he'd start to cry. Bawling in front of the portal was something he didn't want to get started.

Greg Dionne's brother, like the rest of his family—like all the families waiting there—wanted to know anything he could find out.

It was Greg's partner, Tony Sabala, who helped the Dionnes piece together what had happened on May 2. Sabala was a fifty-four-year-old veteran of the industry, though in all his thirty-six years working he'd never actually mined an ounce of ore. Working as a pipeman's helper on Tuesday, Sabala had met up with Dionne at the pipe shop on 3700. He'd poured himself some coffee and sat down. Before he got too comfortable, the drift shuddered with an explosion. It sounded as though someone had blasted close by, but Sabala knew no one was setting charges around there. It could be a cave-in. He took a quick sip and considered going to investigate, but never got the chance. A minute or so later, a brownish black tornado raged through the drift, eclipsing all lights like a shield. His eyes watered and his lungs constricted and burned.

"Call the blue room," he called over to Don Beehner. "Tell them to go check. We've got a bad fire someplace."

Beehner made the call, and both left for the station. Sabala considered escaping by heading down the drift, but he doubted he'd make it out alive. *Either get out on the cage or die right here,* he thought. He saw some men stumble and fall in the smoke. They jumped on the cage with Dionne and some others and made it to 3100, where Gene Johnson met them kneeling by the gate. Sabala thought it was because the layer of smoke was heavier at the top of the drift, and somewhat clearer lower, down along the track. It also passed through Sabala's mind that Johnson was taking five.

"You boys head right for the Jewell," the foreman said.

As the group fought its way off the station, Sabala turned around to check on Dionne. He took out his mouthpiece to speak.

"How you doing, Greg?" he asked through the smoke.

It was Don Beehner who answered. "Greg isn't here," the nipper said. "Johnson asked him to go down below and help cage men out."

Sabala didn't think Dionne was in any better shape than he was. They'd both inhaled a bunch of smoke. He wasn't up to caging anyone. It was true that Dionne was half his age, but the smoke was so bad, the pipe helper doubted anyone could survive what they had breathed in back there. The station was a smoldering cauldron.

The last words someone heard Dionne say were, "Let's go get them." Then he disappeared onto the cage.

Sabala didn't think it was right that his young partner had stayed behind. He almost certainly would have gone on to the Jewell with the others if Johnson hadn't asked him to run the cage. If Dionne had gone to the Jewell, he'd have survived. His wife wouldn't be widowed; his daughter wouldn't be fatherless. There was no denying that he was some kind of a hero, but wasn't his own life worth something, too?

Greg Dionne's older brother, Doug, absorbed everything Sabala said. In doing so, he couldn't help but wonder what kind of man *he'd* have been if he'd been underground the morning of the fire. Some had scuttled out as quickly as they could and never looked back once. Others had stayed to fight the fire they couldn't see. A few, like his brother, stayed to help others get out alive. Doug Dionne believed all men would like to think they'd be the kind of man who'd risk his life for others, but he wasn't sure he was one of them.

The Dionnes weren't the kind to stir up trouble—not in the face of such tragedy. They mostly talked among themselves about why it was that pipe crewman Greg had put on a self-rescuer and yanked men to safety, while cager Byron Schulz had left his assigned post and made it out alive.

One of the Dionnes told Bob Launhardt that Schulz "didn't have a grasp" of what had to be done and Greg had "no choice" but to step in.

"You stay up here, and I'll go down and get the men," Dionne had reportedly said, the self-rescuer's mouthpiece in his hand, as a black cloud billowed around the station. He vanished into the smoke and rode the cage a thousand feet down and brought men back up before doing it all over again.

"People in the mine told me how Greg went down and helped them on and off the cage on 3100. Schulz just sat up there doing nothing! He'd thought only of himself. He left Greg there to die," the family member said.

Byron Schulz was written up as a hero. Greg Dionne died being one.

Those feeling the emotion can't always see it, but resentment is like a leaky faucet that never stops. Drop by drop, it builds from a puddle to an ocean. Many of the Sunshine miners had it in for the state and federal men. Sunshine wasn't some hole in the ground. To the men who worked there, and those who loved it, it was home. Some thought the state mine inspector was the most annoying of the lot. He'd been there just a week or two before the fire, and now he was prancing around as if the Sunshine folks were incompetent and only he knew best. And, worse, he was itching to prove it. Randy Peterson, the cager who'd taken his crew from the smoke of the station through the black of a drift and on to safety, sat with his shifter and a USBM employee at the Jewell station on 3100. While waiting for rescue orders to come down from topside, a beam from the USBM man's lamp hit his eyes. Peterson blinked back the light. Most miners understood one of the first rules of the underground: *Never blind your buddy.* When a man sits across from another on a motor or lagging, he turns off his lamp.

"Turn your light out."

The man flatly refused. "You don't turn your light off in a mine," he said. "It's a safety rule."

"Hey, turn your light out!" Peterson repeated, his voice increasing in anger with each syllable.

"You *don't* turn your light out underground," the outsider said. It was as if he were reading from some stupid procedure manual and didn't know how things were down in the subterranean world. Peterson was seconds from taking his pipe wrench and smashing the man's lamp.

"You're not my boss," Peterson said. "And you're not gonna fire me. Now turn your fuckin' light out!"

MIDDAY, MAY 5
Topside, Portal

WHENEVER THE FAMILIAR SOUND OF THE DOUBLE-DRUM clattered through the yard, hopes rose. *Someone's coming up. Someone's getting out.* Marvin Chase allowed access to some of the surface working areas to give the waiting families something to do, and an opportunity for each to see that everything possible was being done to get their men from the mine. It was a short-lived public relations move. A woman came into the Jewell double-drum hoist room and told George Moore, who was in the midst of lowering a rescue team, that her husband had been working on the 1900 level at 10-Shaft when the fire broke out.

She asked how the hoistman knew where the skip was as it descended down the shaft.

"Right now," Moore said, indicating a gauge, "they're about twelve hundred feet down." He told her that a rescue team was on its way to 3700, traveling at about a thousand feet a minute.

"Where's it now?" she asked.

"About fifteen hundred."

She leaned closer. "And now?"

"Eighteen hundred."

Without warning, the woman lunged for the controls.

Moore was in shock. "Hey, what are you doing?"

She tried to push him out of the way, but he managed to thwart her. But she jumped him a second time. The cage kept moving downward. Moore balled up a fist and slugged her hard enough to knock her away. The lives of the men on the skip were literally dangling on the cable. Moore clutched out the hoist and stopped it just past the 3700 station. Another eighty feet, and the skip would collide with the bottom of the shaft with the force of a head-on wreck. The woman had convinced herself that if she could get the hoist to stop at 1900, her husband could get on the skip and come back to her. Security kept visitors out of the hoist room after that, which hoistman Moore thought was a good idea. He didn't want to deck another woman.

Forty-one

TIME UNKNOWN, MAY 5
4800 Level Station

Ron Flory felt uneasy about pilfering the dinner buckets of the dead men on the tracks. It wasn't grave-robbing, of course, but it sure didn't feel right. He and Wilkinson knew there was no guarantee that anything would be edible anyway. Several days of 80- to 90-degree heat surely hastened spoilage. But the pair had lived on nothing but water and cigarettes for days. Water fills a man's stomach, but it doesn't really slake desire for food. Hunger is at once mental and physical. When a man's stomach aches and his bowels constrict and writhe like a sack of snakes, he thinks not of the pain but of finding something to eat. Flory and Wilkinson talked about food as much as anything. What they would eat when they got out of the mine. What they wished they'd had right that minute.

Tom Wilkinson insisted they had no choice. They needed food.

"I don't know," Flory said.

"If it was the other way around," Wilkinson said, "I'd want them to eat whatever I left behind to survive."

Flory's sensibilities gave in to his empty stomach.

The pair doused their T-shirt face masks and hustled down the drift, dodging bodies and keeping their eyes on the goal—black dinner buckets left by fallen friends. They had already lost weight by then, and both could feel the difference, a waning physical strength. Just before the station, they saw the buckets sitting where they'd been left. With their free hands, they grabbed three and instantaneously spun around to return to the Safety Zone. The air seemed breathable, but neither had a self-rescuer. Flory doubted a T-shirt was really enough protection. Hunger had driven him and his partner to take the risk.

It turned out they had risked a lot for very little. A can of Hunt's chocolate pudding, an Idaho Spud candy bar, and a tuna sandwich were all that could be had. If the smoke had passed through the mine a half hour earlier, the buckets would have been full.

The tuna sandwich was the rankest thing Flory ever smelled. Nearly gagging from its odor, both men ate small bites because desperation and a kind of manic hunger had taken over. At that moment they'd have eaten anything. They decided to save the remainder for the morning, just so their stomachs would have something to grab hold of, and settle down. The rest of the day would be gulps upon gulps of water.

Wilkinson regarded the pudding and made a suggestion that was half a joke.

"Let's save it for the end," he said.

Flory grinned and put the little can back in the bucket and fastened the hasp. When it got really bad, when there was no more hope they'd get out alive, they'd toast their last moments alive with chocolate pudding. The day held one more major event. The hum of the mammoth chiller on 4600 went silent, and the refrigerated air it had pushed toward the survivors went stagnant. It wasn't as if the chiller was really making things all that much cooler—Wilkinson thought the air was somewhere between 90 and 100 degrees in their pocket. But the men wondered why. The water line still flowed, but for how much longer?

AFTERNOON, MAY 5
Big Creek Neighborhood

TO LOSE HER DAD IN THE SUDDENNESS OF THE FIRE WAS A horror unto itself, but to see her mother fading before her eyes was killing Peggy Delange. Betty Johnson always carried a kind of fragility about her, but she was also very pretty. She reminded Peggy of one of those movie actresses from the thirties and forties, Joan Crawford without the pencil-line eyebrows. After the disturbingly cruel call from Farris, her mother's energy drained from her, moment by moment. She stopped eating. She drank only coffee. She occupied every moment smoking by the phone, waiting for a call from Farris that he'd been wrong, that God had made a miracle. When small sores appeared around her mother's mouth, Peggy took her to a doctor. He prescribed sedatives, and told Peggy that her mother had to eat something.

"She won't touch anything," Peggy said. "We've tried."

"At the very least," he said, "get her to put milk and sugar in her coffee."

Her eyes hollow and her lips beginning to crack, Betty promised she would. But it was a lie. She didn't want to eat because she didn't want to live.

All she could think about was Gene and how he'd done everything for her and how much she missed him. He had been her strength. *I don't want to be here no more without him,* she thought one night, curled in a fetal position on the davenport. She went into the bathroom and retrieved some pills to end her life. She sat back down in the living room and examined the bottle. She felt she was so weak, so undeserving. She wanted to die.

"Betty!" She heard a voice call out. "Betty?" It sounded like a neighbor.

She dragged herself to the back door, but no one was there. It came to her that it was Gene telling her not to die. She started to weep.

I will raise the kids for him, she thought. *But I'll do that more for him than for me.*

On the east end of the district, Wava Beehner was beside herself. She paced the floor trying to remember. She knew that Don wanted "Red Sails in the Sunset" sung at his funeral service. He'd told her so. But there was another song and she couldn't think of it. Just the week before, Don had mentioned a second tune that he found particularly meaningful. *Why can't I remember?* Her inability to bring it to mind was killing her. *He asked this of me.* She broke down and cried as hard as she ever had. *What was that song?* On top of that, something more compounded her swelling grief. Don had never been baptized. Wava worried that her husband wouldn't get into heaven; or, worse, that he'd go to hell. And if he didn't make it to heaven, they'd never see each other again.

"Don't worry," her pastor told her, "Don was baptized by fire."

LATE EVENING, MAY 5
Pinehurst

SMUDGE POTS GLOWED AROUND THE RESOLUTE AND THE DIS-tressed throughout Friday night at the portal. And every once in a while, absolute silence set in, only to be broken by a child's whine or a woman's cry. Late that night, just before Bob Launhardt went home to Pinehurst, rescue men lowered a ringing telephone down the borehole to 4800. It rang and rang, but no one answered. It was just another disappointment in what Launhardt and those closest to the rescue effort considered a doomed operation. Before trying to sleep, he unfolded the pages of the day's edition of the *Kellogg Evening News.* His eyes fixed on a photograph of Duwain Crow with his funeral notice. He stood against a paneled wall, his muscled arms folded across his chest. His smile was slight. He was a man at his peak, strappingly built, tough as any man. And yet he was gone. Launhardt inspected the black-and-white image. Duwain had been one of the reasons he'd come to Kellogg and ended up at Sunshine. They had mined together at Talache. They'd roomed together at his folks' place in Kellogg. He passed Duwain's Big Creek house every day on his way to work. Launhardt was struck by the tragic irony of Crow's demise. He'd escaped death once before. Having finished serving his country in Korea, Crow and three dozen other enlisted men had boarded a small Army charter plane from Washington, D.C., to Spokane. The plane ran out of gas over southwest Pennsylvania, and the plane crashed into the waters of the Monongahela River. Crow was one of fifteen to survive.

When Crow and Launhardt reconnected in Kellogg, he recounted how he'd slung his boots around his neck, stripped off his woolen coat, and fought his way from the sinking aircraft through the frigid water.

"I was getting so cold so fast," Crow said, "I didn't think I would make it. Some guy was on the shore and waded out in the water and put out his hand. He dragged me out."

There had been no one to haul him out of the mine Tuesday.

Launhardt's father-in-law, Bill Noyen, logged his May 5 entry in his house in Smelterville: "All sorts of rumors persist. Such as there has been audible contact with the men. Bob said they did have vocal contact right after the fire started, but not since. And that thirty-five bodies were at the bottom of the shaft and rumors of different guys down there. . . . We're all hoping yet—but as time goes on, the hopes are getting more and more remote."

SUNSHINE MIGHT HAVE HAD A HOT DEVIL'S BREATH, BUT outside the portal it was cold. Although Red Cross volunteers distributed blankets and coats, in reality they did little to stave off shivering, especially among the growing number of children accompanying their mothers and grandparents. It was fear as much as icy weather. Not only were miners' kids unsure what was happening underground with their dads, but they were frightened that their moms would break into pieces and disintegrate before their eyes. Frances Phillips, an eighth-grader named for her father, Francis, pulled a blanket around her shoulders and fell suddenly, and inexplicably, to sleep only to wake in a panic. Her little brother, whom she had been watching—the one thing she could do for her mother—was missing. A few frantic moments later she found the four-year-old curled up on a cot under a mountain of coats. His face was pink. She let him sleep, safe and unaware just how bad things were. A song her father, a forty-two-year-old repairman who'd been working 5200, had written could not escape the girls' troubled mind. *When my earthly days are over, please heed my last request. Take me back to Butte, Montana, when you lay me down to rest. Where the river shines like silver.*

In addition to handling the main office phones, Red Cross worker Oradell Triplett, thirty-five, was given another responsibility at night. One of the Sunshine managers informed her that a handful of prostitutes had come over from Spokane to work the crowd. Triplett could scarcely believe her ears.

"Watch out for these women," he said. "Let us know when you see one."

"What will they look like?" she asked, finding her nerve.

"You can tell more by their actions than anything," he said. He also said some of the women were wearing Red Cross armbands.

Later on, Triplett notified security. A redhead out in the mine yard seemed a little too friendly consoling some men. With attack speed, a couple of guys from Company A escorted the woman across the creek bridge.

A person can't be that money-hungry, Triplett thought.

Forty-two

WHEN THE GRAVEYARD-SHIFT RESCUE CREW ARRIVED AT the 3100 hoist room, the air was strange, a kind of translucent, smoky fog that hung like moving drapes. The scene reminded Lucky Friday's Art Brown of the old movie *Phantom of the Opera*. All around was a surreal and frozen scene of the horrific moment when everything stopped at once. Lifeless faces looked up into the beams of light from the cap lamps of each member of Brown's rescue team.

"He doesn't look real," said a miner, looking closer at one of the dead.

"He looks like he's made of plastic," Brown agreed, wishing it were so.

Some of the crewmen jerked their lights away whenever they met the gaze of a dead man. Flesh had puffed up and lips had split. Ears

313

seemed to have melted. Brown radioed topside what they'd found. Somehow, despite what he was feeling, his words were matter-of-fact. He was all business.

A few yards from the station, it appeared that one man had used the air compressor to live a bit longer. How much time the man had bought, or what terrifying things he'd witnessed, no one could guess. Art Brown knew even a minute was too long. He bent down and picked up a muck-dusted dinner bucket. It had been packed four days before by some woman who now was wondering if her man would ever come home. Inside, he found a wallet. It held a few dollars and pictures of the miner's family. Those faces were the other side of the tragedy. Although Brown could have taken the wallet topside and told the woman her husband was gone, Marvin Chase insisted all names be kept confidential. He wanted the women to know the rescue effort was the primary focus, and no one was wasting precious time allocating correct names to dead men. Their air supply halfway depleted, the crew returned to the surface. No one was disappointed to leave. They brought with them the news of more dead, more unbelievably disfigured men. Men who no longer looked as they had in life. It was a problem no one could have imagined.

Putting names to bodies fell on those who had the most contact with the crew. Marvin Chase and Al Walkup, bosses at the top, didn't know everyone working underground. Launhardt knew many, but he was caught up assisting the USBM with the continuing ventilation problems. The initial identification team included accountant George Gieser, union man George Gipson, hiring agent Bill Steele, and the dry man, Dick Terrill. A three-man FBI identification team was on its way from Washington, D.C.

The group assembled in the back of a Kellogg funeral home and was briefed by the Shoshone County coroner, another town doctor, and a pair of volunteer morticians. It was grisly and startling. Steele expected stiff bodies, but rigor mortis had come and gone.

"They'll smell bad," a mortician said. Though the bodies had been zipped inside bags, there was some seepage of the acrid odor of death. No one used a mask or air freshener to allay the putrid odor.

The coroner offered another word of warning, telling the others that the bodies should be considered *remains,* not the men themselves.

"Think of it as just a body and we need to put a name to it."

Steele could barely bring himself to pull the zipper on the first corpse. One of the morticians stepped in and peeled back the black pupa-like casing that had molded like a vacuum seal to the corpse. An appalling stench burst forth and flowed across the room. The smell was as acrid as a mix of battery acid and roadkill, multiplied a million times. The room constricted and everyone breathed in shallowly. Steele peered at the body. It was blackened and featureless. The shirt looked as if it had been soaked in the darkest wine. He couldn't make out a face, and said so.

"He's on his stomach," the coroner said.

A couple of men reached under the slippery corpse and rolled it over.

Even right side up, this doesn't look human. The face had flattened to fit the level plane of the floor on which it had settled. A closer look revealed elements of a human face, but it sure didn't look as though it could ever have been a real man.

"Jesus Christ," someone muttered.

The stink was so overpowering that with the first unzipped cadaver, it became obvious that the gruesome task couldn't continue at that funeral home. The stench would kill the mortician's business. After that, bodies were dispatched to the Shoshone Inn Nursing Home in Kellogg. The not-yet-opened nursing home would serve as a temporary morgue, but a more discreet location would be needed.

An examiner wrote: "We knew most of these men for many years, yet some unexplained mechanism seemed to dull over our emotions and we were able to function almost normally."

MORNING, MAY 6
Shifter's Shack

A TWO-WAY RADIO CRACKLED UNDERGROUND, AND THE reporter with the Red Cross armband, Jerry McGinn, overheard descriptions of tragic tableaux discovered by the helmet crew: a fallen father with his arm wrapped around his son's shoulder; a man holding a sandwich, frozen in the moment. From each pocket of the dead, a story emerged of men trying to get out, or dying before they knew what hit them. McGinn also heard the names of the dead. One was the husband of a woman he'd been talking with while delivering blankets and coffee. After that, whenever she asked him if he knew something, he said they were still sifting through the mine. He didn't give her any hope. He avoided a direct answer.

As McGinn hunkered in the shifter's shack Saturday morning, word circulated in the yard that there was a reporter hiding out as a rescue worker or Red Cross volunteer. The man was using a disguise to infiltrate the inner circle of the rescue effort and to cozy up to families waiting at the portal.

They're talking about me, McGinn thought, his pockets full of toilet tissue scrawled with notes. He wished himself invisible. No one in the shack said a word to him.

Correspondents from other media outlets had wised up. They started asking about the UPI reporter who kept pushing a higher body count. The *Wallace Miner* published an article about the unidentified undercover reporter, and someone from the AP pinned the tearsheet on a wall where the press congregated. On the top of the paper, someone had scrawled, "We want to meet this fella."

Topside, as the temperature dropped, the waiting families were weary, damp, and cold. Some of the Army reservists pitched a huge tent to shield people from a pinprick rain that stopped and started in a rolling rhythm. That day, the waiting families found some comfort in their government representatives. Idaho senator Frank Church once more urged Nixon to ease the district's burden with financial assistance. With Sunshine shut down, unemployment rolls were expected to double in Shoshone County. The Steelworkers demanded a congressional probe. None of its members trusted the USBM or the Department of the Interior to do the job without trying to cover their own asses.

In addition to the USBM's high-sensitivity geophone listening system—a microphone and walkie-talkies—a crew prepared to lower a video camera into the borehole. The camera was state of the art, similar to what had been used to record the famous images of the Apollo spacecraft on the moon in July 1969. The camera was an eye that could see in the dark. The reconnaissance of the borehole to 4800 was important to determine whether or not it could accommodate one of the AEC capsules. It was slow going down the 1,100-foot drop.

It was a common misconception that a shaft or a borehole was a perfectly constructed rock tube. It was straight to the extent that the passageway was vertical, but there were bumps and bulges, and nicks of a size sufficient to hold a truck camper. The crew needed to "bar down" part of the passage. Hammers and heavy steel rods splintered off any fractured and loose rock, letting it fall to the bottom, rather than onto the cage or a man's head. By the end of the day, the capsule had only reached 4400. Provided the anomalies associated with the rough stone channel were not insurmountable—the clearance for the capsule was about five inches on each side—a two-man team would ride the capsule to 4800 and work its way back to 10-Shaft, looking for survivors. The video feed was viewed on a monitor on 3700.

The two capsules from Nevada, courtesy of an AEC subcontractor, Reynolds Electric and Engineering Company, were scheduled to be in Spokane by 8:00 a.m. the next day.

Crews tackled the smoke from the top of the Jewell, removing two sections of the three-piece ventilation stack so a 240-horsepower Buffalo Forge fan could be mounted there to draw out carbon monoxide and smoke from the mine's interior.

Air leaks and excessive heat at 3100 station once again delayed complete recovery and use of the hoist room. Operating any equipment in the heat was dubious; a fan was ordered down to 3100. It would take another twelve hours to get it to the point where the hoist could be used. Curiously, the men in the command center had let go of some of the frustration and tension that had colored every moment. It wasn't that they were giving up, but more that they had become accustomed to a rescue effort that met obstacles at every turn. The hard way, it seemed, became the *only* way. The bureau tried to procure more breathing units, but neither manufacturer of the government-sanctioned breathing units— McCaa nor Draeger—had any surplus. All other mines that had any spares had already sent them. The bureau turned to a London manufacturer of mine-safety equipment. Instead of the high-pressure oxygen cylinder of the Draeger and McCaa, the Aerolox employed an evaporator filled with liquid oxygen. They were also lighter and cooler. An Aerolox face mask supplied oxygen at 65 degrees Fahrenheit—the others could get as hot as 120 degrees. For the beleaguered helmet crew toiling in the depths of hell, it was as though they'd been breathing through a hair dryer. Within a couple of hours of the request, thirty-five British Aerolox units were packed on an Air Force jet headed for Spokane.

AFTERNOON, MAY 6
Osburn

ACROSS THE DISTRICT IN OSBURN, THE SEVENTH-DAY Adventist church, with its high-peaked A-frame façade, had never seen a funeral like Don Beehner's. So many people came that the blue upholstered pews could only accommodate half the mourners. A loudspeaker piped the service to the overflow crowd outside. A fragrant spray of roses and feathery ferns was mounted on a tripod facing the mourners. A pink satin ribbon was pinned across the arrangement with the words *To Daddy* written in glittery cursive script. Wava and her children sat in the front row, her youngest daughter, Nora, in a pretty red dress her mother had borrowed. The pastor told the mourners how Beehner had taken his kids hunting with only a single bullet because he never wanted to kill anything. He had been a gentle guy, one who had worked hard to provide for his wife and children. Don Beehner, a man who grew up with a boozing father and without two nickels to rub together, had done all right with the thirty-eight years God had given him. The service lasted twenty minutes. Don had always said not to make a fuss, and a good funeral was a short one.

After Don Beehner was laid to rest at Nine Mile Cemetery, the little green house on Burke Road was jammed with more people than on any single day in the dozen years the family had lived there. Matthew Beehner counted nineteen cars parked outside. He stood in the kitchen watching various family members embrace each other, balance teetering plates of food on their knees, or just mill around. He looked up at their faces, all red and tear-stained. It seemed like a sad little party.

TIME UNKNOWN, MAY 6
4800 Level

THE SURVIVORS IN THE SAFETY ZONE HAD WAITED FOR HELP for more than four days, more than one hundred hours, and with each hour the idea that they might not ever get out became more vivid, more frequent in their discussions. It was startling how quickly and completely the implausible had become possible. They knew that eventually the rescue team would find them. They were, after all, on a level that was prime silver country.

"They aren't going to seal off the mine and forget about us," Wilkinson said.

"Yeah, but what's going to happen to us?"

Flory slumped on his bedboard, looking small and defeated.

"Are they gonna get to us before we starve to death?"

Wilkinson saw Flory sinking into depression.

"We're gonna get out of this," he said.

To put the focus on anything other than their situation, Flory taught Wilkinson how to square-braid yellow blasting wire, and for hours in the shadows they said nothing as they spun out chains of yellow. At one point Flory made a checkerboard of lagging, and the two men played checkers until they could no longer stand it. And they talked about fishing trips they'd taken and ones they would take if and when they got out. Wilkinson said that the guys on the surface were just biding their time playing pinochle and waiting for the smoke to clear out of the mine.

"And our wives are planning on how they're going to spend the insurance money," he said.

Yet, even as they labored for distraction in the Safety Zone, neither man could ignore hunger gnawing with sharp little teeth at their stomachs. The rotten tuna sandwich had offered no relief. They had tried to trick their stomachs into a false fullness with gulps from the water line. And it had worked for a while; the first four days hadn't been completely unbearable. But by Saturday their stomachs had wised up and would no longer fall for the ruse. Hunger stabbed at them. How much longer could they go without food?

LATE EVENING, MAY 6
Sunshine Portal

THE *KELLOGG EVENING NEWS* STAFF DISTRIBUTED FREE COPIES at the mine on Saturday. Papers fluttered in the chilly night air, the front page screaming, SUNSHINE MINE DEATH TOLL NOW RISES TO 40. Near a Red Cross tent where they waited, Garnita Keene began to wonder if Myrna had deluded herself to such a degree that if Ron had died, she'd be unable to process it at all. And even after she allowed those thoughts to take root, the words never passed her lips. She couldn't be the one to say them to Myrna. She had been the one to help her kid sister with a slathering of Day-Glo orange Mercurochrome on skinned knees. Garnita had been there when Myrna needed help with her son, Tiger. Myrna had been through a lot in her life and was a young mother, but she still was a kid. She needed hope, not a dose of reality.

"He'll come out," Garnita said, concealing her doubts.

Myrna's confidence remained steadfast.

"I know," she said.

The sisters tangled their arms around each other and stayed back from the portal as others learned the bodies of their men had been located. Garnita caught herself with a lump in her throat, over and over, when names were made public.

"I never thought *he'd* die. I thought for sure that he'd make it out."

Myrna held her ground. "Ron *is* going to make it."

Garnita saw the faces of women who had told themselves the same thing, but who now knew otherwise.

She put her hand on Myrna's shoulder. She felt so thin, so tiny. *How much longer can she go on?* Garnita thought.

"If anyone comes out, it will be Ron," she said.

Later that night, Myrna's heart was tested again when a friend came running to her.

"I saw Ron in town! He must have got out!"

"What do you mean, you saw Ron?"

The friend's excitement could barely be contained. "In town. In his truck."

"No," Myrna said. "Ron can't be driving around Kellogg. He's in the mine. I'd know if he'd got out. I've never left this spot."

Myrna learned later that one of her brothers-in-law had taken the keys out of her husband's hanger in the dry. It seemed as if the Florys were acting as though Ron was dead.

Fuck them for that. Damn all of those Florys, she thought bitterly.

NIGHTFALL, MAY 6
Big Creek Neighborhood

THE BIG CREEK NEIGHBORHOOD WAS QUIET AS THE HOURS melted into Sunday morning. Marvin Chase came home late, huddled with his wife and children, and tried to sleep. Bob Launhardt called his wife, Janet, in Seattle to say he was doing all right, though he clearly wasn't. Betty Johnson silently stared from her place on the davenport. The last of the miners drinking at the Big Creek Store had left for home, drunk, but no wiser as to what had really happened at Sunshine. The Shoshone County coroner said all the men had perished within forty to sixty seconds of exposure to the toxic air, and all at 11:50 a.m. Betty thought the designated time was more convenience than science. She, and many others, refused to accept that all had died at once. Surely the men on the lowest levels had survived longer. Wives wondered if their husbands had suffered, and for how long?

In her empty bed in Big Creek, Joanne Reichert, the common-law wife of welder Jack Reichert, woke up in a panic. *I should be at the mine where I can help Jack if he needs me. Maybe he needs me right now and I'm not there.* Some women are unable to stay away from the men they love. Anyone who knew Joanne knew she was one of those. The long days and empty nights had eroded her already fragile mental state. She threw on some clothes, locked their dogs in the kitchen, and drove up the road toward the mine. A sliver of dark sky revealed a swath of stars beyond the clouds over the Bitterroots; a few windows beamed light across the roadway. Her heart pumped in time with her hurried pace. Out of breath at the portal, Joanne Reichert felt immediate relief. Jack hadn't come out yet. *Good.* She didn't want to miss him when he did.

She slipped between the clumps of people, thinking of how Jack was probably standing around somewhere in the darkness, waiting for the smoke to clear so he could come up, go home, and eat dinner. She pulled herself up on the platform backed with the huge safety sign and looked at the crowd. Their mouths were moving, like cattle chewing, with nothing intelligible emanating. Her hair was an unkempt mess, and dark circles dominated her weary, pale face like mascara smudges on a white pillowcase. She was erratic and emotional. She told people that she'd kill herself if Jack didn't make it out of the mine. Several reported their concerns about her, and Jim Farris tapped out a note for Jack Reichert's file: "Common-law wife stated she will commit suicide if Jack is pronounced dead. This threat should not be taken lightly in this case. . . . Her name is Mary Joanne and she has been seen in the yard constantly since the accident. She uses the last name Reichert."

Forty-three

C ARLOADS OF MEN CLOAKED IN SUPERIORITY AND THREE-
piece suits arrived on Sunday in search of motel rooms. Some
were lawyers. They had briefcases, and secretaries they could dial to
type their notes. Their hands had likely never seen really hard work.
They were softer versions of those who mined, and they were concerned more with ensuring that the interests of their clients were preserved than with saving any lives. Others had an agenda that, at least
on the surface, appeared to represent the miners. This was the union
contingency, made up of men who were supposedly on the side of the
miners who'd escaped, and those who were still underground.

Not everyone was happy with the United Steelworkers of
America—locally *or* nationally. Ace Riley was among many who had
long contended that hardrock miners were the bastard children of
the Pittsburgh-headquartered Steelworkers. It wasn't called, for

Christ's sake, the Hardrock Miners Union. It was named for men who worked on the surface, who hadn't a clue about the dangers of the underground. Riley stewed. Not only had the father of five narrowly escaped a fire that killed dozens, but also, just two years prior, he'd seen a partner fall down a chute to a mangled death. As the smoke continued to pour from Sunshine Tunnel and the shortened blue steel stack, hope was ebbing toward resignation. Riley was pushed to the brink. When he was called to give a deposition, he went because he wanted to get some things off his chest.

By the time a Steelworkers representative introduced himself, the man from Butte was ready to blow.

"Let me tell you," Riley said, standing tall and extending his index finger to punch out each word, "you sons of bitches, you sat on your asses and let things happen." He railed against the inspection process. It was a sham, because warnings were always given that inspectors were on the way to the mine. A little clean-up here, move the powder from the station, check the cables of the hoist for any sign of wear, and sit back and follow the damn guy with a clipboard as he goes from topside to each working level. Don't tell him that you gob with rags, old boxes, and other combustible trash that should be hoisted out.

Topside, standing in the yard, physician Keith Dahlberg was still hopeful. Once men were rescued, they would be in need of medical attention—beyond smoke inhalation or any burns. One of his greatest concerns was starvation. Rescue crews carried Gatorade in ten-ounce cans and were admonished to give survivors the sugary liquid in very small amounts. The doctor distributed a memo:

"I suggest a quarter of a can every twenty to thirty minutes. Do not leave the [Gatorade] with the patient because he might not be able to use good judgment and would drink the whole can at once."

He also worried about the impact of days of total darkness on a man's mental state. He expected a form of hysteria. He wrote: "We don't know how five or six days alone in darkness will affect a man.

Morphine injection may be supplied to the first-aid man on the crew to administer if necessary...."

The absence of light could send a man to the loony bin, or even to his grave, but there were tales of men surviving after lengthy periods of darkness. Speaking with reporters out in the yard, Marvin Chase pointed out that a Virginia coal miner had once survived an astounding three weeks without any light.

"The man was mentally and physically in fine shape when found by rescuers," Chase said.

AFTERNOON, MAY 7
Sunshine Mine Yard

THE ASTRINGENT ODOR OF PINE-SOL AND LYSOL WAFTED through the floorboards of Sunshine administration offices. In the basement below the office was the shifter's dry, and the men down there who'd been on body recovery were dousing everything that had to be cleaned—hardhats, rubber boots, slickers. Clothing was bagged and burned, with a new supply being issued by a mini–JCPenney store set up in the timekeeping office. The concern about contamination was genuine. At least four rescuers had been treated for rashes on their necks and backs. Whenever a whiff of fetid pine passed through the air, those who smelled it figured it was probably what death smelled like. Some would never be able to use pine-scented cleaning products at home again.

Word had gotten out through miners drinking at the Big Creek Store that the mine's hostile environment was exceedingly cruel to the dead, and because of that, few bureau or district men had the stomach for the recovery detail. Miner Johnny Lang volunteered because he didn't have any kin among the missing. Lang had seen dead bodies before, too. As a nineteen-year-old merchant marine in Algiers, he'd followed the sound of machine-gun fire wanting to see what a war looked like. He had climbed a hill and looked out over the scene of death. A row of dead men, bloated and bleeding, lined a stone-paved lane; the smell of their rotting flesh pummeled the sea breeze.

Lang drew on that experience as he kept his eye on one of the mine supervisors who'd been called to work in his crew. They met on 3100 to inspect breathing equipment before retrieving bodies. The supervisor looked green.

"You think you're gonna be able to handle this?"

The man said he wasn't sure, and Lang pushed him.

"You know what?" Lang asked. "If you throw up in your mask, you got to eat it. If you take the mask off in there, you're dead. If you don't think you can handle that, go back up there. There's nothing to be ashamed of. If we go back there and you panic, you'll endanger all of us," Lang went on. "And you know what? I'm not gonna give you my air. None of it."

The green-faced man turned around and departed. That astounded Lang. A real miner would have pressed on rather than look like a coward.

It took balls and a lead-lined stomach to do the job that no one wanted. Their buddies had ceased to look like men, their features exaggerated far beyond the bounds of recognition. Eyes bulged grotesquely. Teeth seemed to push forward, as if they were wrong-side-out. Ears had swollen to twice normal size. The steel grommets on tool belts pinched so tight that a couple of guys were nearly cut in half. When Lang tried to position a corpse into a bag, the flesh gave a little. It shocked him. *This fella's arm might come off,* he thought, and slid his hands under the torso to loosen the suction that held it to the floor of the drift. Wherever the leather of his gloves touched the dead man's skin, wide strips of darkened flesh peeled off. Lang's mind messed with him as he worked. He could smell the putrid odor of the decomposing flaps of skin, yet he was breathing contained air. *It wasn't possible to smell anything.* It took him back to

Algeria and the dead soldiers he'd seen there when he was nineteen. A phantom stench recirculated through his face mask.

The corpses were packed into two-handled zippered black bags with whatever had been scattered around—lamps, dinner buckets, or equipment. A few still had BM-1447s stuck in their mouths—one last breath before falling. Self-rescuers were within arm's reach of many. Some could have fallen as they staggered across the drift, but Lang recalled what some of the mine escapees had told him on Tuesday. *The thing got so hot, I sucked a little cool air from the side.*

It was that cool air that had killed them.

One crewman had to puncture a corpse with a pick to drain the gases and fluids so it could be put into the bag. The body hissed like a leaking tire.

Lang somehow found a way to do his work without allowing emotion to creep in. He looked at the placement of the bodies and imagined their last moments. He studied three fallen miners on 3100 and imagined a courageous, then desperate scenario. One was separated from the others by a few feet. It appeared the first two had been walking together with the third, and the smoke got so bad that the strongest of the three had to let the others fall to the ground because he couldn't help them anymore. In some movies, men ran off and left their comrades behind. *Every man for himself.* It wasn't like that at Sunshine on May 2.

Nobody went off and left his friends, Lang thought. *None of them guys panicked. Pretty tough men, them miners.*

TIME UNKNOWN, MAY 7
Wallace

IN WALLACE, A TALE OF ARSON WAS, IN FACT, SMOLDERING. Nervous and exhausted, Joe Naccarato's wife, Georgia, was about to be sucked into a scenario spun by Ace Riley's partner Joe Armijo's wife, Delores. Both women had husbands trapped in the mine. Armijo was positive her husband had intentionally torched the mine. She rambled out a convoluted tale of good and evil twins, incendiary devices, a book that recorded a disastrous mine fire that had acted as a blueprint, and, in the worst of it, she implicated Ace Riley.

"You had better not tell anybody about this or I will get this guy," she told Naccarato. "His name is Riley and I'll have him follow you around."

Later, a buddy of Riley's was in a Wallace bar when a sheriff's deputy came in asking a lot of questions. The cop wanted to know how much Riley drank, whether he was a decent fellow. When Riley heard about it, he went looking for the deputy. Riley wasn't good at concealing his anger, nor was he adept at waiting out situations to cool off.

"You want to know anything about me, all you got to do is ask me," he said. "You keep messing with me and I'll have your goddamn badge."

The deputy said the county prosecutor had put him up to it. Local law enforcement was investigating information that his partner, Joe Armijo, had intentionally set the fire.

"There's no goddamn way in hell," Riley said. They had taken the cage to 5000 together that morning. Never was there a moment when he wasn't aware of his partner's whereabouts the day of the fire.

"There's no way he could climb up to set the fire and come back down."

Riley got the message. *Sunshine and the Bureau want someone to blame for the fire.* Spontaneous combustion sounded feeble, and the bureaucrats and bigwigs knew it. The mine was hot, of course, but it wasn't hot enough to ignite timbers and gob. When some crazy woman came in with a ridiculous story, those who needed a scapegoat pounced.

Yet among those who seriously doubted the arson theory was mine superintendent Al Walkup.

"Some guys were bitter about the company, all right," he said when the subject came up. "But Armijo didn't seem that way. I know the man. He didn't do it."

Walkup thought racism might have made Armijo a target. *Mexicans are always getting blamed for everything around here,* he thought. *Even if it isn't their fault, they get blamed.*

It wasn't until Sunday that the fans on 3400 were finally shut off. Launhardt was nervous about the shutdown, even though it had been discussed since the first day of the fire. The cardinal rule of fighting a mine fire was to do nothing to a mine's ventilation system until you knew what would happen. With the circuitous drifts and leaky bulkheads scattered throughout the enormous Sunshine, no one could be sure about anything. But leaving the fans operating only served to blow smoky toxins to the 3100 and 3700 levels. When the fans ceased, so did the smoke. It was the only good news there'd been in almost a week. Now, Launhardt told himself, there was a chance to get to 10-Shaft and then on down to the men.

Throughout the day, May 7
Sunshine Mine Yard

Black wings circled the outtake channel over the mine. None who noticed the flock of crows wanted to say why the scavengers were there, what it was they smelled that brought them. Up at the mine's collar, softhearted miner Jim Gordon, who once drove ore trucks to Sunshine's processing plant or to rail cars in Silverton, transported bodies to Uncle Bunk's warehouse in Smelterville—the only place other than the nursing home where they could be hauled. With scarcely a word, men loaded the back of a Trojan Powder Company red-and-white truck. Gordon didn't think about his cargo, but only about the advice given by a boss as he turned the ignition.

"Best keep the windows rolled down and drive as fast as you can."

Elizabeth Fee, the high school Latin teacher, resumed her place on a bench near the portal. A lavender-and-yellow sign mocked her breaking heart, its message in a hippy-dippy floral graphic scheme, LOVE SAFETY. Mrs. Fee had chain-smoked cigarettes to the filter, her skin ashen, her cheeks concave. She had been through hell, and she knew her prayers weren't going to be answered.

Army reservist Lee Haynes approached his former teacher in what felt like the longest walk of his life. He started to break down even before he spoke. He had a promise to keep.

"Norman's gone, isn't he?" she asked, sparing him from saying the words. A cigarette dangled from her trembling hand. She held Haynes like a baby, and they cried. Richard Lynch, the boy who'd lived with Haynes to finish his senior year, was also among the confirmed dead.

And for the pessimists or those who'd just flat given up, the mine indeed seemed cursed. Those who trusted their faith were repeatedly taunted by a fire they couldn't see, one that shouldn't be burning in the first place. Frustration escalated when a surface fan whirled to a dead stop and more smoke streamed through the mine. Although the fan was quickly repaired, disheartened crews discovered that not only had the fire resurged in the 910 raise where Harvey Dionne first saw smoke boiling behind the bulkhead, but the 13,800-volt power line that snaked eastward from the Jewell along 3700 had been severed in the process. Once again, the ever-beleaguered 10-Shaft hoist was without power. The drive to get the capsule down the borehole to 4800 was stymied by the debris fall that came with the rekindled fire. A twelve-inch air line had been cut, causing air to bleed and dropping pressure from 80 to 30 psi—inadequate to run the crane the USBM men were using to lower the capsule. A larger compressor was sent for from another mine.

And way down on 4800, the water line, once a gusher, slowed to a trickle. Flory and Wilkinson's worries escalated. Given the heat they endured all day and night, water was keeping them alive. Even a single day without water might lead to serious dehydration and death.

LATE EVENING, MAY 7
Cataldo

THE LAST MOMENT SPENT WITH A LOVED ONE OFTEN TAKES on increased importance in a grief-burdened heart. In the shadow of Cataldo's historic Jesuit mission, Doug Dionne sat with his family and unspooled his last visit with Greg. The brothers hadn't seen each other in three years. With his Army service completed, Doug returned to the district the last week of April, just a week before the fire. His first glimpse of Greg was a messy-haired, stubble-flecked grown man with a slight scowl. Greg had just been rousted from his bed—and so had his wife, Jackie. Greg teasingly chewed out his older brother for the intrusion, in the half-serious, half-kidding manner brothers tend to relish. Now, as Doug Dionne grieved, an image from that reunion surfaced. Greg was holding his tiny daughter, Dusty, in hands as large as oven mitts. The fuzzy-headed baby swayed like meadow grass. Greg directed his gaze at the baby, not at his wife or his brother. How he loved his little girl. Instead of fading, Doug Dionne's final visit with his brother was flash-frozen.

Betty Dionne's thoughts were fixed on Greg, too. Like all women with sons trapped underground, she would rather die than outlive her boy. Men like Bob Follette, the father of missing Bill Follette, held another view. Certainly he loved his son. But Bill had become a man in the mine. From the first day he rode the cage, Bill was a miner first, a son second.

Never in a million years could a mother make such a distinction.

Forty-four

BOB LAUNHARDT DID WHATEVER WAS ASKED OF HIM. Monday morning he was in front of reporters to answer how a simple fire had become one of the worst mining disasters in American history. Sunshine lawyers had pushed him front and center to combat media reports questioning the mine's safety program. But Launhardt's argument—accurate as it was—did little to placate detractors. The company had done what was required by Idaho and federal law—and more than most metal mines. Some criticisms were specific and obviously sharpened by 20/20 hindsight. Hoist operators in metal mines did not work in sealed-in compartments with oxygen, as was required in coal mines. And once the hoistman was down, no one was getting out of the mine. Period. Launhardt also took more hits on the self-rescuers. Federal law required coal-mining operations to provide one unit per man. Metal mines had no such requirement. Words failed him when a reporter asked why so many had failed, when he said he'd inspected them personally.

And fire drills? Also not required. But the escape-route issue was a problem. The Silver Summit route was on 3100, a level to which most never ventured. There were signs posted, but as smoky as it was May 2, no one could read them.

Launhardt put the onus on the employees. They needed to be responsible for their personal safety.

"I don't believe it is fair to the industry to put the entire burden on management and nothing directed toward the individual," he said.

Such statements, not surprisingly, didn't win him new friends among the growing legion of widows and partnerless miners.

The USBM left Launhardt to twist in the wind. Some charged flat-out incompetence, claiming that Launhardt wasn't up to task for the safety job. The USBM also suggested that since Launhardt reported to the personnel director and not the mine superintendent or general manager, Sunshine didn't consider safety significant. That contention offended Marvin Chase, but it was also further proof that the feds didn't know what they were talking about. Chase knew having a safety man report to the operations boss was a terrible idea. There was too much pressure to push aside safety rules to make production.

If Launhardt was falling apart, no one outside of his family knew it. Besides a slight weight loss that drew his long face further downward, there were no outward signs of what was gnawing at him every minute of the day. He kept everything bottled up. It couldn't have been easy, but he was a man with greater reserves than he might have known before May 2. He faced the fire head-on to determine what had gone so wrong. *Why hadn't his safety program protected his men? Yes, mining was dangerous, but what else could have been done to spare more lives?*

Launhardt could have retreated from the mine and the district, but he didn't. He stayed right there. Digging in, in search of answers. Some might have thought it was about seeking atonement. But for Launhardt, the reality was that it was about being called into service.

And while Launhardt and Sunshine were getting hit hard, long-time employees like Ray Rudd were pissed off by reports heralding the USBM as paragons of heroism. It irked him how absent the names of Sunshine rescuers had been in news reports—and how the USBM's leaders never mentioned them. When the USBM took a series of photos to provide the media with an inside look at the rescue effort, it only served to increase tension. Sunshine employees were asked to step out of the frame, or were cropped out later. Sunshine miners were referred to only as "victims." No one bothered to say that dozens of Sunshine boys were doing all they could to get their buddies out of the mine. And they weren't giving up.

"Why do they make it seem like all our guys just ran away?" Rudd, his face red and hot, asked a friend. "We *don't* run."

The feds worsened relations by comparing the lethal conflagration at Big Creek to the *Titanic* disaster—a cautionary tale of man's greed and hubris. Instead of an opulent and gargantuan luxury liner, the target was a vast mine that surrendered future luxury in the form of silver ore. Sunshine Mine superintendent Walkup groused about the government's blatant grandstanding. Other locals were outraged by the shameful and casual disregard they were shown by a few of the outsiders from back East. Some had no business—no real interest—in being anywhere near Big Creek except to boast in graphic detail about their supposed conquests of the young wives of trapped miners. That wasn't even the worst of it. When Walkup went underground to check the progress of a ventilation repair, the USBM escorts who had seemed so cocksure topside turned out to be 'fraidy cats. *These guys are scared to death most of the time*, he thought.

MIDDAY, MAY 8
3700 Level

THE DOUBLE-DRUM AT 3700 10-SHAFT WAS WITHOUT POWER, and the only way to reach the lowest levels was once again stymied. Chase, Walkup, and Launhardt knew that as long as that was so, the men on the lower levels would never see daylight. Launhardt knew the toxicity of the air. It was hard for him to pretend he held any hope. One breath, he knew, and a man was dead. Not everyone was so fatalistic or pragmatic, however. Electrician George Clapp, the older brother of the young miner who'd warned Flory and Wilkinson of the fire, wanted to believe there were survivors so badly that he accepted no other alternative. The five-man crew with Clapp, now at the front of the line, and former boxer Johnny Lang at the rear, went down 3700 and under the 910 raise that the other crew had been shoring up and reinforcing with timber, rubber bladders, and polyurethane foam. As they passed under the fire zone, embers fell on the track, leaving a scattered trail of topaz glowing off into the darkness. Clapp and Johnny Austin, the lead man from Bunker Hill, separated from the other three to get to the hoist room. Their packs swung with their hurried steps, pulling the shoulder straps sharply into their skin. A mantra played repeatedly in Clapp's head: *Gotta flip that switch.*

Just past the raise, they hit a blast of fresh air before entering smoke once more. Condensation had collected on overhead pipes, and a scalding rain fell on their heads and bare arms. A little farther on, they stepped over bodies as they moved in on the hoist room and the electrical panel. A row of oil switches faced Clapp like five guys giving him the finger. He had to pull down the primary switch, and then reset it to reenergize the hoist. Adrenaline was a river through his veins. This had to be quick, and they had to get the hell out of there. Smoke, embers, and toxic gases filled the space. He pulled down. Too fast. The switch didn't trip. He did it again with the same result. His heart raced. He was pulling on the switch with force and haste, and though he knew better, he couldn't pull himself together to slow it down. He tripped the switch just fine, but resetting took some finesse, and in his nervousness, that was eluding him.

Johnny Austin kept barking at the electrician to get on with it.

"Hurry! *Hurry!*"

Clapp returned an irritated look. "I am!" he said, his remark muffled somewhat by his face mask. He stopped for a split second and slowly pulled the switch until it reset and latched.

"Got it," Clapp said, facing down the drift. Embers lit up the trackline by the raise. They were past the fire zone, and had to go back through it to get out. "Let's go," he said.

Clapp knew no man should find himself on the other side of a fire. *Always hit the fire from one side, and push it away.* Linked together again, Clapp, Austin, and the rest of the crew passed the 08 pipe shop. There, just days before, Greg Dionne had machined coupling threads and stacked finished pipe for delivery. Austin stopped. All around were bodies, bloated and black. Clapp didn't want to look. But Austin jabbed his finger in the air and started counting.

"Seven here," he said.

It was the first time Clapp had really seen any of the dead. He'd heard body counts and names, but communication between those who knew and those who might have wanted to know was almost nonexistent. The smoke was a veil. But even if it was clear, he couldn't have named those men scattered around. There was no story to tell about what might have happened, except that it had been quick.

"Hurry, let's go!"

It was Austin again, and the link line stretched taut as the five began to retreat. Clapp felt someone take hold of his line, and he nearly jumped off the track.

"What the—?" he said. "Who grabbed me?"

No one had. His tag line, the tail of the rope, had caught on the track. Clapp was spooked. He unhooked the line and off they went. This was no place to be. He looked up at the raise from where, only moments before, the smoke had boiled. For the first time he could see what the crews had been doing. Three-quarter-inch plywood had been hammered into place, and yards of burlap had been stapled along the edges where the panels met timbers. Foam had been sprayed.

After a second or two, Austin let out his familiar refrain: "We gotta get out of here." And the link line grew taut once more. A moment later they were on a motor heading back to the Jewell station. When they arrived, the phone was ringing.

"You guys okay?" a shifter topside asked.

"We're fine," Austin answered.

"Something tripped the main breaker up here."

A little while later, the answer came. The raise that the crew had passed under just minutes before had collapsed. Carbon monoxide levels dropped in the mine, and some incorrectly assumed that the cave-in had put out the fire. No one knew that the cave-in had also crushed the compressed-air line feeding 4800.

TIME UNKNOWN, MAY 8
4800 Level

"JESUS! IT AIN'T MOVING!" TOM WILKINSON SAID, LOOKING up, his mouth agape. The grimy paper towel on the fan line, the one that functioned like a ribbon on an air conditioner and confirmed that bad air was moving away from the Safety Zone, paused. It hung limp, no longer fluttering at a thirty-degree angle. Both men sat up and strained to make sure what they were seeing in the dim light was real and not another bad dream. Not only had it stopped, but the paper towel then did the unthinkable: it curled in their direction.

"We need to get the hell out of here."

"Get what you can and let's go."

Flory grabbed his boots and belt; Wilkinson followed. They had to move closer to the borehole and the good air. But moving from the crosscut meant leaving the motor and their best source of reliable light. Wilkinson's lamp still worked, but it wasn't going to last much longer. As the smoke crawled at them, the paper towel reversed itself again. Something was happening somewhere in the mine. Someone was doing something. It was possible that pressure had built up down on 5000 where the smoke had been fed down through the crosscut. The guys set their stuff down. They could stay. Dripping from the heat and the blast of panic, Flory pulled out his powder knife and a piece of wood and proceeded to whittle a toothpick. They both needed thinking time. It was getting close to do-or-die. The only two alive on 4800 sat on their bed boards in the dim light of the motor's headlamp, a single eye staring them down. Conversation had dwindled not only because they were weak from hunger, but because they'd exhausted every subject for discussion ten times over: girls, mining, and—a favorite—how their wives would spend their life insurance money. But other things were making the situation more desperate. Wilkinson wondered about Flory's mental state after his insistence that he could climb out of the mine, a half-crazed and determined effort that was wholly out of character. Flory had never acted with such stupid reck-lessness. The only thing left to eat was the Hunt's pudding, but for some reason neither could quite understand, food wasn't as appealing as it had been. They were shutting down, in both body and spirit. And they were probably going to die. They'd be found there, God knows when, and it would be obvious, by the little home they'd created in the Safety Zone, that they'd survived the initial poisoning of the mine's air.

ALL DAY, MAY 8
Sunshine Mine Yard

SUNSHINE'S MINE YARD WAS SWARMING WITH GOOD INTEN-
tions and dismal failures. The capsules from the AEC were deemed
too small to ferry back survivors, and the smaller of Sunshine's own
capsules was put on a flatcar and brought from the topside machine
shop down the Jewell to 3700. Once in the borehole, it took more than
half a day to get the walls barred down. Some wondered if the air
pressure would be enough to haul the men up and down. It was asking a lot of a hoist designed to lift small machines, supplies, and heavy
tools. And then there was the cable from which the capsule would be
suspended. At a half inch thick, was it really strong enough?

But there was something worse. It was the sudden and unexpected
rekindling of the original fire that had caused the cave-in. Crews
working their way down 3700 were forced to turn back; increased
heat and skyrocketing carbon monoxide readings made it too dangerous there. The men working that section reported that the heat
was so brutal that their packs became too hot to touch. All were
ordered out.

Despite the setback, Marvin Chase still held hope they could get
the hoist going.

"I can't say I am as optimistic as I was before," he told the press.
He also quietly amended the figures the papers had been reporting
since the first day. There were ninety-three men trapped, not eighty-
two, which meant with thirty-five known dead, fifty-eight, not forty-
seven, were missing.

Jerry McGinn, the reporter who doubted Sunshine's figures,
heard a voice call out across the yard. "That guy's the reporter!"

McGinn had been identified, and in an instant the mine yard
turned into the angry villagers scene from an old horror movie.
The faces of those he'd been writing about surrounded him—

union men, wives, and shifters. All were pissed off. He'd betrayed them all. One guy kicked him hard where it counted. McGinn went down and doubled up. His red face matched his hair.

One of the reservists grabbed him by the shoulders. "Is that good enough for you?"

Another shouted, "You won't make it out of town alive!"

McGinn was escorted from the yard by a guardsman and some miners, knowing who'd probably fingered him. *Damn AP,* he thought.

Charlie Clapp's brother, Dennis—the young miner who'd alerted Flory and Wilkinson—completed a shift on body detail and went straight home. He'd bagged Ace Riley's partner, Joe Armijo—also the first guy with whom Clapp had mined. He'd recognized Armijo by his diggers and his boots—not his face, which was cracked and bloated. He and another miner spread a body bag over the body, flipped it over, and struggled to zip it up. Fingers slipped and stumbled, and the zipper pull snagged. Clapp almost vomited. When he got home, he knocked back some whiskey. The hideous odor of the day rooted itself in his nose and throat, and only booze seemed to lessen it. The trunk of a body-detail buddy's prized Chevelle was another matter. Clapp had made the mistake of stashing his stinking diggers there. Despite hours of crazed scrubbing, the stench had an astonishingly enduring staying power. *Never again,* he thought.

ALL DAY, MAY 8
Osburn

THE WORLD WAS PAYING ATTENTION. PAUL ROBINSON'S DESK at KWAL was covered in a two-inch-deep shower of confetti from heaven. Most of the letters sent to the station had a dollar or two tucked inside, along with notes wishing the best for "the children of the miners of the Kellogg disaster." Robinson was flabbergasted by the response from the Salt Lake City radio station. The missives were from all parts of the country. The Long Valley Forkettes, a 4-H club in McCall, Idaho, planned a fund-raiser; the children and faculty of Highlands Elementary School in Boise collected $376.73. Also from Boise came $90 from the French and Spanish classes at West Junior High. A lawyer from Libby, Montana, sent $25; a Spokane florist sent $100; the ladies' auxiliary of a transit union in Seattle collected almost $30. A widow from Meadow Vista, California, whose son-in-law had just died and left a ten-year-old girl fatherless, cleaned out the man's change box and sent it to KWAL. With an official relief account open and growing at the bank in Wallace, JCPenney astounded Robinson with generosity that none could have imagined—a check for $10,000.

Forty-five

Topside, a crew member caught up with Bob Follette and confirmed that his son, Bill, had been found among some barrels and benches near 10-Shaft on 3100. The basketball player's frame was contorted in a crouching position as if he had been fighting for fresh air along the drift floor. His partner, Louis Goos, was just a few yards away. They had come up in the cage seconds after partners Bob Follette and Howard Markve jumped onto the motor for the Jewell and fresh air.

Maybe he was there, but in the smoke I couldn't see him? Follette asked himself.

Bob Launhardt stayed away from the body detail, but no one had to tell him how gruesome it was. He'd heard stories of coal-dust explosions where bodies had sat for days, and had bloated like dead cattle on a sun-soaked pasture. He'd heard, too, how miners used

343

their picks to poke holes in a body before stepping on it with their boots to deflate the corpse like an air mattress.

Outside Launhardt's safety office window, light rain had fallen. The chill it brought made the masses of people in the yard constrict as a defense against the shivers. It was a devastating scene.

When would it end? How would it be resolved?

Launhardt scribbled a short note for personnel director Jim Farris.

"Mr. Chase says we should contact Mrs. Beehner and tell her it is OK with us if she wants to interview with *Life* magazine."

He hesitated a moment and added a postscript: "I will meet with her and tell her exactly what happened to Don if she wants this info."

The stress of the week had been taking its toll, day by day, hour by hour. It was so subtle that someone might have missed it. But Bob Launhardt was so pressed, so crisp, when he first faced the TV cameras. His words, even in the shocking hours just following Beehner's death, were sharp and clear. He was the picture of a safety man in whom any miner could entrust his life. A man in charge. But as the days of the tragedy wore on, the tall, lanky man seemed to shrink as though he were fading away, just a little at a time, until he'd just blow away.

EVENING, MAY 8

4800 Level

FLORY AND WILKINSON HAD BEAT ON PIPES, CALLED FOR HELP until they were hoarse, and braided a mile of blasting wire. Neither could understand what would keep the rescue crew from coming after them. Every day since they were trapped, they'd made an attempt to get to the station, but the smoke had been too caustic. Nothing was going to stop them Monday afternoon. To wait any longer was to concede right then and there that they would die. They were without food. Digestive juices in search of something to dissolve were consuming their insides. The pain rolled and passed in waves of agony. *This is what it feels like to starve to death.* Making it worse was that there was no end in sight. It seemed that no one was coming for them. They doused their shirts with water and took off. The smoke was a whisper by then, but they could still taste its acrid tang. Passing the men on the tracks was always the worst of their hurried walk. They had swollen like balloons. Shirt buttons had popped. Wilkinson doubted that their identities could be matched with photographs anymore. They looked nothing like they had in life. Stepping past them was like maneuvering through the most difficult obstacle course.

Lights flooded the station. It was empty, but for one man. He was slumped by the phone, still clutching the receiver in his hand. His face had inflated into a monster's. Damp T-shirts still covering their mouths and noses, Flory and Wilkinson exchanged horrified looks and kept away from the man. Wilkinson went for the cord and belled for the cage, using the emergency nine-bell signal. They craned their necks and looked up the shaft and hollered into the darkness.

"Hey! We're down here!"

But it was quiet.

Flory fastened his eyes on the man with the phone. The closer he got to the dead man, the sicker he became. The man's skin had split, and coagulated body fluids were oozing out. Flory grabbed the cord and pulled on it to extricate the receiver from the dead man's grip. A gooey film covered the receiver. In his hunger, it reminded Flory of tapioca pudding.

He took the T-shirt from his face. "Hey!" he called out again. "We're down on forty-eight!"

The line was dead and without static. Flory balled up his fist and banged on the box. Neither man knew about the cave-in that had crippled the communications link to their level.

They were captives, and the futility of their situation was making Flory crazy.

"I'm going to climb up the shaft," he said. "I'm gonna get the hell out of here."

It was Wilkinson's turn to cool down his partner.

"You are *not*," he said, his words a command. "You'll never make it. You're going to stay here. We're going to get out of this."

Though mentally foggy from hunger and full of fear, Flory immediately retreated from the irrational idea of a thousand-foot climb through darkness.

"It's been too long since we had a good meal," he said. "We'd never make it. It would be a long climb without a good meal. I think the Lord wants us to stay right here and wait until somebody comes."

Ron Flory was sure he and his buddy were close to the end. Certainly they had the will to survive and the drive to make it out of the goddamn mine, but they had no food, water was in short supply, and the hours were piling seamlessly into days. Flory promised God he'd go to church every Sunday if he ever got a second chance.

Forty-six

Around 3:00 a.m. on Tuesday, a four-man USBM crew rode the capsule to 4800, laying phone lines as they descended into the dark. They traveled in pairs, but one man had to remain in the capsule, talking to the hoistman on 3700 so he'd be able to navigate through the rough channel. The first man out of the capsule pointed out footprints in the muck. There was no way of telling when they had been made, but their proximity to the telephone was either curious or coincidental. When the four had assembled at the borehole, they worked their way west into the dead-end drift. The air was 92 degrees and breathable without apparatuses. Methodically moving toward the face of the drift, some three hundred feet away, the crew saw evidence that men had been working there on May 2. A pair of jackleg drills rested in the muck. The diffuse beams of their cap lamps sprayed light over the rock face, revealing fuses draped

347

from drilled holes. No miner would ever leave live charges if he had thought for one minute he wouldn't be back. No one abandons explosives for some other guy to find with the end of his drill. The crew went east, looking for any signs of life. But fifteen hundred feet down the drift, their lights began to fade.

"Hello, *hello* . . . anybody there?"

They stopped to listen, but there was only silence. Sunshine men were dead at the station or bulkheaded in someplace where nothing could be heard. Disappointed, the rescue team returned to the surface. Another crew would take over.

Ron Flory and Tom Wilkinson had been a thousand feet from rescue, but nobody knew it.

DAWN, MAY 9

Bunker Hill Warehouse, Smelterville

LAMP NUMBERS FIRST, THEN CLOTHING, SCARS, AND TATTOOS were the first indicators of who was who as the identification crew sifted through the bodies in the Smelterville warehouse. Most miners wore the same jeans, hats, shirts—or no shirt at all—every day of the workweek. They'd hose the muck off at the station, go upstairs, and strip down and hang everything in the dry until the next shift. Most brought diggers home once a week for washing, but some never did. The men scanning the remains worked with a rhythm that, once going, fueled them into the long hours of the night. Victims who had been sealed in body bags for a longer period had looser skin. It was as though they'd been in a crockpot all day, and the heat of the mine and the fluids of their bodies had softened tissue to fall-from-the-bone goo, making it easier for examiners to slide off fingertips for inking and printing. The bodies that had remained in the mine the longest, those at the deeper levels, however, were more difficult. Their skin had hardened; patches seemed plasticlike, or leathery. In those cases it was impossible to pull off fingertips. FBI men used a pair of steel cutters and snipped through the bone, then the digits were daubed in ink and pressed on paper.

Although their faces were gone, there were clues to pinpoint identity. In the most gruesome task on a hideous list, dentures were pulled from disfigured mouths. Some men had personalized their hardhats with automotive or powder supplier stickers. One had stenciled green racing stripes on his hat. Most smoked, so a brand of cigarettes—a pack tucked into an inner-tube hatband—was also a clue. One miner carried his eyeglasses to and from the station that way. Tool belts also held potential. Some guys had special wrenches or expensive Snap-On tools.

When a bag holding one of the larger dead men was unzipped, a flare of yellow contrasted sharply against the black morass of decomposing remains. A closer look revealed that coils of yellow blasting wire had been used to fasten the victim's overall shoulder straps.

Seeing that, Bill Steele knew instantly who it was.

"This is Custer Keough," he said. "He's worn his overalls like that for years. No doubt. It's him."

An FBI agent stripped the skin from the fifty-nine-year-old miner's fingers. Steele didn't think it was necessary. Only Keough had that yellow wire. Once a name was paired with a body, it was turned over to the FBI for fingerprint confirmation. Fingerprint records, thankfully, were not hard to come by. Many of the dead had been printed in the military; other comparisons came courtesy of arrest records from the Shoshone County Sheriff.

Identifying Joe Armijo was also relatively easy. He was a tall man, just under six feet, with a lean build and shiny black hair. In addition to the Navy tattoos on his chest and both biceps, Armijo had a heavy scar that spilled down his right shoulder, the remnant of an accident at Bunker Hill. A BM-1447 self-rescuer had been tucked inside his body bag. Armijo was one of the thirty-one who made it to the 10-Shaft station on 3100, only to die.

When identity still remained in doubt, bodies were weighed and measured and set aside as John Does. Five men were designated as such—one of whom would be later identified by a wedding band.

Something else registered as peculiar. Four of the five John Does came from the same pocket. All the men there had removed their lamp belts. Why had those particular men taken them off? The FBI didn't know, but Steele did. Belts were heavy, loaded with battery packs and ten-inch pipe wrenches. Whenever a man ate lunch or waited at the station, he routinely dropped his belt. The men on that level had been waiting for the cage.

Throughout the night, fluorescent tubes buzzed like a chorus of wasps and cast a shadowless light. When it came time for a break, Bill Steele found a place to eat a TV dinner, though after a moment it dawned on him that he was sitting on a stack of body-bagged remains. Others were doing the same thing. If someone had told Steele he could ever get so used to the unthinkable that he'd do something like that, he'd have said they were crazy. Somewhere between working on the handful of bodies at the funeral home in Kellogg, and the ever-growing heap in Smelterville, Steele became immune to the horror.

Forty-seven

"TOM, DAMN, I JUST SAW A LIGHT OUT THERE," RON FLORY said, looking in the direction of the borehole.

Wilkinson thought the worst. *Now Ron's lost it for sure.* It made absolutely no sense that anything or anyone would come from *that* direction. Everything came from 10-Shaft.

Wilkinson remained calm. "You're seeing things. There's no light."

"Yeah, there is."

"No, there isn't."

The two argued a little, and Flory put on his boots and turned off the motor light. A black shadow descended over everything.

And a wash of light spread over the drift.

Wilkinson sat up. There *was* a light reflecting over the water line.

Flory hit the water line with his wrench, hammering out as much noise as he could. Wilkinson went for the motor and flashed the light.

351

Flory kept pounding, a steady hammering that said, *We're alive back here.* Wilkinson yelled for help.

Then a beam moved in their direction.

"Stay right where you are," a man's voice called out. "We're coming."

It was more than a week after they'd been trapped. Outside at the portal, news swept through the crowd and hope poured over everyone like rain.

Ron Flory, twenty-eight, and Tom Wilkinson, twenty-nine, had been found. It was not delirium, but reality. They had dreamed about it and discussed it over and over since the smoke stalked their crew and left them alone. The two survivors of 4800 had no idea how many others had died. In their time underground, they assumed their level had been the one in trouble. They'd seen the other cages whiz past the station on May 2.

"How many of you?"

"Two. Just two."

Becker and Kanack came into the Safety Zone, where they met a pair of miners as grungy and bewhiskered as men could be. Although their features were hollowed by weight loss, they were in surprisingly good physical condition. Their mood was even more striking. Never in all their lives had the rescuers seen such unabashed joy. Even Wilkinson, who kept his emotions more private, couldn't help but let it show. *They'd been saved.* Flory's eyes flooded. They were going home.

Wilkinson asked for a smoke. A second later, when he took a drag, he nearly fell to the floor. *Man, that was strong.* Flory had a cigarette in his mouth, too. Their promises about quitting after they got out of the mine had been abandoned in two seconds. They'd pledged to go to church, and to be better husbands and fathers. Only time would tell on those promises.

Both wanted to know how severe the fire had been, and why rescue had taken so long. Becker indicated the death toll had been substantial, but there were no definitive numbers.

"You're the only two we've found so far," he said, adding that they were hopeful that the guys on the lowest levels would be all right. They just hadn't made it down there yet.

Flory's head spun, and adrenaline pumped. Wilkinson also felt the surge of energy and emotion. They picked up their dinner buckets and some of the braided blasting wire and walked toward the borehole where the capsule would take them to the surface. Flory would go first, then Wilkinson. They were told the borehole was dangerously narrow and their ascent would be slow. The capsule would take them to 3700, to the spot where Kenny Wilbur had removed the lagging cover that allowed fresh airflow to 4800 and created the Safety Zone.

On the surface, the public address system that until then had only brought news of food and cigarette distribution gave hope that lifted hearts to the sky: *We have found two men alive and in good health on the 4800 level.*

7:45 P.M., MAY 9
Sunshine Bridge

MYRNA FLORY WALKED FROM RON'S DARK BLUE CHARGER to the bridge over Big Creek. Her bell-bottoms were loose at the waist, her hands numb from gripping things so tightly. She was tired, sick, and afraid that God might actually renege and let her down. She wondered if she'd have to raise Tiger on her own, after all. She heard other women were planning funerals and futures. A group of network TV people loped across the yard, light stands and cameras with power cords dragging like maypole ribbons. *They're after another story.* The memory of the reporter who had told her that her husband was dead was still fresh. But they didn't come for her. They backed off.

A preacher touched her shoulder. It was 7:40 p.m.

"Mrs. Flory, your husband's alive. Come with me."

Is this a dream? Myrna felt the emotion of the week close in on her, and started to cry. She had a bad cold and a throat raw from coughing. She was sicker than she'd been in a long time, but she was overjoyed. A few more men were around her, and before she really knew what was happening, she was in a small room adjacent to the payroll office.

Frances Wilkinson was already there, having stayed most of the week in her sister's camper, crumpled on a metal folding chair. She, too, had been crying.

"They found Tom, too," she said. "They're both alive." She and Myrna held each other and sobbed.

Mine officials backed off to leave the women alone in the most joyous moment since the fire broke out.

Outside, the pack moved closer to the Jewell, compressed by their excitement and the need to be at the front of the group. And they were shivering. The early-evening air brought a bite from the mountainside.

"Two so far!"

AFTER 7:00 P.M., MAY 9
3700 Level

WHILE RON FLORY WAITED FOR HIS PARTNER ON 3700, SOMEone handed him a can of Gatorade. He poured it down his throat, and a USBM photographer recorded the moment. As a Wallace doctor checked his pulse, Flory was lost in the thoughts of a hardworking man. He only wanted two things: for Tom Wilkinson to get up the borehole, and to get out of Sunshine. While it was true his wife and boy had been on his mind, there was nothing more important than breathing the fresh air of a world not shut in darkness.

Flory asked for a cigarette and messed with his lighter. It hadn't worked since he'd been trapped. A miner struck a match. He mentioned that he was going to quit smoking.

"How you holding up?" the doctor asked.

"Oh, I feel great," Flory said, though the ordeal's toll on his body and mind was obvious.

"Don't keel over, here," the doctor said. "You'll embarrass the whole goddamn outfit."

The other guys laughed. This was the moment all of the men had dreamed about as they'd battled day upon day of disappointment and the unbelievably cruel fire.

"Did it seem like seven days down there? Longer or shorter?" a Sunshine rescue man asked.

Flory didn't have to think. "It seemed like seven years," he said.

When he arrived to take his place with his buddy, Wilkinson had considerably less patience, and no taped voice recording was made. Someone offered him a coat, and he took it for the walk out into cool, fresh air. But when the doctor attempted to take his pulse, Wilkinson jerked his arm away.

What the hell's he doing? Wilkinson thought. *Let's get out of here.*

Two stretchers were set to the side of the station. Wilkinson refused to have anything to do with them.

"We walked in," he said. "We're going to walk out."

The survivors were told their wives would be waiting for them outside the portal, as well as a couple of hundred well-wishers, along with television cameras and correspondents from the news magazines and major East Coast dailies.

"Before we go out there, you want us to run them off?" one of the rescue men asked.

Neither did. They were focused on getting outside. No delays. *Just get going.*

And up the Jewell Shaft and out of the portal, they walked to the most blinding lights they'd ever seen. A Sunshine shift boss followed behind in case either slumped over. Ron Flory had felt okay before the light, noise, and chilly air from the outside blasted at him with almost overwhelming force. There were so many people there, cheering and clapping, his legs went weak. He fought hard to keep from hitting the ground.

"Thank God," he said, stepping into air moved by wind, not by a compressor. He looked astonishingly fit, his blue T-shirt stretched over a leaner frame. His beard, no longer neatly trimmed, was the only hint that he'd been away for more than a week. A cap lamp borrowed from another miner and affixed to a dirty yellow hardhat sent a beam into the crowd of three hundred. Hand after hand reached out to greet him. Disoriented by the commotion, he walked right past Myrna. She lunged for his arm. He turned and hugged her so hard the breath was squeezed out of her. For the first time in more than a week, his muscles relaxed and he just let go and cried.

Right behind Flory, Sonny Becker held on to Wilkinson's arm, steadying him for the walk out. Wilkinson, squinting back the glare of the movie lights, looked for Frances's coat to pick her out of the crowd. He didn't see her. In truth, he couldn't see much at all. He needed his glasses. Also, he didn't know that Frances had borrowed her sister's navy peacoat. Not a very big man to begin with, Wilkinson looked small standing next to Flory. In many ways he had been the stronger of the two underground, but he appeared frail in the light of the TV cameras. The crowd parted to let Frances through, and she held her husband and sobbed. A smile broke out on his heavily whiskered face. He thought that he and his buddy were just going to get into their cars and go home. He had no clue they'd need to go to the hospital. Wilkinson had no idea how extraordinary his survival had been.

The cheers were deafening, and suddenly the world was big again. As the survivors and their wives climbed into the front seats of the ambulances, a pastor near the portal led the families in a hymn, "Praise God from Whom All Blessings Flow."

A rabid caravan of reporters followed Shoshone County Sheriff cruisers and the two ambulances down the gulch to the highway, and on to Kellogg and West Shoshone Hospital. Driver, wife, and survivor all rode in the front seat, talking on the radio to the other ambulance. The survivors talked about food and drink and the crowd outside the portal, but mostly about food. Ron Flory wanted a steak and a cold beer, and that sounded damn good to Wilkinson, too. As Myrna gripped him, her big bear of a husband cried.

Robert Flory drove his mother and sister, riding the accelerator with such a heavy foot that it passed through his mind that he was going to crash. If others at the mine were buoyed by the discovery of his older brother and partner, Robert's feelings were somewhat dark and mixed. He had been told by the rescue crew that there were no others alive on 4800, and probably none in the deeper levels. There were others who were desperately needed by their families. Many others. He loved his brother, but Myrna, young as she was, was a fighter. She would have been able to get by. He wondered about others with households full of children and no man to bring home a paycheck.

Myrna's sister, Garnita, stood at the hospital entrance crying as the ambulances pulled up. Her brother-in-law was a big man, but he'd shrunk down to mortal size. Flory had dropped nearly twenty pounds and Wilkinson had lost around fifteen. But with a wool blanket draped over his shoulders, Flory looked especially small. Garnita's concern shifted to Myrna. She held on to her husband and they walked in lockstep toward the door. Myrna had also withered over the week, existing on nothing but coffee and cigarettes.

Which one is thinner? she asked herself.

A reporter called out a question about the survivors' need for treatment and rest.

"They aren't about to lie on a cot," an ambulance driver with a broad smile shot back. "I'll tell you that. No cots for these boys."

Flory wasted no time announcing that his days underground were over.

"I won't be a miner again," he said, "if I have anything to say about it."

Myrna nodded. "No, no way."

Wilkinson, however, was less committal. "I don't know," he said, "I couldn't say. I might go back in the mines. If I find something else, I might go to it."

Frances Wilkinson let her tears go. "If he wants to go back, he can," she said. Inside her purse she carried a piece of the braided blasting wire. She'd make it into a key chain and would keep it with her forever—as if she needed anything to remind her of what happened at Sunshine.

MAY 9

Pinehurst

MEANWHILE, THINGS WERE QUIET AT THE FIRKINS PLACE IN Pinehurst. Lou Ella dressed to go to the mine. Days of hope and anguish had melted her small frame; the Jaycee's wife had lost at least fifteen pounds. Nerves had bunched up her intestines like a clenched fist. The children urged their mother to eat, but even with the renewed hope that came with finding Flory and Wilkinson, food stayed on her plate, congealing. She still had no idea that Don Firkins had fallen on the concrete floor of the hoist room, feverishly trying to activate his BM-1447. No one told her how Don's life had sputtered from his body as Byron Schulz looked on, frightened out of his mind and unable to do anything. In the end, Lou Ella didn't make it to Big Creek that day. She didn't have to. A brother-in-law gave her the news that Don's body had been identified. Tears, always at the edge of her eyelids, fell down her hollowed cheeks, and her voice was a soundless scream. The sky had finally fallen.

Forty-eight

MORNING, MAY 10
Coeur d'Alene Mining District

WEDNESDAY'S MORNING NEWS DEFINED THE TIMES. AN IRA sniper had killed a British soldier; the prosecution was nearing the end of its case against radical activist Angela Davis; and a U.S. blockade of North Vietnamese ports had begun. But amid all of that, there was good news from northern Idaho. The *Los Angeles Times* trumpeted it with two-inch letters on the front page: TWO FOUND ALIVE IN BURNING MINE. Nearly every paper in the country ran the story on page one.

In a shared room at West Shoshone Hospital, it was a nonstop celebration. Flory and Wilkinson started their day with New York strip steaks and interviews from media outlets across the globe. The men had shaved and their wives had freshened up. Myrna Flory had put on a short skirt, and Frances Wilkinson had curled the ends of her hair in a flip. Idaho senator Frank Church sent his best wishes by

Western Union: REJOICE WITH ALL IDAHOANS AND THE NATION AT NEWS OF YOUR SAFE RECOVERY FROM SUNSHINE MINE, AND PRAY THAT OTHERS WILL FOLLOW YOU TO SAFETY. Idaho governor Cecil Andrus arrived with a six-pack of Lucky Lager, and photographers snapped images that wire services dispatched across the country. The nurses wouldn't let the guys smoke in their room, but when Andrus showed up, all rules went out the window. It was the best beer Wilkinson had ever tasted. The governor promised that if they didn't want to go back into mining, the state would retrain them for new jobs. He'd personally see to it.

Flory credited his survival to a guardian angel. "I'm not a praying man," he told a reporter, "but I prayed a lot down there."

Later that day the survivors were discharged, and the world beat a path to their doors. The *London Express* phoned Flory. So did the *National Enquirer*. A life insurance company offered sales positions within hours of their exodus from 4800: "Relating your experience to our customers would be worth thousands of dollars to you in sales." A flurry of mail crammed their mailboxes. Many praised God for sparing their lives: "I'm sure you and your families have thanked the Lord many times for your narrow escape, but I'm wondering if you have asked the dear Lord for what purpose he spared you two...." Others, from across America, from England, and from South Africa, shared the joy: "Our oldest daughter was in her room in the basement doing homework when she came running up the stairs and said she had just heard on the radio that two survivors had been found. I don't mind telling you, Tom, that there was not a dry eye in this house as we thanked God for your safety...."

But throughout the mining district the joy was tempered with grief, blame, and bitterness. At the Big Creek Store, conspiracy theorists insisted Flory and Wilkinson hadn't been survivors at all, but that the company had planted them on 4800 as a public relations ploy.

"How else could they have survived and the others die?"

"Yeah, and did you see that they didn't look as bedraggled as they should have?"

In disasters like the Sunshine fire, truth frequently yields to emotion. Sour grapes taste sweet when pain becomes impossible to bear. Garnita Keene put up with nasty remarks from women who thought their husbands and boyfriends should have been the ones to survive. *Flory was a drug addict and Wilkinson was a drunkard. They were lazy sons of bitches who didn't know a whiz-bang from their own assholes.* She knew the bitterness came from sudden, unbearable grief and an overwhelming sense of unfairness, so she said nothing.

Yeah, both boys drank their share, she thought to herself. *But so did everyone else. And drug addict? I doubt Ron ever used drugs in his entire life. He's too damn cheap. For God's sake, Myrna went to the Laundromat because Ron didn't want to open his wallet to buy a washer and dryer.*

"Why did God save them and not the others?" one woman asked.

"I don't have the answers," Myrna's sister said. "Only God knows."

Among those who questioned God's choice was Don Beehner's widow, Wava. Others had told her that neither of the survivors was any good; they were druggies or lazy or any number of things her husband had never been. She'd heard they were sleeping behind an air door. *They weren't even working like the rest of the men.* For a time, bitterness supplanted the sadness she felt for her own loss.

"It is unfair," she told her pastor. "What right do they have to live when so many good guys died?"

"Wava, it *is* fair," he said. "Don was ready to meet God. He gave his life for another man. These men have been given a second chance. If they don't do something with it, they'll be condemned to hell."

"I don't like them," Wava said. "If not Don, then why not another man? There were so many good men that could have done so much."

"I don't want you to hate them," he said. "It's okay not to like them, but don't hate them."

She promised to try.

Meanwhile, Garnita didn't tell Myrna, but sometimes she believed it would have been better if Ron and Tom had died. She knew Ron was having nightmares, and she expected that it hadn't been easy for Tom, either. Everybody wants to live, but living after something so terrible, after something that took so many others... what a dreadful gift it was. And each camera flash or congratulations card only served to remind Flory and Wilkinson of their good fortune and the immeasurable grief that had overtaken the mining district. Although the pair had been alone together for eight days, they wanted to get away from the hordes of people, the media, the letters, and the funerals. They needed to get away from the whole damn thing. They planned a camping trip.

MORNING, MAY 10
4800 Level

THE SKIN COVERING THE BLACKENED TORSOS OF THE DEAD was rigid, like a leather glove that had been soaked in water, then kiln-dried. Nothing remained to suggest their former humanness other than the oddity of their tongues, protruding from mouths that looked like open knotholes. Among the dead on 4800, Johnny Lang came across his opposite shift partner, Davy Mullin. Mullin was slumped near the phone. Only a distinctive collection of blasting company stickers on his hardhat gave away his identity. Of the six others, Lang couldn't determine which one was Gordy Whatcott, his other partner; all were too far gone. Through the creepy smoke veil, he ventured toward the half-drilled face on the stope where they'd last worked. Mullin or Whatcott had halted in the midst of drilling— just flat-out stopped. *They expected to be right back,* Lang thought. Everything was set up to grind that rock for blasting at shift's end.

By late Wednesday all the bodies on 4800 had been accounted for, and Lang went home, where he answered a call from partner Gordy Whatcott's wife, Wilmyra.

"Did you hear anything?"

"Why hasn't the mine called you?" Lang was thunderstruck, then furious.

"I know that Flory and Wilkinson got out. Somebody told me that the other men they found could have been some engineers that were dead down there. Gordy and Davy could be back in their stope waiting for help."

Her words were strung together with a thin reed of hope.

Lang confronted Al Walkup at the mine.

"What's the deal here? How come you haven't told them women what's happened to their men? Giving them hope when there really isn't any—it ain't right."

"We can't tell them until it's official," Walkup said.

The young boxer from Texas could barely rein himself in. "Jesus! Flory and Wilkinson were down there. They knew all them guys. And they went back to the station and they knew that nobody was alive!"

"We can't tell anyone until it's official."

"It's a damn fact! I'm telling Gordy's wife."

Lang drove right over to the Whatcotts' place in Kellogg and waited on the steps, rehearsing what he'd say, how he'd tell her. He was good with words, but he couldn't find any that would provide both truth and comfort.

Wilmyra Whatcott came to the door, her face pale, her skin tissue-thin.

"He's not coming home," Lang said. When his own tears fell, he turned away.

Forty-nine

A SUMP PUMP ON 5000 HAD FAILED AND WATER HAD CAS-caded over the station and pooled in the drift before running like a river to God knew where. There were two bodies found on the level. Bunker Hill rescue man Harry Cougher went to the first man, facedown on a mass of pipes on the station. He slipped open a body bag and began to roll the swollen corpse into the vinyl envelope. He'd shifted the corpse into the bag and started to zip it shut when he saw the man's glove floating in three inches of black water. Procedure required that all personal effects be packed in with the body with which it belonged. Cougher reached down and grasped the glove. It wasn't a glove. The man's skin had sloughed off into a single piece.

"Oh my God," Cougher said through his mask. He picked up the skin glove and put it into the bag.

364

A look at each of the dead brought only silence and memories. Many had been boys on the district's Little League team; they had skipped school together, and conspired to get into Delores Arnold's hook house. Some were rivals, but they had grown up together. Lifting a buddy who was nearly a brother with an aluminum snow shovel was probably the toughest thing a man could ever do. The recovery team worked in pairs or in trios, scooping up bodies while another man slid a bag underneath. Sometimes it took up to four men to do it. Miners, of course, came in all sizes.

Corpses were arranged several deep and the cage was belled up, a last ride to daylight at the collar. A thousand feet of steel cable separated the hoistmen from their reeking cargo, but ferrying the bodies still unnerved the men at the controls. They could feel that the weight was lifeless.

The 5200 level was the last chance for survivors, and everyone working underground knew it. The level had access to 10-Shaft, and with good air coming in on 4800 from the borehole, it seemed possible that someone could survive down there. But all hope died at 7:06 p.m. All there were dead, though it appeared they'd survived longer than those on the upper levels. Using brattice cloth, a kind of fire-retardant burlap, they had time to start building a bulkhead on the north tail drift off the station. Three bodies were discovered in a cluster by a motor. One man had been running the motor, and the other two had been passengers. The driver was wedged between the motor and the ribs. Two additional victims were found on the station side of the attempted seal, but the rest had melted into a big, hideously foul pile of cadavers, BM-1447s scattered like seashells on a muddy beach. All but one—the fellow nearest to an open air line—were gruesomely decomposed. Had he lived longer than the others? Long enough to see everyone else die? Some also posited that the toxic cloud had hastened decomposition, and since the last man standing on 5200 was showered by clean compressed air, he had stayed better preserved. Among those victims were the Delbridges, a father-and-son pair; Roger Findley's brother, Lyle; and Garnita Keene's boyfriend, Billy Allen. Twenty-one had died on 5200.

Al Walkup notified topside that all the men were accounted for and it was over. The hope for another miracle had evaporated into the cold, damp mountain air.

LATE AFTERNOON, MAY 10
Sunshine Mine Yard

RAIN FELL IN SHEETS, SENDING MUDDY RIVULETS DOWN THE banks of Big Creek and turning its clear waters to creamed coffee. Susan Markve, whose father, Louis Goos, was never coming home, told her family that God was crying. The remaining rescue men moved about in yellow slickers. Water filled the footprints of the families who had stood vigil for more than a week. With the discovery of each clutch of bodies, the families left the water-soaked tent and went home. Only a handful waited until the end. The pastor of a small congregation formed a circle of some of the remaining, stuck in Purgatory and still hoping. Lee Haynes held the hand of the wife of a man who'd served in his unit in the reserves and they repeated the Lord's Prayer. Marvin Chase almost melted into the muddy ground. He was shaky, and could barely make eye contact. Not for shame, but because seeing hope fade to despair had become too difficult to take in. He told the waiting family members that the rescue crews had made it to 4400 and 5200. There they'd found seventeen more bodies, but no survivors. The only consolation was that the tragedy had occurred swiftly, even down on the lower levels. On 4400, seven bodies had been found. Three were found clustered around an oxygen cylinder that they'd apparently used to keep alive. Others had likely already succumbed. They were around a lunch table, buckets open and sandwiches out.

"Please go home," mine manager Chase told those who'd waited until the very end. He promised to notify family members when there was more news.

A woman found her voice and let out a guttural scream.

"They lied to us! They said they were pumping air into the mine, and they weren't."

A chilly wind blew across the portal. The site had gone from a place of support and shared misery to a ghost town. Joanne Reichert stood on the little bridge and surveyed the yard. The air was icy. Empty chairs and garbage littered the yard like the leavings of an outdoor concert. Chase repeated that there weren't any more survivors. Her legs buckled.

"It's all over," Chase said firmly. "Go home."

The rage of the long wait boiled over.

"You sons of bitches!" she screamed. "You fucking sons of bitches!"

The fury of the outburst jolted her sister. "Joanne!"

"Please go home, ma'am," Chase said.

Her hysteria was a volcano. Someone tugged at her and she started to move back to the car.

It's all over and no one saved Jack. The fucking mine killed him. Killed them all.

"Murderer!" a woman yelled as Marvin Chase turned from the crowd of reporters and the family members who had given up their coveted folding chairs to hear what he had to say. The woman's eyes were all wept out, and family members bolstered her weakened body. The mine manager pretended not to hear. Nothing he could say would make one bit of difference, anyway. The truth was that the relationship between miners and their bosses had always been adversarial. But as the Sunshine body count piled up, it began to dawn on some who'd lost their partners and friends that perhaps all those deaths weren't the cost of the job, but the result of a lackadaisical attitude toward their safety. Sunshine safety engineer Launhardt could preach all he wanted that the mine was as safe as the laws allowed, and he could have been absolutely right. Launhardt's concern was genuine, but that didn't mean that the laws in place were adequate enough to protect the men. Where were the teeth to the law? In Pittsburgh, the president of the Steelworkers called for a repeal of the Federal Mine Safety Act. Union president I. W. Abel charged that the USBM was in bed with mine operators. "A nation that affords the ultimate in protection for its astronauts and their collection of moon rocks must likewise see that the miners who extract vitally needed earth ore are extended the same protection," he said.

No argument from the people of Kellogg.

LAUNHARDT'S FATHER-IN-LAW WROTE IN HIS DIARY, ON THE saddest day: "The final curtain has been drawn on the Sunshine Mine disaster and 91 of the 93 men have been found dead.... Bob was here for the first time since the fire broke out. There are the usual rumors of inefficiency in the mine, and this might be so, but Sunshine is no different from any of the other mines in the area...."

Fifty

MORNING, MAY 11
Coeur d'Alene Mining District

THE LOBBY OF THE SHOSHONE INN NURSING HOME resembled a car lot of coffins, all gleaming and orderly: rounded corners and burnished steel on the better ones in the front; plainer ones that looked more like boxes in the back. Cager Roger Findley came to inquire about making a visual identification of his brother. Lyle Findley had a peculiar patch of white pubic hair, and no matter how badly his body had been pumped up in the heat of the mine, nothing could alter his bull's-eye spot. In what surely was a kindness, a funeral director told Findley that his request would be denied. Findley didn't even think of arguing. He wanted to remember Lyle as he'd been on elk-hunting trips up the Coeur d'Alene, or even as the big brother who'd kicked him in the butt when he went on a three-day drinking binge.

Joanne Reichert also came to be convinced. It took everything she

369

had to show up when Jack Reichert's family had let her know in both direct and subtle ways that she wasn't welcome. Reichert's father approached her with visible disdain.

"You have no right to be here," he said. "You aren't his wife."

She kept her mouth shut and went to talk to a funeral director.

"I want to see Jack," she said, her voice splintering.

"I'm sorry, but that's not possible," he said.

She persisted, and the man turned off his compassionate, kindly façade. "The bodies are all bloated," he said as directly as he could. "You don't *want* to see him. They had to identify the men by their lamp numbers."

Joanne returned to Big Creek wanting to bury herself on their bed and cry. Everywhere she looked—from his clothes in the closet to the guitar stashed in the corner of the front room—all of it was *him*. She didn't want to leave. The house *was* Jack. Joanne bitterly watched June Reichert and other "real" wives swoop into town to get what was theirs. In some cases those "real" wives had thrown their men out for drinking or carousing, or because they'd just had enough of being a miner's wife. Yet there they were, sitting in the catbird seat with their purses wide open. Joanne Reichert found out that the piece of paper that was a marriage license held more power than promises when she went up to the mine office to inquire about Jack Reichert's insurance. He had told her that he had made her his beneficiary. "As my *wife*," he had said.

Joanne spoke with a woman in the office.

"I'm sorry," the clerk said. "Your name's not on it."

"But he told me I was."

"Sorry. His son is listed as his beneficiary."

The news crushed her. It wasn't the money, though she really needed it. It was because he hadn't done as he'd promised. Before Reichert died, everyone thought that he was married to *her*. All of a sudden, everything about them had turned into something very ugly.

She was a whore, a shack-up who had tried to pawn herself off as something better than she was. One day she was a woman in love, the next day she was a small-town pariah.

New York photographers for *Life* magazine arrived at the Kitchen home in Hayden Lake to take pictures. Donna, just out of the shower, had her hair wrapped in a towel in each image. Delmar Kitchen smiled faintly, but his expression was a mask. In less than two years he'd gone from being one of the Kitchen men to being the sole survivor. Before the *Life* people finished, the Kitchens handed over family photos that showed both father and son in better times. Dewellyn, with his dark hair and intense eyes, had a tough-guy persona that even the cheesiest Instamatic camera could capture. The photographs, of course, didn't show the story behind the man, a father who'd blow his entire paycheck on taking his kids to a carnival, and tell the utility company to take a hike when its bill was past due. A photo of patriarch Elmer Kitchen showed him exultant with a first-place ribbon from the county fair for raising the biggest cabbage that year. No one outside of the family, and certainly no man in the mine, knew that twenty-seven-year mining veteran Elmer Kitchen was a gardener. No one knew that when his children were small, he always came home from the mine or the woods with a treat in his dinner bucket. He would chug through the ryegrass field toward the front door, but he'd never make it all the way before his pack of children rushed to see what he brought them. One time, when he was working in the woods logging, he brought home a baby rabbit. Another time he showed up with a swan. The kids put it in a pond and kept it as a pet.

Over in Woodland Park, Wava Beehner put on a brave face, got in the station wagon, and drove up Big Creek Road to see about workmen's compensation and Social Security benefits. In the Sunshine personnel office she found Jim Farris behind his desk, sorting through claims and adding names to a growing ledger. He was obviously dismayed by the figures and the complexity of some of the men's marital lives. A widow with no children would receive about $230 a month; a widow with children would get a maximum of $306. Social Security would pay up to $440, depending on the number of dependent children.

"Thank God I don't have to worry about you, Wava," he said. "You were married to Don. You were his only wife, and he didn't have any kids with anyone else."

All morning Farris had been trying to sort out an unbelievable mess. So far, six women had come forward to make claims—wives no one had ever heard about.

"You wouldn't believe the mess I got here," he went on, pointing at papers. "I've got this one who came from down south and showed up to get this guy's life insurance, and he's been with this other woman for ten years. They've got four kids. But he never divorced the first one. I had to give the other woman the money. The kids don't get anything."

Wava left the office with paperwork outlining the money she and the kids would receive. The benefits would end when the youngest, Matthew, turned eighteen. It amounted to less than $8 a day. That and $5,000 in life insurance didn't seem like much, but Don Beehner's family was better off than most. His tightwad tendencies and his wife's part-time cleaning job at the bowling alley had allowed them to build a nest egg of more than $2,000. Outside of a $25 monthly payment on a '59 station wagon purchased the month before the fire, the Beehners didn't owe a penny. Wava wasn't getting calls from motorcycle shops or the car dealerships demanding payment before the men were in the ground. She didn't have to add insult and financial worry to her thoughts—at least not right away.

Norman Fee's mother, Elizabeth, was unique among those qualifying for death benefits. She was a dependent mother. She'd have given anything to have another woman receive her son's benefits.

She wrote to Sunshine, "You have no idea how much I wish that he had been married, that he had had a child."

.Like many of the survivors, shell-shocked Buz Bruhn also stumbled through memories to make sense of the fire. His thoughts remained fixed on Mullan carpool buddy Casey Pena. Two weeks before the fire, the fifty-two-year-old World War II Purple Heart and Silver Star recipient had been saying that he was "ready to die." He brought it up several times, in the way men sometimes do when they are disgusted by something over which they have no control. The words, of course, by themselves might have held no special meaning beyond a man letting off steam. That's what Bruhn had believed when he first heard them. He knew uneasiness sometimes came with the morning drive, and a feeling of impending doom was a part of mining. But Pena had seemed to hint at more than that. He'd announced that he had finally taken care of some paperwork that he had put off for almost a year—he'd put down his new wife's name as his insurance beneficiary. Bruhn began to believe Pena had had a premonition.

Out of the four men with whom he carpooled May 2, Bruhn was the only survivor.

Inside the little house in the shadow of KWAL's signal tower, a parade of food arrived on an endless conveyer belt from everyone who knew, or had ever heard of, Louis Goos. Homemade pies, pasta-packed casseroles, and Jell-O salads practically spilled from the refrigerator and made a food mosaic of the countertop in Howard and Susan Markve's tidy kitchen in Osburn. It was a bottomless buffet line with no takers.

Why, Susan wondered, *do people bring food when eating only makes the grieving vomit?*

Partially because he'd told her his wishes, but also as a final way of making that lost connection with her father, Susan took charge of the burial. Her dad's body would be transported to Sturgis, South

Dakota. Louis Goos, the man who everyone thought would be the sole survivor of the fire, the fellow who'd survived fourteen car wrecks and a dozen serious mine mishaps, would be planted in the dark Dakota soil that looked and smelled like fresh-ground coffee. Not long after they learned he was dead, Goos's landlord told the Markves that his live-in girlfriend had ransacked his house. Every single photograph, every personal item, was gone—guns, cowboy hat and boots, everything all the way down to his underwear—gone. Susan Markve broke down when she saw the mess. Her father had many roles in his life: miner, Army sergeant, husband, and father. But after May 2, any tangible proof that he had existed vanished.

Howard Markve contended with more than the loss of his father-in-law, Louis Goos, or the death of partner Bob Follette's son, Bill. Not only had the men died, they'd *vanished*. Markve understood why the grieving needed to see the bodies of their men. People needed to see for themselves to make it real, otherwise a mind played games. Markve caught himself thinking about heading over to his father-in-law's place in Wallace. *Let's go drinkin'.* And if Markve needed help, he didn't ask for it. Instead, on his own he fought to suppress the mental pictures of Norman Fee on the floor of the cage, or Bob Goff staggering across the station. He worked at washing it all away with beer and silence. Even so, he planned to return to the mine. Miners faced everything head-on. *New guys are coming. If you don't claim your stope or your raise, you just might find yourself looking for a new job.*

A string of funerals ran throughout the brokenhearted district. Two were double services with side-by-side caskets; one was a triple, with a father, son, and cousin. Elaine Bebb told her daughter Lou Ella Firkins that she couldn't survive the agony of two separate funerals. Mrs. Bebb had been in bad shape since the fire; she'd even passed out in front of the Jewell. So Lou Ella mourned her husband, Don, and her stepfather, shifter Virgil Bebb, at a double funeral in Shoshone Memorial Gardens.

And over in Coeur d'Alene, Delmar Kitchen said good-bye to his dad, Elmer, and his brother, Dewellyn. They, too, were side by side, together always. Kitchen knew he could no longer handle the drive from Hayden Lake after the fire. There was too much time on that drive to listen to the thoughts in his head. There was too much time in a car that was no longer chilly from keeping an open window to let out his father's and brother's cigarette smoke. Donna agreed that they'd have to give up their house and move back to the district, to a mobile home in Pine Creek. No more two-car garage; no more two baths. She could reason that it was okay, though. Great as the family's loss had been, she still had her husband. Her dream home, well, it had only been a dream. It just didn't seem right to dwell on that kind of loss.

Bob Launhardt was missing among the pallbearers at Duwain Crow's funeral following services at the United Church of Kellogg. Neither did Launhardt stop by to see Lauralee Crow. His absence was strange, considering the friendship he had shared with Duwain, dead at thirty-nine. Mrs. Crow didn't hold it against him. Launhardt needed to find out what had caused the fire. Crying over old times could wait.

Tom Wilkinson joined an overflowing congregation at the United Church of Christ–Congregational in Wallace to mourn the death of Johnny Davis. It was the only funeral he attended. Wilkinson let a what-if mess with his head. *What if I'd been more persuasive and Davis had dumped shift to celebrate his birthday?* Ron Flory also would attend a single funeral, Clapp cousin Mark Russell's. The Sunshine survivors said there were too many memorials and they couldn't get to all of them. Some didn't buy the excuse. They thought Ron and Tom were embarrassed about living when so many had died.

And over in the big white house in Big Creek, Marvin Chase contended with a few threats: phone calls motivated by grief and the need to place blame. One caller warned Chase not to stand too close to the shaft. Lee Haynes and a few of his fellow Army reservists led a reconnaissance operation of sorts, surveying the perimeter of the property and peering under the family's cars for bombs. A few nasty letters came through the mail, one in the guise of a cheerful Raggedy Ann and Andy card. Viola Chase could never stand the sight of those two rag dolls after that.

Two hours before sunrise, May 13

Sunshine Portal

THE LAST OF SUNSHINE'S DEAD WERE REMOVED FROM THE mine on May 13 at 3:38 a.m. From darkness to darkness. The last body was that of Mark Russell, Ron Flory's best friend. The young man was just thirty. He'd always described his job as "working in the black." It was so true.

A couple of days later Garnita Keene slipped into a spot in the rear of Kellogg's Lutheran church and listened to the minister eulogize the short life of Billy Allen, a local boy, Army reservist, and Sunshine miner trapped on 5200. Billy's mother, Winnie, melted into a pew as her own personal what-if scenario continued to plague her. The morning of the fire, she'd run out of their Pinehurst home with Billy's diggers. Having missed shift on Monday, he'd forgotten them on Tuesday. If only, she told herself, she hadn't done that, he might have gone to work and turned around and come back home, and just maybe stayed there. He might never have been down on 5200 on May 2. Myrna Flory's sister lingered in the back of the church because the estranged Mrs. Allen and her two children had arrived from Arkansas. She looked around at their faces and felt it was selfish to hold on to grief as if her loss were as great as theirs. She knew it wasn't. Even so, the what-ifs hold great power. She followed the funeral procession up the road to Greenwood Cemetery.

And on and on the funerals continued. The toll of the tragedy was greatest on Kellogg. The town had lost twenty-five men. Wallace had also been hit hard, with eighteen gone. And tiny, tiny Big Creek had lost six of its fathers and sons. The oldest victim was pumpman Floyd Rais, sixty-one; the youngest was Michael James Johnston, nineteen. The Sunshine fire left seventy-seven women widowed and more than two hundred children fatherless. Three were yet to be born and would never know their dads. The dead had shared much beyond a love for mining and the tragedy that took their lives. More than half had served their country; twenty-eight were Army veterans. In all, it was the worst disaster in Idaho history, supplanting the historic forest fires of 1910 that killed eighty-five people.

After the fire, men blamed themselves for surviving when their partners had perished. Widows felt resentful of friends who received more aid and attention than they did. Children were angry because their dads never came home again. Girlfriends of married miners grieved in silence. Cads looking for widows with insurance bankrolls moved in. The district had been turned upside down.

And a safety engineer named Bob Launhardt was dealt a dark and heavy burden.

Epilogue

AFTER GENE JOHNSON'S BURIAL, BETTY CONTINUED TO SET a place for him at the dinner table. She removed knickknacks and whatnots from tabletops and replaced them with photographs of her husband, taken at all times of his life. She hung his miner's hat on the gun rack of his pickup and swore to God she'd never take it down. The new Dodge Power Wagon, with its special tri-tone paint scheme of white, blue, and green that Gene had so loved, had become a tribute to his life. For many around Kellogg, Betty was a tragic figure, like Miss Havisham in Dickens's *Great Expectations,* a woman who had consigned herself to wait out the hours of her own life, living with a memory. Uncomfortable with her never-ending tears, friends avoided her.

When Johnson's $15,000 insurance payoff arrived, it came with a note from Jim Farris. The personnel director signed it "with kindest personal regards." Betty would rather have killed him than take a dime that passed through his hands.

Once while shopping at the Osburn IGA, Mrs. Johnson saw Farris in the checkout line. She went to her pickup and waited behind the wheel, engine running. *I'm going to run over that son of a bitch. I hope he goes to hell. He treated us like we were nothing. Like them guys was nothing,* she told herself. She tried to follow, but she was so deep in her thoughts she lost him. Later she sent a note to him along with her marriage certificate and birth certificates for the two youngest girls. "Mr. Farris: I want to thank you for the phone call telling us about Gene's death. I can't think of anything as brutal as what you did to me. It will always be remembered."

Betty Johnson went missing the afternoon of what would have been the Johnsons' silver wedding anniversary. Her oldest daughter, Linda, called Peggy at the bank and told her she'd been all over Kellogg but couldn't find her. Peggy suggested they go together to the cemetery. Their mother had been there every day since the funeral.

The sisters drove up the narrow road toward a big white cross fashioned from a telephone pole on a hillside above downtown Kellogg, past the Italian section, and farther on up the hill before turning toward the place where their father had been buried. Shepherd's crooks held plastic flowers, and some graves were marked with little wrought-iron arches; a few spelled out names, others only initials. Their mother had ordered an arch with the letter *J* and a double headstone. The date of her death waited for the mason's chisel.

The sisters found their mother sprawled out on the grass, red roses scattered beneath her tiny frame. Betty Johnson was convulsing with tears. Next to her was a little banner: *Happy Anniversary Honey.*

"Why can't I go with him?" she asked. "I don't want to be here by myself. I don't want to live this way."

"I think we've lost her," Peggy told her sister. "She's never going to let go."

Betty Johnson was not alone. Across the mining district there were other wives, sons, brothers, and best friends who were never going to let go. No one really could.

❖

INDEED, ALL LIVES IN THE DISTRICT WERE REWRITTEN IN the smoke of May 2, 1972. In both direct and subtle ways, many would never get over the fire. And no matter the outcome of myriad state and federal lawsuits that sought to fix blame and responsibility, only Bob Launhardt would devote himself to discovering what had caused an impossible fire. Whether he was motivated merely by a personal and professional need to know, or by undeserved guilt, it did not matter. With ninety-one dead, answers become a necessity, and for Launhardt they were an obsession. A congressional probe spotlighted blame and the cause of the fire, but did not answer why a fire had ignited in Sunshine Mine. Hundreds of men testified, and throughout the proceedings, emotions remained on high boil. Driven by the USBM and the Interior Department, the testimony had the distinct feel of scapegoating rather than fact-finding. The House Labor Subcommittee heard damaging and bitter testimony from cager Byron Schulz and Lavern Melton, president of the local Steelworkers. Melton claimed management had not only ignored safety concerns, but had frequently retaliated whenever any were brought to the attention of the company. He told about Don Beehner's complaint of a safety violation concerning accumulated garbage in drifts: "He was rewarded for his effort by being required to clean it out."

Outsiders who'd pushed themselves into the story grabbed headlines. Nader's Raider Davitt McAteer divided culpability by telling the subcommittee that not only was Sunshine criminally negligent, but the USBM was blameworthy for its lax manner of dealing with violations. Sunshine, the twenty-eight-year-old lawyer told the panel, had the worst safety record of all metal mines, but had *never* been fined or assessed any penalties.

The Kellogg doctor who volunteered at the mine, Keith Dahlberg, sent a letter to his family back East. He was irritated by those grandstanders: "A lot has been said by Ralph Nader and others about the deplorable safety conditions at Sunshine, which is always easier in retrospect. One wonders why if he's such an expert on safety, he did not warn us a couple times."

Most of Sunshine's management testified locally, so they could remain at the mine to help fight the fire, which continued to burn for weeks. Launhardt went before the investigative committee in the auditorium of the Washington Water Power Company in Kellogg. He faced a wall of lawyers and experts from Interior and the USBM. He answered each question coolly and professionally.

Sunshine's lawyer pushed the point that the government had done a poor job of educating mining companies.

"Did the Bureau of Mines ever advise you that all old workings should be sealed?"

"No," Launhardt replied.

"Did they ever advise you that the hoistman should have oxygen apparatus for survival and be trained to use it?"

"No."

"Did they ever advise you that there should be a self-rescue unit for each employee?"

"No."

"Did they ever advise you that you should have an accurate record system to determine what employees were underground at all times?"

"They never advised us of this."

The only time emotion flickered was when he had to answer questions about Don Beehner.

"Do you know why he would have removed his face mask?" a lawyer asked.

"I can't answer that," he said, hesitating slightly. "I don't think anybody knows. An act of heroism."

After two hours, Launhardt finished what would be the first of seemingly countless depositions that in many ways would consume his life.

Certainly during the initial investigation, Launhardt was convinced the catastrophe was mostly a product of ignorance, bad timing, and poor ventilation, none of which he could have done much about. Always a great student, Launhardt was the kind of man who devoured every detail on a subject of interest. The USBM and the Department of the Interior had conducted the biggest investigation in the history of mining, and Launhardt supported their efforts in every way he could. But they had their own agenda as the governmental agencies responsible for ensuring that mines comply with federal law. For Launhardt, to comprehend what happened on May 2 was to dissect what had led to the mind-set that had everyone in the district asking the same thing: *What can burn in a hardrock mine?* But there was also one other question on Launhardt's mind: *Why was the smoke so toxic?*

It didn't take long for him to find some answers. The USBM had recently sent two ventilation experts to Big Creek, first in November of the previous year, and then a follow-up a couple weeks before the fire. Launhardt believed the USBM should have recognized the potential for a short circuit of the mine's ventilation system, which ultimately led to poisonous outtake air being pumped in with fresh, breathable intake air. They had been through Sunshine at the exact location where the exhaust airway intersected with the old workings, and had seen firsthand the ventilation fans that were in place upstream from those mined-out vein structures. They'd walked right past the leaking bulkheads. They'd seen it all and never remarked about it. They'd never said, *Hey, Sunshine, move the fans downstream from 09, so that if a fire ever occurs in those bulkheads, the smoke and gas will be blown out of the mine—not back through it.*

Everyone knew that Sunshine's ventilation system was completely inadequate.. The deeper the working levels, the hotter the temperature and the greater the need for enhanced air movement. The dead-end stopes with dangerous gases or low oxygen levels were found below 4800. The USBM knew that, and recommended in its preliminary report that the company straighten out and enlarge sections of the exhaust airway on 3400 to allow greater airflow.

Sunshine's ventilation engineering staff had met with the USBM's Warren Andrews and Ralph Foster on April 24, just nine days before the fire. Launhardt held Andrews and Foster in high regard. They were not, by his estimation, government hacks occupying space until pension time rolled around. The USBM team measured air volume and calculated leakage into the old workings. Andrews and Foster understood the ventilation system of the mine as well as, if not better than, the company's own experts on airflow. The USBM men knew how a short circuit of the mine's ventilation system could lead to serious, if not fatal, consequences for the men underground busting rock.

FBI AND USBM CHEMISTS EXAMINED EVIDENCE COLLECTED from Joe and Delores Armijo's basement where the deluded woman insisted her husband's evil twin had conducted experiments with incendiary devices. The samples were inconclusive. Neither the Interior Department nor the FBI could rule out that arson had been the cause of the fire. Interior's assistant director Stan Jarrett, however, kept pushing the arson angle. He doubted the thoroughness of the Shoshone County investigation. The FBI responded in an internal memo that "the U.S. Attorney felt no active investigation warranted by FBI... various parties having vested interest are trying to shift blame and/or responsibility for this disaster."

A while later, other reasons for the investigation appeared to emerge. According to another FBI internal memo: "He mentioned that there are political implications which indicate to him that the Department of Labor is attempting to take from the Bureau of Mines (Department of Interior) the functions of that Bureau."

Nevertheless, assistant director Jarrett continued his crusade and met with an FBI special agent in his USBM office in Arlington, Virginia. The FBI filed another report, and this time Jarrett laid the fire at the feet of the union: "Jarrett speculated that there was a militant type group in the union at this mine, which caused the company and the Bureau of Mines to be very cautious in their dealings with union representatives."

When the federal government's *Final Report on Sunshine Mine Fire* was released in 1973, Launhardt disputed much of its content, including the following passages:

"The emergency escapeway system from the mine was not adequate for rapid evacuation."

Launhardt considered that charge the most ridiculous of the purported factors, as it played out in Sunshine Mine or any other deep, multilevel mine. The poisonous gases in the air left no time for escape. Shaft repairman Robert Barker had been found with his arms folded behind his head, lying on some lagging, a coffee cup resting nearby. It was as if he was waiting for the smoke to pass, as though it was only a temporary inconvenience. Barker, like many others, had no idea there was any real urgency to evacuate.

"Top mine officials were not at the mine on the day of the fire and no person had been designated as being in charge of the entire operation. Individual supervisors were reluctant to order immediate evacuation or to make a major decision such as stopping the 3400-level fans."

Launhardt agreed the evacuation could have been better facilitated, but he doubted Chase or Walkup could have resolved the issue of the 3400-level fans. No one knew how the fans would affect the atmosphere, because no one knew where the fire was burning.

"Company personnel delayed ordering evacuation of the mine for about 20 minutes while they searched for the fire."

Many debated that charge. There had been a search for the source of the smoke, and confusion about who could make the call for an evacuation. Launhardt didn't find out about the smoke for at least a half hour, and by the time he dumped the stench, many of the men were already trapped. Launhardt supported the search. In order to determine which way to send his men out—through the Jewell or Silver Summit—the foreman needed to know where the smoke originated.

"Most of the underground employees had not been trained in the use of the provided self rescuers and had difficulty using them. Some self rescuers provided by the company had not been maintained in useable condition."

It was that charge that hit him the hardest. It was the worst kind of finger-pointing because Sunshine was the first hardrock mine in the district, maybe in the country, using self-rescuers at the time. Neither federal nor state laws required them. Launhardt had brought them to Sunshine in 1963 because he thought they would be a good safety measure. Although testimony from many of the survivors indicated that some of the units were in poor shape, or completely unusable, Launhardt felt that there had been enough to go around. Without them, at least forty-three more men would have died.

"Mine survival training, including evacuation procedures, barricading, and hazards of gases, such as carbon monoxide, had not been given mine employees."

Sunshine was a metal mine, not a coal mine. Launhardt had followed the letter of the law for safety training. He was also a realist. He knew the resistance the men felt toward the subject. Most thought they'd never need to escape a fire at Sunshine, because Sunshine wouldn't ever have one.

"The controls built into the ventilation system did not allow the isolation of No. 10 Shaft and its hoist rooms and service raises or the compartmentalization of the mine. Smoke and gas from this fire was thus able to move unrestricted into almost all workings and travel ways."

Launhardt couldn't argue that one because it was a fact. But the USBM had a role in that scenario. The USBM ventilation experts didn't recommend such system controls following their 1971 ventilation survey.

And though the report had been the culmination of hundreds, if not thousands, of hours of testimony, research, and analysis, it did not address what Launhardt considered the most important issue: Why did the Sunshine fire spread more rapidly and produce more toxic gases than a normal hardrock fire?

According to the *Final Report,* "*a fire smoldered in the abandoned area, filling it with smoke before the smoke was expelled and detected. The sudden release of a large volume of smoke and toxic gases was not characteristic of the normal growth of an open fire.*"

SOMETHING WAS MISSING. THERE WAS NO WAY A FIRE WAS going to smolder in those sopping old workings, building an enormous toxic cloud, and go unnoticed. In early spring of 1973, the legal team connected the dots when a Minnesota pig farmer successfully sued a foam manufacturer after his sheet-metal pig barn became engulfed and killed his animals. The fuel that fed the blaze was the supposedly nonburning, self-extinguishing polyurethane foam. The foam sprayed on 3400 near the 09 crosscut in Sunshine Mine was nearly identical.

The insulating product had long been promoted by the industry. *Mining & Quarrying,* a trade magazine, reported in an August 1962 article titled "Knocks Fire Cold":

"A revolutionary method of insulating and sealing passageways in coal and metal mines by applying sprayed-in-place urethane foam to exposed underground surfaces was demonstrated by the U.S. Bureau of Mines for the American Mining Congress in Pittsburgh. . . . Since the foam will not support combustion, it can be used to insulate combustible materials in the mine and makes possible the quick erection of emergency, flame-retardant curtain walls to localize an outbreak of fire underground. . . . "

It turned out that polyurethane foam had a deadly past. In 1957 a fire in a British coal mine killed twenty-nine men. During the post-fire investigation, the polyurethane foam that had been used as a sealant became suspect when evidence indicated that the purportedly inflammable product had burned. At first the investigators zeroed in on the possibility that the foam had been improperly mixed, rendering it unsafe and flammable. Graham Wilde, head of the Mine Fires Section of the British Health and Safety Executive, conducted a series of laboratory tests and found the rigid foam could ignite; in fact, surprisingly easily. A report indicating the inherent dangers of the sealant was dispatched to the United States with a letter from Graham urging the USBM to join England and other western European nations in banning the foam for use underground.

Donald Mitchell of the USBM responded to the British report and conducted his own tests at the Bureau's test mine in Brewster, Pennsylvania. Little, if anything, was relayed to the industry, but Mitchell's test results indicated that the foam was in fact flammable, even in a strong air current. He also confirmed Wilde's findings that the product burned with such intensity that once ignited, it was difficult to extinguish. And yet nothing in USBM literature indicated mining companies should remove what was sprayed into mines and railway tunnels. Even more surprisingly, polyurethane foam continued to be promoted and used.

Almost a decade after the British banned the foam, American mines still used it. For Sunshine, it was viewed as a timesaving and cost-effective way to stop leakage and channel airflow in a mine's ventilation system that was becoming increasingly deeper and more difficult to manage.

In 1966 the USBM's own publication, *Fire Hazards of Urethane Foam in Mines,* said:

"After two years of research on sealants and coatings, the Bureau of Mines published a report on urethane foam. Fire hazard from foam exists if flame propagates beyond the ignition source or penetrates the foam.... Foam on the ribs and adjoining roof presents a fire hazard.... Flame propagated in all tests with foam on the ribs and across the roof."

Launhardt was flabbergasted. How could the USBM ignore what was so patently obvious? The research in England was incontrovertible, and the USBM's own findings backed it up. Why was the information dismissed? Why hadn't Donald Mitchell heeded his own concerns? Even in the piss ditch, down low from the test inferno, Mitchell's hair and eyebrows were singed. Why hadn't the government called for the removal of all underground foam? And why, during the rescue and recovery effort in May 1972, had USBM crews allowed the use of gallons of spray foam to seal the leaky drifts?

The foam had seemed so innocuous that Launhardt never paid it any mind. It sprayed on a creamy white, but in time the dust and grime of the mine coated it and it looked like the mud of a wasp nest—a bubbly form wrapping timbers and rocks and bulkheads in a smothering sheath of hardening goop. Launhardt came to believe the benign miracle insulator was a killer. He knew that it didn't take a lot of heat to get it to burn, and once it started, it burned like solid gasoline. Had the foam not been sprayed all over 3400, Sunshine's safety engineer believed, the fire would not have played out as it did the morning of May 2. What was there to burn, anyway? The marine plywood was as soggy as a rowboat at the bottom of a lake. The hot, wet mine took its toll on timbers all the time—which was why timber-repair crews were among the busiest crews. Launhardt dismissed the Bureau's theories that the crew cutting rock bolts with acetylene torches had hauled off for lunch around 11:00 a.m., leaving behind chunks of hot steel to rest against the bulkhead. Maybe careless, maybe stupid, but it shouldn't have been a big concern in any case because the timbers were wet there and the men had been told that the foam didn't burn. Had it not been for the foam, nothing would have come of it whether it was an errant cigarette or a hot rock bolt. And he knew it couldn't have happened that fast. If the foam hadn't been there and it was a small wood fire—all fires start out small—it would have smoldered a little and the smoke would have alerted someone before things got so out of hand. The fire just wouldn't have flashed to consume an entire bulkhead in less than a minute.

Launhardt was also bothered by USBM ventilation inspections in the fall of 1971 and a little more than a week before the fire. Both times the Bureau's experts passed through the polyurethane-foam-sprayed airways. No one could have missed the massive amounts of foam, it was so pervasive and obvious. And at the time the Bureau knew that the foam was a potential fire hazard. Instead of informing Sunshine that it ought to scrape that toxic foam out of there, they didn't even remark on it.

It was, of course, a combination of factors that led to the disaster. Without the short circuit of the ventilation system, most of the combustion by-products from the burning polyurethane foam would have gone harmlessly to the surface. But it was the velocity of the fire and the magnitude of toxins in its smoke that were so crucial to understanding what happened on May 2. Many, including Launhardt, believed—as subsequent tests concluded—that polyurethane foam acted as an accelerant akin to solid gasoline, which led to rapid combustion. That, in turn, gave rise to the torrent of smoke and deadly gases, the likes of which had never been seen before. The scenario was what experts called a "fuel-rich" event. The difference between flame-spread rates in timber fires and polyurethane foam fires was the essential clue. British researchers of fuel-rich mine fire scenarios later reported that fire in a timbered mine advanced at a rate of 2.3 to 17.1 yards per hour. Burning polyurethane foam advanced at 0.7 to 2.5 yards per *second*.

Mine Safety Appliances Company and Dow Chemical had developed the product, called Rigiseal, with the research support of the USBM. The Bureau not only promoted Rigiseal, but even sent its own employees to demonstrate the product at various mines, including Bunker Hill. For some reason—ownership, incompetence, whatever—the people pushing the product at the mines were unaware of its dangers. Launhardt and others close to the Sunshine case were suspicious. They felt that the reason the foam had been overlooked during the initial investigation was to keep the government out of potential lawsuits. By then several suits were pending, including fifty-two wrongful death claims on behalf of miners' survivors, and the company's own legal claim to recover damages and lost production. The government was a defendant in both scenarios. The key issue in the litigation was the premise that, but for the combustion of rigid polyurethane foam at the 3400–09 intersection, the fire would not have been a disaster.

As expected, the lawsuits to place blame and accountability took their sweet time to make it to trial. Widows did not sue Sunshine. For some that was out of loyalty, but also because by accepting the $25,000 paid over ten years from workmen's compensation, they were precluded from taking legal action against the company. By the time the primary case was heard in a U.S. District Court in Boise, six years after the fire, in 1978, many of the litigants had dropped out or settled. A consortium of chemical companies that had had a role in the manufacture of the foam settled for $6 million, to be divided among lawyers and the two-hundred-plus heirs of represented families. Sunshine was also a plaintiff seeking damages from the USBM, the Pittsburgh firm that manufactured the self-rescuers, and the makers of the foam, Mine Safety Appliances Company. The chemical companies, however, did not settle with the mine. The government argued that no blame could be placed anywhere because the facts were unclear about when the fire ignited, where it started, and the role, if any, of the polyurethane foam. The government lawyers also tried to prove that Sunshine was more focused on production than on safety and therefore was to blame. After five months of testimony, including five days with Launhardt on the stand, Judge Ray McNichols ruled in favor of the defendants. Judge McNichols was unconvinced about the role of the foam. He said that even if the polyurethane foam had been the cause of the catastrophe, the federal government couldn't be liable under the federal Tort Claims Act. Many disagreed with the judge's ruling, but in the end it stayed firm. The only proof that polyurethane foam was recognized as dangerous was that after the Sunshine fire, no American mines continued to use the product underground.

AND FOR DECADES, THE FIRE PLAGUED THOSE WHO WERE THERE May 2.

Delmar Kitchen thought he'd dealt with the fire, but in time he came to understand that he'd only become a good liar. After the sole survivor of the legendary Kitchen men buried his father and his brother, he found himself drowning in anxiety that went on for years. His hands would grow numb when he was driving, forcing him to pull over and wait it out. It was as if his own sadness wanted to choke the life out of him, like clenched hands around his neck.

Though the bodies were tucked into pockets of earth for all time, many still found it impossible to accept. Lou Ella Firkins's children would swear on the family Bible that they had seen their father's silhouette in an upstairs window watching as they played in their backyard. Once, Don Firkins's widow heard footsteps coming from her son's second-floor bedroom. She set her ironing aside and crept upstairs to catch him playing hooky. She heard the sound of Levi's pantlegs brushing against each other as he walked.

"You little shit," she said as she pushed the door open, "I caught you!"

But the room was empty.

Lou Ella knew it was the spirit of her beloved.

For a long time after the fire, whenever Bunker Hill hotshot Harry Cougher saw someone sprawled on a towel sunbathing, he'd have to fight the compulsion to stop his car and stare hard. *Is that person dead?*

Although touchy subjects were never broached in the Launhardt home, Julie, a perceptive thirteen-year-old at the time of the fire, had a vague understanding of the May 2 disaster. But all of it came from her mother. Simply put, it was that "it wasn't your dad's fault." There were so many questions, unasked and unanswered. Julie knew her father was associated with the safety program, but was unsure to what degree. Was he solely responsible for the safety of the men? Or did he report to someone else who was? She also knew the fire was an accident, the result of something possibly preventable. When Janet and the children moved back to Pinehurst a few weeks after the fire, they faced a man more distant than ever, a man whose darkest moment was locked up and private. A mystery. Julie sensed the pain of the fire in her father's eyes, but he never said anything directly about it. He had liked to shape things a certain way, organize problems like socks rolled into little fabric eggs and placed neatly in a drawer. After the fire, he couldn't do that. Julie knew what thoughts were going through his mind. *Why was I unable to prevent this? And, once it did happen, why couldn't I have saved more?*

The two oldest could see that their father was holding himself together by burying himself in his work. He couldn't let go of the fire and its cause. In a way, they believed, he was a victim along with the other ninety-one. Bob junior had a gut feeling that his dad felt the fire wouldn't have happened if he'd never left the mine for the insurance sales job in Spokane.

Whatever went through their father's mind had become a bone-crushing burden.

THE UNDERGROUND PRISON OF 4800 REVISITED RON FLORY every night for weeks, even years. Myrna would wake him from a bad dream and nuzzle him back to sleep, telling him that he'd be all right. But he was locked into dreams that had him walking in semidarkness, trying to avoid stepping on men who had been changed by time and heat into something inhuman. Tom Wilkinson didn't talk quite so much about what troubled him; he was always better at holding things inside. But big Ron Flory carried the 175 hours in the Safety Zone like a heavy stone. One night in a Kellogg bar, a woman teetering on spike heels and sloshing a drink slapped him as hard as she could.

"You!" she said. "I know who *you* are." Flory resisted touching his burning cheek. "My husband would be alive if you hadn't stolen the food out of his bucket."

Flory hoped the slap made her feel better. He said nothing and turned away. What the woman and the other mourners didn't know was that there was also a heavy price for being a survivor. Flory paid it every time he caught the eye of one of the widows or their children.

Those who lose a loved one often console themselves with the hope that something positive can come from the tragedy. The deaths of the ninety-one Idaho miners were the clarion call that not only changed the hardrock mining industry's safety practices and restructured the federal government, but opened America's eyes to the dangers inherent in really hard labor. A year after the fire, the USBM was out of business and the Mining Enforcement and Safety Administration was the new governing agency. MESA was the first federal agency with sole responsibility for assuring miners of a safe working environment. New rules were set for American mines. A check-in and check-out procedure was mandated. Hoistmen now worked in sealed-in compartments with oxygen tanks and a separate ventilation supply. Self-rescuers were no longer optional in hardrock mining, but were required to be carried by each man underground. Regular evacuation drills also became mandatory. No miner—new hire or old hand—could ever say that he didn't know his way out.

In March of 1977, MESA was transferred from the Department of the Interior to the place where most thought it belonged, the Department of Labor. There it was renamed Mine Safety and Health Administration.

Exactly what started the fire remains unknown.

IT HAS BEEN MORE THAN THREE DECADES SINCE THE FIRE killed ninety-one men and Bob Launhardt was left haunted by what had happened—and what could have been done to prevent it. Sunshine Mine closed in February 2001, ironically marking the day with a fire drill. Its deepest levels are now filled with water, submerging the hoists, the trackline, and the footprints of the men who'd worked there for more than a century.

Ron and Myrna Flory divorced, and as much as he didn't want to, Ron returned underground to work in the mines. Though he is unemployed and on disability now, having suffered serious burns in a car accident several years after the fire, he still sees himself as a miner. Tom and Frances Wilkinson left the district and never looked back. Rumormongers at the time of the fire had it that the Wilkinson marriage was so shaky that Frances went to the dry to take divorce papers from his street clothes. Still married, they deny the story, but in the end, did that matter? Now living in St. Maries, Idaho, Wilkinson returned to Sunshine only briefly after the disaster. He has since enjoyed a long career with the Forest Service, working in the fresh air and the light of day.

Like several Sunshine widows, Wava Beehner remarried within a year of the fire. When that marriage failed, she turned bad luck into pragmatism. She told herself it didn't matter. When she got to heaven, she was sure, Don would be waiting for her. He'd understand. Betty Johnson lives alone in her Kellogg home, away from Big Creek and the mine, though it never leaves her mind. Her bitterness toward Jim

Farris, now deceased, has not lessened, and she maintains little or no contact with any of the friends she once had—though she sees many every day. Joanne Strope Reichert became the central figure in a legal case that made it all the way to the Idaho State Supreme Court. As Jack Reichert's common-law wife, she sought to keep his Buick Skylark. She lost. Devastated by the tactics of attorneys who painted her as "the biggest tramp" in the district, Strope left the area for almost thirty years. She only returned to Kellogg recently.

The sole survivor of his crew, Bill Mitchell still believes that it was an angel that reached out through the smoke and saved his life on May 2. The angel's name is Greg Dionne.

Janet Launhardt left Bob Launhardt a decade after the fire. Now remarried, Bob Launhardt lives in the same tidy house in Pinehurst, overlooking the golf course. He suffers bouts of depression that he concedes are likely tied to the events of that terrible Tuesday. Obsession both fuels and fights his depression. Clearly, when so many die on your watch, it isn't easy to let go. Now in his seventies, he is an old man with perfect posture and piles of information to prove that what happened so long ago could have been averted, that it hadn't been his fault. He has spent his life examining the Sunshine fire from every angle.

"Every day is how often Bob thinks about the fire," Launhardt's second wife, Barb, explains. "It almost killed him, too. He almost had a nervous breakdown."

Even now, whenever he gets the opportunity, Launhardt preaches safety and the role polyurethane foam probably played in the disaster. There are more believers today, but he wonders why so much of the dangerous and combustible foam remains in American mines, hotels, restaurants, and tunnels. Had Launhardt's message been heard, the death of 177 miners in South Africa's Kinross gold mine in 1986 might have been prevented. Launhardt can still hear a survivor's voice over the static of the radio clip: *"They told us it wouldn't burn!"* The words were an echo of what the USBM told Sunshine in the mid-1960s when polyurethane foam was sprayed over drift walls as a ventilation sealant.

"What's important here," he says, "is that we make sure this doesn't happen again. It could. It really could." His words are not a salaried man's memorized script, but a speech that came from the heart of a miner.

The places and the people of the Coeur d'Alenes are no longer as they were before the day the men died. Many of the tough young miners who fought their way out of the mine that day are now crippled old men, though only in their sixties. Wallace's hookers turned their last tricks. Kellogg's Uncle Bunk left town. The towering stacks that gave Smelterville its name and pumped untold tons of lead into the sky are no more. In 1985 the feds tagged a twenty-one-square-mile area around Bunker Hill as the nation's second-largest Superfund site. Many of Kellogg's businesses are shuttered, and the town's Chamber of Commerce now pushes tourism as the area's savior. And though it is impossible to know if anyone truly believes the brochures that tout the place as a Bavarian-style ski village, its people and those of the other mining towns of the district are hopeful about the future. Optimism still runs in their blood. Mining has always been about doing better the next day. Far beyond the hardhats and carbide lamps that embellish thrift-store walls, the industry's impact remains profound. It will always be so.

IN MEMORIAM
MAY 2, 1972

Robert Alexander, 50

Billy Allen, 24

Wayne Allen, 39

Richard Allison, 37

Arnold Anderson, 48

Robert Anderson, 37

Joe Armijo, 38

Ben Barber, 31

Robert Barker, 42

Virgil Bebb, 53

Don Beehner, 38

Richard Bewley, 40

George Birchett, 40

Wayne Blalack, 35

Robert Bush, 47

Floyd Byington, 35

Clarence Case, 55

Charlie Casteel, 30

Kevin Croker, 29

Duwain Crow, 39

Rod Davenport, 35

John Davis, 28

Richard Delbridge, 24

William Delbridge, 55

Roberto Diaz, 55

Greg Dionne, 23

Carter Don Carlos, 47

Norman Fee, 27

Lyle Findley, 30

Don Firkins, 37

Howard Fleshman, 38

William Follette, 23

Richard Garcia, 56

Richard George, 20

Robert Goff, 35

Louis Goos, 51

John Guertner, 54

William Hanna, 47

Howard Harrison, 34

Patrick Hobson, 57

Melvin House, 41

Merle Hudson, 47

Jack Ivers, 44

Gene Johnson, 45

Paul Johnson, 47

Wayne Johnson, 43

James Johnston, 19

Custer Keough, 59

Sherman Kester, 60

Dewellyn Kitchen, 31

Elmer Kitchen, 54

Kenneth La Voie, 29

Richard Lynch, 24

Donald McLachlan, 23

Delbert McNutt, 48

James Moore, 29

David Mullin, 34

Joe Naccarato, 40

Orlin Nelson, 32

Richard Norris, 24

Donald Orr, 50

Hubert Patrick, 45

Casey Pena, 52

John Peterson, 57

Francis Phillips, 42

Irvan Puckett, 51

Floyd Rais, 61

Leonard Rathbun, 29

John Rawson, 27

Jack Reichert, 45

Dusty Rhoads, 57

Glen Rossiter, 37

Paul Russell, 30

Gene Salyer, 54

James Salyer, 51

Allen Sargent, 38

Robert Scanlan, 38

John Serano, 37

Nick Sharette, 48

Frank Sisk, 31

Darrell Stephens, 20

Gustav Thor, 38

Grady Truelock, 40

Robert Waldvogel, 50

William Walty, 29

Gordon Whatcott, 37

Doug Wiederrick, 37

Ronald Wilson, 41

William Wilson, 41

John Wolff, 49

Don Wood, 53

Acknowledgments

THE DEEP DARK IS THE SUM OF COLLECTIVE MEMORIES OF many who lived through the events of May 2, 1972, and a vast, and mostly untouched, historical record. Consider those records—archived reports, diaries, letters, news accounts from the time, and legal papers—the backbone of this book. Over the past four years, I conducted more than two hundred interviews for this book and did my best to reconcile the historical record with the memories of the men and women who lived through the tragedy.

I am grateful to so many of the people of the Coeur d'Alene Mining District, who helped in direct and indirect ways, for their contributions to this narrative. Among the many I'd like to acknowledge: Ron Flory, Myrna Kinnick, Tom and Frances Wilkinson, Marvin Chase and his sons Rob and Pete, Larry Hawkins, Mel Jaynes, Ray and Rita Rudd, Randy Peterson, Lou Ella Firkins, Paul and Margie Robinson, Len Bourgard, Linda Daugherty, Lee Haynes, Johnny Lang, Susan Goos Whipple, Patty Goos Long, Howard Markve, Kenny and Judy Wilbur, Lee Morgan, Johnny Cordray, Wilbur and Ginny Bruhn, Ken Riley, Terry Jerome, George Clapp, Steve Knoll, Bob and Lois Follette, Jack Harris, Betty Larsen, Keith

Dahlberg, Al Walkup, Bill Mitchell, Bill Steele, Art Brown, Ed Adams, Gordon Miner, Jerry McGinn, Joanne Strope, JoAnn Babcock, Edna Davenport, Mary Jean Hinkemeyer, Lino Castenada, Dennis Clapp, Ben Sheppard, Doug Dionne, Richelle Crumm, Shirlene Flory, Pat Allen, Don Capparelli, Harry and Linda Cougher, George and Patty Moore, Jon Langstaff, Stan Taylor, Scott Baille, Garnita O'Neal, Frances Phillips, Jim Gordon, Dale Furnish, Ray Alexander, Roger Findley, Bobbie Findlay, Bob Flory, Mary Barber Grondin, Ed Adams, Peg Geiser, Bill Dellbridge, Laverne Melton, Larry Hoven, Keith Collins, Mary Woolum and Kathy Wolfe Ebert.

A large group of historians, archivists, and mining experts proved invaluable to this project. I greatly appreciate the contributions of John Amonson, Oradell Triplett, Carol Roberts, Nick Clapp, David Bond, Gene Hyde, Elaine Cullen, and Jerry Dolph. Special thanks to Susan Karren, Director of Archival Operations for the National Archives and Records Administration for the Pacific Alaska Region, and her associates John Fitzgerald and John Ferrell and Richard C. Davis, Manuscripts-Archives Librarian at the University of Idaho; Alan Virta and staff at Boise State University's Special Collections Department; and Terry Abraham and staff at University of Idaho Library, Special Collections and Archives.

Out of some forty boxes of archived materials from the United States Bureau of Mines (correspondence, depositions, charts, and photographs), nothing was of greater value than the "Final Report" in its various iterations. I appreciate the hard work of the men and women of the USBM and the legacy of their efforts. I'd be remiss if I didn't mention the work of Dick Gentry, a writer who conducted several dozen taped interviews a decade after the fire. Those tapes provided a voice to many who are no longer with us.

On the publishing side, I'm indebted to a pair of brilliant, talented, and wise women. Literary Agent Susan Raihofer of the David

Black Literary Agency, for making the business fun, collaborative and meaningful; and Rachel Kahan, my editor at Crown, who stepped into this project with grace, heart, and wisdom. Also, thanks to Emily Loose, *The Deep Dark*'s acquiring editor who handed off the project to Rachel's capable hands. I also want to acknowledge copy editor David Wade Smith and attorney Amelia Zalcman for their contributions. Others helpful to this project include researcher Gary Boynton, reader and advisor Kathrine Beck, map designer Francois Houle, copy editor Julie O'Donnell, and friends Tina Marie and Nelson Brewer.

Special mention must be made to Bob Launhardt, without whom I doubt I'd have been able to write this book. Bob provided a small mountain of source material, cheerful guidance, and an enduring friendship that means more to me than he'll ever know. In addition to Bob, I'd like to acknowledge the rest of the Launhardts (Janet, Bob Jr., Julie, Jeannie, and Bill and Hazel Noyen), the Beehners (Wava, Matt, and Nora), and the Johnsons (Betty Johnson and Peggy White).

Without exception, there is a significant story associated with everyone who worked at Sunshine during the time period covered in my book. I know that because I heard so many. But a book can tell only a fraction of what happened. For those who lost men that day and their names do not appear in the narrative, please accept my apology. The exclusion is the result of limitations of the author and the medium.

Finally, I want to thank my wonderful wife, Claudia, and our daughters, Marta and Morgan, all of whom traveled to the district over the years as I conducted interviews, sought out material, and learned what it was to be a miner. My love and thanks forever.

About the Author

GREGG OLSEN is the author of the *New York Times* bestseller *Abandoned Prayers* and author of *Bitter Almonds, If Loving You Is Wrong, Confessions of an American Black Widow, Mockingbird,* and *Starvation Heights.* A journalist and investigative author for more than two decades, Olsen has received numerous awards and much critical acclaim for his writing. The Seattle native now lives in rural Washington state with his wife, twin daughters, cat, and six chickens.

Also by *Gregg Olsen*

In this haunting true saga of medical murder, Gregg Olsen reveals one of the most unusual and disturbing criminal cases in American history.

In 1911, two wealthy British heiresses came to a sanatorium in the forests of the Pacific Northwest to undergo the revolutionary "fasting treatment" of Dr. Linda Burfield Hazzard. It was supposed to be a holiday for the two sisters. But within a month of arriving at what the locals called Starvation Heights, the women were emaciated shadows of their former selves, waiting for death . . .

"A fascinating turn of the century story of medical malpractice and murder. If you liked *The Alienist*, you'll find *Starvation Heights* all the more gripping because this story is true."
— MICHAEL CONNELLY

STARVATION HEIGHTS

A True Story of Murder and Malice in the Woods of the Pacific Northwest

GREGG OLSEN
NEW YORK TIMES bestselling author

1-4000-9746-0
$12.95 paper

Available from
Three Rivers Press
wherever books are sold.